WINNER OF NATIONAL MAGAZINE AWARD FOR BEST FICTION

Zoetrope
ALL-STORY

CONGRATULATES
ROBERT OLEN BUTLER, REBECCA LEE, AND STACEY RICHTER
ON THEIR AWARD-WINNING STORIES

Call Zoetrope: All-Story at 212-708-0400 for subscription information, or visit our Web site at *www.all-story.com*

D0192131

GRANTA 76, WINTER 2001
www.granta.com

EDITOR   Ian Jack
DEPUTY EDITORS   Liz Jobey, Sophie Harrison
US EDITOR   Kerry Fried
EDITORIAL ASSISTANT   Fatema Ahmed

CONTRIBUTING EDITORS   Neil Belton, Pete de Bolla, Ursula Doyle,
Will Hobson, Gail Lynch, Blake Morrison, Andrew O'Hagan, Lucretia Stewart

FINANCE   Margarette Devlin
ASSOCIATE PUBLISHER   Sally Lewis
CIRCULATION DIRECTOR   Stephen W. Soule
TO ADVERTISE CONTACT   Lara Frohlich (212) 293 1646
PUBLICITY   Jenie Hederman
FULFILLMENT MANAGER   Richard Sang
SUBSCRIPTIONS   Dwayne Jones
LIST MANAGER   Diane Seltzer

PUBLISHER   Rea S. Hederman

GRANTA PUBLICATIONS, 2-3 Hanover Yard, Noel Road, London N1 8BE
Tel 020 7704 9776 Fax 020 7704 0474
e-mail for editorial: editorial@granta.com
Granta is published in the United Kingdom by Granta Publications.

GRANTA USA LLC, 1755 Broadway, 5th Floor, New York, NY 10019-3780
Tel (212) 246 1313 Fax (212) 586 8003

Granta is published in the United States by Granta USA LLC and distributed in the United States by
Granta Direct Sales, 1755 Broadway, 5th Floor, New York, NY 10019-3780.

TO SUBSCRIBE call toll-free in the US (800) 829 5093 or 601 354 3850 or
e-mail: granta@nybooks.com or fax 601 353 0176
A one-year subscription (four issues) costs $37 (US), $48 (Canada, includes GST), $45 (Mexico and
South America), and $56 (rest of the world).

Granta, USPS 000-508, ISSN 0017-3231, is published quarterly in the US by Granta USA LLC,
a Delaware limited liability company. Periodical Rate postage paid at New York, NY, and additional
mailing offices. POSTMASTER: send address changes to Granta, 1755 Broadway, 5th Floor,
New York, NY 10019-3780. US Canada Post Corp. Sales Agreement #1462326.
Printed in the United States of America on acid-free paper.

Copyright © 2001 Granta Publications.

Front cover photograph: Bettmann/Corbis
Back cover photographs: top: Brandon Jones by Richard Mulcahy; bottom right: Dock Boggs
courtesy Mike Seeger collection and Dock Boggs

ISBN 1-929001-06-1

Discover
the Writer's Life
in New York City

Master of Fine Arts in Creative Writing

Over more than six decades of steady innovation, The New School has sustained a vital center for creative writing. The tradition continues with our MFA in Creative Writing, offering concentrations in fiction, poetry, nonfiction and writing for children. Study writing and literature with The New School's renowned faculty of writers, critics, editors and publishing professionals.

Faculty 2001-2002: Jeffery Renard Allen, Hilton Als, Donald Antrim, Deborah Brodie, Peter Carey, Jill Ciment, Jonathan Dee, David Gates, Lucy Grealy, Zia Jaffrey, Jhumpa Lahiri, David Lehman, Pablo Medina, Honor Moore, Geoffrey O'Brien, Dale Peck, Robert Polito, Francine Prose, Dani Shapiro, Laurie Sheck, Jason Shinder, Darcey Steinke, Benjamin Taylor, Abigail Thomas, David Trinidad, Susan Wheeler, Stephen Wright.

Visiting Faculty: Ai, Martin Asher, Frank Bidart, Joshua Clover, Margaret Gabel, Glen Hartley, Dave Johnson, Phillis Levin, Thomas Mallon, Glyn Maxwell, Robert Pinsky, Sapphire, Lloyd Schwartz, Jon Scieszka, Ira Silverberg, Julia Slavin, Tom Sleigh, Peter Trachtenberg.

Director: Robert Polito

Fellowships and financial aid available.

For a catalog and application
Call: 212-229-5630 ext. 302
Email: nsadmissions@newschool.edu
www.nsu.newschool.edu/writing

New School University
 The New School
66 West 12th Street New York NY 10011

Riffs and Choruses

A New Jazz Anthology

ANDREW CLARK, EDITOR

"**Wide-ranging and exhaustive . . . .** There is lots of good material here. To paraphrase Helen Gurley Brown, you can never be too rich or too thin, or have too many books about jazz."
—*Booklist*

Now Available | $29.95 | paperback

Song & Dance Man III

The Art of Bob Dylan

BY MICHAEL GRAY

"Michael Gray's **monumental, endlessly illuminating** *Song & Dance Man III* most successfully places Dylan in his cultural context . . . resourceful scholarship."
—*Rolling Stone*

Now Available | $35.00 | paperback

A New History of Jazz

BY ALYN SHIPTON

"As jazz underwent a renaissance of sorts in the 1990s, jazz criticism flooded the publishing market. But **few of those books were as nuanced or readable as British critic Shipton's,** which spans the entire history of jazz . . . Shipton's detailed treatment seeks to rebut some of the more popular myths about the origins of jazz, many of which have been accepted as fact, especially following the release of Ken Burns' *Jazz* documentary. The author makes a convincing case for several new theories about the origins and spread of jazz . . . . Those who want the true history of jazz should definitely jump into this impressive work."—*Booklist*

Now Available | $35.00 | hardcover

Available in fine bookstores everywhere
1-800-561-7704
www.continuumbooks.com

CONTINUUM
CONTINUUM
CONTINUUM
The Continuum International Publishing Group Inc

 **76**

Music

"If fate is merciful, this Hedda will soon be coming to Broadway!"

- Ben Brantley, The New York Times

SHE'S HERE!

KATE BURTON

HEDDA GABLER

Photo: Richard Feldman

Kate Burton
Harris Yulin

David Lansbury   Jennifer Van Dyck
Maria Cellario   Angela Thornton
and
Michael Emerson
in
HEDDA GABLER
by
Henrik Ibsen
a new adaptation by
Jon Robin Baitz
directed by
Nicholas Martin

TELE-CHARGE® (212) 239-6200 www.telecharge.com ⓢ AMBASSADOR THEATRE, 219 W. 49TH ST.

SOLJAS
Nik Cohn

Brandon Jones (third from left), 1005 Saint Claude Street, Treme, New Orleans, c. 1982

RICHARD MULCAHY

On his twenty-ninth birthday, Baby Williams gave a party for two or three thousand in the New Orleans Superdome. Baby and his older brother Slim ran Cash Money, the hottest rap label in the city, and they liked to live large.

Every birthday Slim and Baby tried to outdo each other in the extravagance of their gifts. Baby, a man shaped like a 300-pound butt plug, had high expectations. 'It better not be a helicopter. I don't need a motherfuckin' helicopter, I already got one,' he told his entourage. But he needn't have worried. This year his gift was a Ferrari 360 Modena Berlinetta.

To show his appreciation, Baby jumped on the car and started to leap up and down. He was wearing combat boots and left a dent each time he landed. He reached into his jeans and pulled out two thick fistfuls of banknotes, tens and twenties and fifties, and started to fling them in the air. 'I am the number-one stunna!' he cried. 'Money ain't shit to me.'

When the notes began to flutter overhead, Melvin was in the first row of the crowd, perfectly placed. A cluster was heading right at him, all he had to do was reach out, but he was stampeded. A wave of people slammed into his back and sent him sprawling. Melvin went down hard, face first. Someone kicked him in the skull, someone else trod on his chest. He rolled up into a ball, arms curled over his head. He was calling on Bobby to help him, but Bobby wasn't there.

He could hear Baby Williams yelling, 'Money ain't shit to me, money ain't shit,' and the Hot 8 Brass Band blasting 'Back that Azz Up'. There was a floating feeling in his head, he may have lost consciousness. Then Bobby was shouting in his face. Bobby held his arms and dragged him along the floor till they were clear of the crowd. Melvin lay flat on his back, looking up at the lights in the roof, far off. His pants were wet.

Bobby had come away loaded: two fifties, a bunch of twenties and tens. And Melvin had nothing. Bobby kept thumbing the notes and calling him a bitch, and Melvin didn't have a word to say. A shorty, maybe ten years old, was standing next to his face in brand new Reeboks, his shoe a few inches from Melvin's eye. When he lifted his shoe, there was a crumpled twenty underneath. All Melvin had to do was reach out his hand.

Afterwards, he and Bobby hit a Popeye's on Canal Street, and Bobby ate three family dinners. Bobby was eighteen, five months older than Melvin, but he was close to Baby Williams's weight class and getting closer every day. He sat by the window with his big greasy hands and grease all over his face, and he wouldn't stop thumbing the banknotes. Two cops were outside and Bobby waved the notes at them. In Melvin's eyes that was purely stupid.

He was staying by his Uncle June's on Euterpe. June was the one who'd raised him, more or less. He wasn't really an uncle, but when Melvin was five, Melvin's mother had got herself sidetracked and couldn't keep him. He went to live with his grandma, but she got a cancer and died. After that he was fostered out. The first family couldn't handle him, they said he was too wild. The second family put him in a cage. They said it was the only way to stop his row, so they shut him up in a chicken coop with a tin roof over it. They took the chickens out first, but not the chickenshit. When Social Services found out, they put him in the House. He was eight years old, and he wouldn't speak. When he used to live with his moms he was never quiet. The way he chirped all hours of the day and night drove her crazy. Now he didn't say a word. The people at the House didn't know what to do. They sent him to a psychiatrist; it didn't help. They hit him; it didn't help.

The only person who could reach him was his mother's sister Maxine. She had a house on Orange Street, close to the St Thomas projects, she shared with Uncle June. Sometimes she came to visit Melvin in the House and one day she took him home with her. She was a big fine woman with children of her own. They didn't want Melvin in the house, but Maxine wouldn't let them harm him. Once, when her kids were at school and Melvin was sick with the flu, she baked him peanut-butter cookies and they watched TV all day. Then Maxine lost the house and moved in with her boyfriend. The boyfriend didn't want Melvin, so Uncle June took him. June had two friends like himself, he-shes, who had a room to rent. It was just a closet, but it had a window and a bunk bed. Melvin slept on top, and Uncle June was the bottom.

Uncle June was almost young then, but shapeless and lumpy like a sack filled with mashed potatoes. He dressed like a man but he had a little girl's voice. One time when Melvin walked in on him naked, it looked like there was nothing down there, just shadows.

He was cool, though. There were men and women in his life that disrespected him, and this made him get evil at times, but he never got evil with Melvin. They moved in and out of projects, most often the St Thomas. At some point, Melvin began to talk again. It turned out he had a stammer.

He couldn't say where the stammer came from. He didn't have it when he was in his mother's house. Maybe it was rust. But he never got rid of it.

When he was ten he topped five foot. Four years later he was the exact same height. The St Thomas soljas gave him a hard time. They used to whale on him and imitate his stammer. The worst was 'Rilla. He was younger than Melvin, but he had a lot of gold chains and gold teeth, gold all over his person. He was tight with some heavy dealers, moving up the ladder, and one day he backed Melvin up in a breezeway and pissed on him. Melvin went back in the house and took Uncle June's Glock and walked over to 'Rilla's house and shot him. He didn't kill him, just winged him. He meant to kill him but he'd never used a Glock before.

Life was easier for a spell; he had some respect. Then Uncle June moved to the Calliope and Melvin was back in trouble. Calliope niggas made the St Thomas look like church.

Bobby was living two houses down. He was big even then, and he had that winning attitude. His name was Bobby Mabry, but he went by Bobby Murda. Nobody messed with him. Bobby's younger brother Tyree had got killed the year before, and Bobby was still mad about it. The motherfucker that did the shooting got killed himself before Bobby could reach him. That was frustrating to Bobby.

Uncle June didn't take to Bobby. He never did care for soljas. According to June, that street life was only good to get you dead. He kept nagging on Melvin to do his homework and stay in school but Melvin wasn't hearing him. His dream was to be a rap star. Him and Bobby together. Lil Mel and Bobby Murda.

Many times he'd be out on the streets when some of Cash Money drove by. They'd be in their Bentleys or a fleet of bright yellow Hummers, bombing the bass, flossing mad gold and platinum too. When the girls on the street felt that bass, they threw themselves up against a wall and started shaking their booty. Then the Hummers moved on and those girls were left to dangle. Their asses would still be twitching when Cash Money was ten miles down the road.

Melvin planned to write a rap every day but he couldn't seem to have the knack. And Bobby was no big help. He was running the clubs every night and high every day, and sex, he was a pure hog for sex. How many songs had they finished so far? Not one.

Day and night, he thought about hitting big: the Hummers and Bentleys, the house at English Turn. English Turn was where Slim and Baby Williams had bought mansions and kept their families hid. Melvin drove out there with Bobby a few times when they'd stole a ride. There was a gate with a guardhouse and a golf course and landscaped gardens and a clubhouse with white pillars. In the evening you sat on a veranda and looked across a lagoon, and all your neighbours were white.

How you lovin' that? After Melvin walked in Uncle June's house with that twenty-dollar bill, he took it out and looked at it in the light for a long time. It was ugly-assed, one corner ripped, a sorry piece of paper. Used to be Baby's. Now it was his.

New Orleans rap is all about funk. It's lowdown and dirty, the greasier the better, and it has nothing to do with fashion. In the mid-Nineties, when the city first captured the national market, gangsta rap was said to be finished. The music press was full of stories claiming that the killings of Tupac Shakur and Biggie Smalls had reawakened hip-hop's social conscience. But New Orleans must not have heard the news. Instead of toning down, its raps became more brutal, its rhythms raunchier than ever.

The format was simple: unspeakable lyrics, irresistible beats. Slaughter met sex on the dance floor, and the Dirty South was born. Its first ruler was Master P from the Calliope. For two years his label, No Limit, was the bomb. Then Cash Money took over.

The Williams brothers rose from the Magnolia. To begin with, they were street hustlers, scuffling like everyone else. Later they came upon money, never mind how, and went into the music business. They started selling records out of the backs of vans, in the clubs and community centres, in mom-and-pop stores in the projects. They signed up Mannie Fresh, a veteran DJ with a genius for beats, and a stable of neighbourhood rappers, and, in 1997, they dropped their anthem, 'Bling Bling': 'I'm tattooed and barred up/Medallion iced up, Rolex bezelled up/And my pinky ring is platinum plus...'

'Bling Bling', a national hit, was the first of many, peaking with Juvenile's 'Back that Azz Up', the hottest rap record of 1999. Depending on whose figures you believe, Cash Money grossed fifty million dollars, or eighty, or over a hundred million.

Master P, meanwhile, seemed to have lost his touch. Maybe the pressure had got to him. A full laundry list of New Orleans rappers— Pimp Daddy, DJ Irv, Yella Boy, Kilo G, MC T. T. Tucker, Warren Mays—had died by the gun. So P and his bodyguards moved away to Baton Rouge, and Cash Money owned the city.

Joyce lived in New Orleans East. She was a homecare nurse, and Edgar, her husband, was a shoe salesman. They had two daughters, Gabrielle and Jalene; the whole family was strong in church. Their home was a ranch-style brick bungalow with its own driveway and a patch of St Augustine grass out front. There was even a palm tree of sorts. More dead than alive, but Joyce gave praise for it. She didn't tell her age. She was in her prime, that's all she would say. She suffered with diabetes and had to watch her weight. This came hard to her, because she dearly loved chocolates and all sweet things, but how could she complain? Everyone had their cross.

When Joyce heard that Cash Money would be shooting a video at Garette Park, right down the block from her house, she was caught in two minds. She had no love for gangsta rap. Glorifying guns and killing, all that *language*, to her it was Satan at work. But Cash Money, well, she had to admit she liked those beats. Mannie Fresh, the man was blessed with a gift, no doubt. And Juvenile too. Don't nobody dare to tell her daughters this, but when 'Back that *Thing* Up' was on the radio all the time, Joyce used to listen out for it.

The video featured Cash Money's rising star, Lil Wayne, known to his crew as Weezie. He was eighteen, and his first album had gone platinum. By Cash Money standards, its lyrics were tame, but that wasn't Weezie's fault. His mother didn't allow him to curse, he said.

13

The video wasn't due to start shooting for hours, but Joyce put on a pair of big old shorts and a Saints shirt, and carried a beach chair outdoors. She wanted to be sure not to miss anything, so she brought binoculars and a thermos. It was a lovely morning, crystal clear, and the sidewalk was crowded with neighbours. Kids were selling lemonade and sodas, it felt like carnival.

A Cash Money bus was already parked down the block. It had an outsize platinum '$' spray-painted on the back and every inch of the sides were covered with publicity for *Baller Blockin'*, the label's movie. According to Mannie Fresh, a baller blocker is 'a nigga standin' in your way of ballin'. In other words, a playa hata, and nothing was lower than that. 'I think playa hating should be made a crime, I really do,' said Fresh.

The painting on the bus showed the Cash Money Army, thugged up in bandanas and full bling bling, exploding out of the Magnolia in a flameburst. The bus had no windows that Joyce could tell. She thought this was strange, but maybe not. If you were Cash Money, you didn't need to look out.

When she turned her eyes to this street she lived on, though, she thought it was something worth seeing. All these tidy houses and tidy front gardens and driveways with cars in them; cars with wheels and hubcaps and working engines; new cars, some of them. It was a far cry from the inner city. Most of New Orleans these days was dead or dying. Tourists called this decadence; they thought it was romantic. Their New Orleans was the Big Easy, the City that Care Forgot. Crawfish and jazz brunches and Hurricanes at Pat O'Brien's, the French Quarter, the Garden District, mansions on St Charles Avenue, the live oaks in Audubon Park. They rode the streetcar and shopped all day, and at night they got drunk and stupid on Bourbon Street. It was one big party to them.

Joyce could have taught them better. She was born and raised in the Sixth Ward, right by the St Roch Cemetery, and she'd seen the city rot on the vine. Oh, there was still beauty all right. Sometimes it could fool you almost. She'd be a riding a bus, when she passed this or that place she knew as a child, it was like a hand clutched her throat. But she didn't get off the bus, no way.

Tourists and poverty, that's all there was. She read in the *Times-*

Picayune where the population of Orleans Parish was close to sixty per cent black, and over half lived below the poverty line. Hundreds of millions of dollars, billions, poured in every year, but none of it ever seeped down. Every cent was gobbled up by the politicians and the banks, old white money and new black money. That's right, black money. The mayor was black, the city council had a black majority, there were millionaire black businessmen. They were as bad as the whites. Worse, to her mind, because they betrayed their own people.

The lies; the bare-face lies. Politicians, black and white, kept announcing schemes to turn things around. Convention centres and casinos, museums, tourist malls. More jobs, they said; more money for education. But nothing ever changed.

Ask Joyce, it was deliberate. The schools were a crying shame, and why? Because they were planned that way. The whole idea was to keep people ignorant. Then they were fit for nothing but cleaning up the tourists' mess. That's what the politicians needed. Menial labour, dirt cheap.

Talking about it made Joyce so mad she forgot about her blood pressure and had to take a pill. She lay back in her beach chair, breathing deep and slow, and wished she could take one quick dip into a box of Russell Stover chocolates, just one.

Her husband was right; she took things too much to heart. She needed to count her own blessings, that she wasn't caught up in the projects, but safe in New Orleans East. This was next best to the promised land. Her own home, her own yard, her very own palm tree. Praise God, Joyce said. Praise Him.

Something was happening down the street. Word spread that Lil Wayne had arrived.

Today's video showcased a cut from his new album, *Lights Out*. To judge by its language, Wayne had managed to tear loose from his mother's apron strings. 'You can look forward to me takin' over,' he told *Da Rude*, a local rap magazine. 'Some eye-opener shit, 'cause niggas be sleepin' on Weezie, and Weezie 'bout to wake niggas up, "good mornin'".'

When Joyce caught sight of him, he was behind the wheel of a mint purple Porsche. The Porsche wasn't moving, being perched on top of a flatbed, but Weezie kept twisting this way and that, as if cornering at ninety. The video crew took some test shots. 'They started filming, they filming right now,' Joyce said, and began to bounce up and down in her seat, but it proved a false alarm. The camera stopped whirring, the crew broke up. After a few seconds, Lil Wayne climbed down to the street.

He was tiny. In a full-length mink coat, with his wraparound shades and his baggy pants pulled low, he looked like a ten-year-old dressed up in his daddy's pimp clothes.

Watching him sashay down the block, Joyce let out her breath through her nose. 'Would you look at that child?' she said. Wayne's new record was playing. People all around were dancing.

'What time is it?' she asked.

'Ricki Lake,' she was told.

For a moment she felt stricken. Ricki Lake was her favourite TV talk show, the highlight of her day. When her sister Carla had a heart attack and was in the ICU, Joyce didn't leave the hospital for two days and nights, but she never missed Ricki Lake. And now? 'Child,' she said, and started to shake that thing.

Soljas lived and died by the G-Code. To be recognized as a G was the highest condition any hustla could aspire to. The G was a big-time gangsta, a godfatha, a don. He had all the cars and hoes and bling bling any man could dream of, yet he stayed true to his roots. He was a mighty warlord, but he had a project soul.

It was a matter of honour. 'As far as what I mean by G-code,' said Juvenile, 'is the way we dress, the way we talk, the way we was raised. Traditions. When I say G-code, I'm talkin' about what you went through where you from.'

Terrance 'Gangsta' Williams, half-brother of Slim and Baby, was a G. Around the Magnolia he was a great hero, though he did not live there any more. He was serving life plus twenty years in a federal pen, for Continuing Criminal Enterprise, solicitation to commit murder, and conspiracy to sell six ounces of heroin.

From jail, he gave an interview to *F.E.D.S*, the magazine of 'convicted hustlers/street thugs/fashion/sports/music/film/etc'. Questioned by the mag's ace reporter, Cold Crushin' Kenny Rankin,

Gangsta didn't deny the charges, though he tried to put them in context. When he was still on the streets, New Orleans had been known as Click Click, murder capital of the world, but he felt its status was deceptive. 'That's only because New Orleans is a very small city,' Gangsta argued. 'Everybody's trying to build a reputation and get their hustle on—the city's not big enough for but so many gangsters. So, somebody had to go.'

'How many people do they say you've killed?' Rankin asked.

'…According to the streets they say I've murdered over forty people.'

'How old were you when they started calling you a heartstopper?'

'I was about fifteen.'

'What does "heartstopper" mean?'

'When you penetrate someone with some iron.'

All in all, he sounded upbeat. 'I do thank God and I will admit that me having this life plus twenty was one of the best things that could've happened to me. It's all love in the federal system,' he said. He was writing a book and planning a movie, warning the young not to follow his path. Meanwhile, he was grateful to be alive, and to have his brothers' support, and most of all to be who he was. 'To Mister Terrance Gangsta Ooh-Wee Magnolia Williams,' he concluded, 'all I can say is, "I'm jealous of myself".'

The source of the G's strength was pride. Pride in his family, in his click, in his own legend. But if he came from a project, as most Gs did, pride in that project came first and last. It was what he represented.

Outsiders found this hard to understand. To them, the projects were dumping grounds. Driving through them, it seemed inconceivable that these tortured labyrinths of dung-coloured buildings, with their scorched walls and boarded-up windows and stench of human rot, could be a source of pride to anyone. Yet they'd started out as model housing. When they were built, mostly in the 1940s, they were seen as a blessed escape. Ten of them ringed the inner city, each a small city to itself, each conceived in hope.

The G-Code was born of the 1980s, when crack first flooded the streets and raised up a new breed of drug lord, more murderous than any before. The projects turned into fiefdoms, ruled by guns and celebrated by rappers like Juvenile: 'Welcome to the section where it's hotter than a bitch/Niggas breakin' up bricks, niggas tryin' to be rich/All day hustle, boocoo scuffle/Niggas huddle, AK-47s muffled/Blood in puddles, people scatter/Flying pieces of human matter...'

The G's gift was to harness the slaughter and ride it. But he needed soljas to protect his turf and run his games. Many of these were children; the younger they were, the less hang-ups they had about shooting people: 'I ain't terrified from nuthin'/I'm young, wild, crazy and disgustin'...'.

Your project was who you were. It gave you a tribe, and a cause. Soljas called that love.

The enemy was everyone outside. New Orleans was an endless maze of rivalries and ancient feuds. Apart from the projects, there were also eighteen wards. Gerrymandered political districts, drawn up in the nineteenth century, their boundaries defied logic, but soljas held them sacred.

Some wards were allied, others at perpetual war. A story is told of a boy called Lawrence from the Sixth Ward, who went to a club in the Fourth Ward. The Fourth and Sixth Wards are friendly, the Fourth and Seventh are not. So when Lawrence got in the club, some niggas asked him his ward. Lawrence held both hands up, one with four fingers extended, the other with two. But he was dancing, and it was dark, and the niggas couldn't see that his thumb was down on the hand with the four fingers out. They thought he was saying seven. So they shot him once in the head, once in the chest and once in the stomach.

To soljas, the incident was regrettable, not tragic. Few of them conceived a long-term future; their life was minute by minute. They slung rocks (dealt crack), robbed gas stations and convenience stores, and served their time in the Orleans Parish Prison. Sooner or later, most likely, they were shot.

Even that was not all bad. When a solja died in battle, he was memorialized on a T-shirt. His image appeared in four-colour glory, usually in combat gear, with the dates of his sunrise and sunset and a line of tribute from his click. In death, he achieved what life had denied him. He was someone; and he had the T-shirt to prove it.

June had trouble in his head. His brain was flooded with heavy water. He could feel it slopping behind his eyes every time he took a step. He needed to go see the doctor.

This new affair with Melvin didn't help none. The call had come in at three in the morning, Melvin phoning from jail. Him and Bobby Mabry had been in a bust-up on Orleans Avenue. Some dudes came out of the projects and tried to rob them. Melvin fought back. There was a maylay and somebody shot off a gun. The bullet hit a woman on the other side of the street. Passed straight through the flesh of her arm. She was lucky.

That was Melvin's story. But June could see the holes. What were those boys doing down on Orleans? And why did he fight back? He'd been robbed enough times before, he ought to know that tune. A man steps to you with a gun, you honour his request.

June saved his questions for later. He called Cheapie Bail Bonds, like he did all those times before, and carried Melvin home. The boy never thanked him, just hit him up for pizza. Heartaches was all it was. If June had a lick of sense, he'd put that boy in the street, but he knew he could never do it.

This morning they went to the courthouse, Tulane and Broad. Lord knows June despised that place. Big old ugly grey building like some kind of fortress, they might as well hang a sign, JAIL STARTS HERE. And the way these children walked the halls. In the time when June came up, he'd say he was black and proud. But these youths over here, that was some other something. Tatted up, slugged up, thugged up, even in the courthouse they strutted and talked that gangsta talk.

Not Melvin, though. He might signify on the street, but in here he walked real light.

Bobby Mabry was brought out from the cells, he had prison wear on. To June's way of thinking, he ought to keep wearing it all the time, save everyone a heap of trouble. The whole case was playtime to him, he never stopped yawning and flapping his mouth, but Melvin he was scared, he didn't want to be no man's wife.

The judge set the case back six weeks, and Bobby went back to jail, and Melvin was out on the street. Soon as he was out of the courthouse he went to laughing, doing that pimp-roll shit, with his pants pulled low to show off his drawers. Everyone he met, he called them nigga.

They had lunch at the Verdict Cafe. June had no appetite, but Melvin ate for them both. This was disturbing to June. Melvin never ate that way, most times he barely picked. It was like he was being Bobby, gluttoning and jabbering both at once, and with his stammer the food flew out as fast as he forked it in.

'What were you doing on Orleans Avenue?' June asked.

'Business,' Melvin said.

June just raised up and left him there. Stood at the corner, waiting on the Broad Street bus, and he couldn't stop shaking. This was what loving got you. He needed to go see the doctor.

Before Master P or Cash Money there was bounce. It started in the late 1980s, a wild mix of rap and Mardi Gras Indian chants and second-line brass-band bass patterns and polyrhythmic drumming and gospel call-and-response. It was raw sex in dance, a music of summer block parties, of swelter.

On Sunday afternoons, when the temperature in the bricks was around 110 degrees and the humidity near a hundred per cent, the top DJs let blast for five hours straight, and the projects turned into giant mosh pits.

Big fine women and slim fine women hogged the spaces next to the speakers, action-ready in shorts and halter tops. Dancing to bounce was called twerking. To twerk meant shaking that thing till the sweat flew and the concrete underfoot was slick as an ice-rink.

The DJ shouted orders—walk it like a dog, walk it like a model, wobble in a circle—and the women jumped to obey. When the DJ told them to shake it on a stick, they bent over till their hands were flat on the ground, their buttocks high in the air, and twitched so fast they seemed plugged into a socket. All you saw was a blur of flying booty. 'Now tiddy bop,' the DJ ordered, and the women raised their T-shirts to shake their breasts. 'Now show the globe,' and the women bared their asses. 'Now pop that pussy till the pussy goes pop…'

In the city's record stores, bounce outsold mainstream rap five-to-one. Since its first great hit, 'Where Dey At' by DJ Irv and MC T. T. Tucker in '91, it had produced a succession of local heroes.

Most of them had died untimely, but their legacy remained: both No Limit and Cash Money had made their fortunes by marrying bounce to hip-hop.

Mobo Joe was a rare survivor from the early days. In his prime he had produced classics like 'Run Dat Shit' by Ruthless Juveniles and 'Straight Up Villing' by Dog House Posse. When he passed by with Kenny, his 400-pound lieutenant, every G in town gave him space. But Joe fell on evil times. He got caught up in drugs, lost his money and his business, and ended up with a two-year stretch.

Now he was out again, and a billboard for his greatest hits, featuring his jail card—IVORY PAYNES, 79353-079—overlooked the interstate, near the Superdome.

In the flesh he looked shrunken, as if his frame no longer filled his skin, but he said he was not beaten. His girl had a job at Cachi Nails ('if your nails aren't becoming to you, you should be coming to me'), and he drove a Malibu, and when asked how much his billboard had cost, he smiled mysteriously. 'I'm still Mobo Joe,' he said. 'I know how to work my jelly.'

Maybe so. But younger bounce kings like Fifth Ward Weebie and Josephine Johnny, who was said to have shot up a bar and wounded two women in the legs to publicize his new album, *Out On Bail*, were stealing his spotlight. 'Back in the day, I was the shit,' Mobo Joe liked to say. Not any more.

Bounce was so all-powerful now that no event could flourish without it. On a Saturday afternoon King George, an uptown ruler, gave a children's party in the Magnolia. He provided free T-shirts and food but no DJ, so nobody came. Well, almost nobody. Some social workers showed up, and women dispensing condoms and Aids pamphlets, plus a few hot girls with video cameras, but they barely made up a quorum.

King George, a mountainous man, held the party in a community playground. He owned a hip-hop clothing store and a record label, and some of his rappers sat around a picnic table, looking bored. Big Slack, the first among them, was short and stout and wore a T-shirt promoting *Ready For Combat*, his new CD. It showed a death's head in shades and a military beret, over crossed AK-47s, and the legend, MESS WITH THE BEST—DIE LIKE THE REST.

This was his first album. 'I been rappin' thirteen years but, due to incarceration, I fell behind my business,' said Slack. Had he been in jail a lot? 'Back and forth.' He paused to reconsider. 'Well, I'll be honest wit' ya,' he said. 'More back than forth.'

King George started serving up turkey necks from a giant vat. Across the playground a small boy, no older than seven, came into view. He wore a football shirt down below his knees, he had a wall eye. As he approached, he could be heard rapping: 'Motherfucka I'ma take you out/Bringin' the pain is what I'm about.'

One of the hot girls, seeing but not hearing him, favoured the child with a dazzling smile. 'Trick bitch,' said the child, 'I'ma let you suck my dick.'

DJ Jubilee would not have approved. His record label called him 'King of Bounce', and he claimed to have created over a hundred dances, among them the Shake It Like a Dog, the Stick Your Booty Out and the Ee Wee Unk. He was also the anti-G.

Born Jerome Temple, he tutored handicapped children, coached basketball and football teams, and said he'd never touched drugs, not even marijuana. He had grown up in the St Thomas and one of his brothers was doing life in Angola, but Jube was not a man who lied. His diligence and rigour were bywords. Even on stage, demonstrating the Shake It Like a Sissy or the Penis Pop, he carried himself like a traffic cop.

His record label, Take Fo', was equally righteous. The owner, Earl Mackie, was college-educated, a family man, church-going and low key. He'd graduated to bounce from *Positive Black Talk*, a local TV show, and was big on self-improvement. Sometimes his minister gave him grief about the lyrics Take Fo' put out, specially those by the transvestite Katy Red, who called herself the Millennium Sissy and liked to rap about cocksucking. Earl Mackie's defence was that it beat killing.

Most nights Mackie's artists gathered in a studio near the courthouse. The studio looked firebombed, with collapsing sofas and graffiti-splattered walls, but the atmosphere was restful. Henry the Man, Mackie's partner, manned the console in hospital scrubs, dandling his infant daughter; Junie B, the Magnolia Pepper Girl, who spat game like an uzi on record, talked about becoming a primary school teacher. Only Choppa acted the star.

He was the label's newest signing, a nineteen-year-old from suburban Marrero, good-looking and brash, dizzy with self-love, but he was hardly a gangsta. His family was a unit, his father worked; at home, he answered to Darwin.

'I'm bad,' Choppa said. He'd got suspended in school, and he was always in the clubs, and he had two gold teeth at $125 each. Unlike Cash Money and No Limit, Take Fo' couldn't afford to hand out precious metals and made do with faux-gold pendants. Choppa wore his on all occasions. When a photographer appeared, he also grabbed up his cellphone and posed with it, speed-talking, though no one was on the other end.

He could never stand to stay home. If he heard that his click was on some street, throwing bricks up against a wall, he had to be out there with them. But a solja? He looked blank. He was a lover, not a warrior. 'Everyone lovin' Choppa,' he said. 'Everyone wantin' me, wantin' me, it'll drive me crazy some day.'

On Saturday night he played a dance at the gym of a community fitness centre in Laplace, an hour's drive outside the city. The night was hot and steamy, and groups of teenage girls sat outdoors at picnic tables, catching any breeze they could. They seemed nice girls, well-behaved. They talked about their nails, and boys, and Destiny's Child, and boys. Then Choppa came on stage, and the girls flew into the gym. 'If you like your pussy ate, say Aaaahh,' Choppa said. And all the nice girls went, 'Aaaahh.'

Brandon Jones was a golden child. There was a light in him; just seeing him made people smile. Everyone in Treme knew that he was chosen.

Treme was a black neighbourhood abutting the French Quarter. Families had lived here for generations. The majority were poor, but many owned their own houses, handed down from parents and grandparents. The houses were lovely to look at, old clapboard shotguns and Creole cottages, but not so lovely to live in. Still, they were homes.

In the late Eighties, many of these homes were razed to make way for Louis Armstrong Park, in hopes of luring the tourists who thronged the Quarter. The people who were put out of their houses to make room for the park were promised housing in New Orleans East but ended up in the projects. Treme never recovered.

The hoped-for tourists never came. A proposed Tivoli Gardens came to nothing; a casino opened and closed. Property speculators bought up homes on the cheap and resold them to white gentrifiers, but few of the incomers put down roots. Crack was taking over the streets. Soon everyone had a gun.

Due to a bureaucratic mix-up, Brandon's legal name was Benson. He was light-skinned, almost honey-coloured. On the streets they called him Red.

His mother Regina was sixteen when she birthed him and already had a year-old daughter, Tiffany. Regina was a riotous woman, with a big laugh and a wild temper and an anarchic sense of humour. People said she should be a stand-up comic, but she was too busy working two jobs and wrestling demons. Brandon's father was up in Angola serving life for four murders. So Brandon was raised by a rotating committee: Regina, his mother's friend Booby, and his grandmother, Miss Rose.

From the time he could walk, he ran the streets. Treme streets were still safe then, you could use them to learn, and Brandon was wild for knowledge. He was also saddled with a sense of duty.

He was nine when he met Nan Parati. She was one of the white incomers, a graphic artist. One day she caught him smashing bottles in the street and told him to stop, because the glass ripped her bicycle tyres. Brandon was furious. Not only had she ruined his pleasure, but now he felt responsible for the safety of her tyres.

He went to work in Nan's studio, and she became part of his raising, too. She taught him history and philosophy, and Brandon taught her Treme. He'd never been outside Orleans Parish, so she took him travelling to Philadelphia and New York, to her family's home in North Carolina. Brandon told her there were mothers, moms, and maws. A mother said, 'Brandon dear, get up'; a mom said, 'Get up'; a maw said, 'Boy, get yo ass outta bed'. So Regina was his maw, and Nan was sometimes his mother, sometimes his mom.

They had many fights. The mood in the streets was changing,

and Brandon started running with Peanut and Dookie and Fat Cory and UDog, who styled themselves the Sixth Ward Creepers. Cory had been shot and was stuck in a wheelchair for life. This was seen as an achievement.

At fifteen, Brandon had been shot at three times and could list twenty friends who'd died. He was arrested for shooting off a gun in the air, and again for breaking into a car. That time he was innocent, but the cops cuffed him so tight he lost circulation in his wrists. When Brandon complained, one of the cops said, 'I hope they cut your motherfuckin' hands off.' Then they beat a confession out of UDog, and Brandon was locked in a cell with a man who'd just killed his best friend for messing with his wife. He felt safer in there than he did with the cops.

On sunny days the Creepers used to sit out on some derelict porch and pose for pictures with their money and guns. That was Brandon's life. Then he would go to Nan and cry, and swear he was going to change. He sent her a letter saying, 'I can't understand how stupid I acted for five years of your helping meracales that you gave me. I owe you so much first of all like a trillion dollars, my freedom.' That was Brandon's life too.

School never agreed with him, but he could write. He started a hip-hop version of *Romeo and Juliet*, retitled 'Homeyo and Ugliet'. The opening scene began:

Corey: Chris, who do you think is the finest girl in school?

Chris: I like [Juliet]. That girl got the biggest tits in the world. I mean that butt! When she's walking up the street in the rain you can use her butt for an umbrella.

The arrests kept piling up, and he felt himself drowning. He checked himself into the Odyssey House, a drug rehab centre that taught self-awareness and taking responsibility for one's own actions. He didn't have a drug problem, but he needed out of his home, out of Treme, so he stuck with the Odyssey programme, and when he emerged, he had acquired a direction. He still hung with Peanut and Fat Cory and the rest, but he got a job bagging groceries at an upscale healthfood store on Esplanade Avenue. This made him, in Treme, a high-flyer.

He learned therapeutic massage, read any book he could lay

hands on, wrote poetry and journals. He also wrote raps, hundreds of them; his rap name was B-Red. With two other rappers, G-Sta and Casual T, he formed a group named Certified Hustlaz. Like every other click, they flashed bling bling for publicity pictures, but their music was politicized and self-aware, and Brandon's verses raged with an apocalyptic preacher's fire: 'How many niggas you gonna kill before yo twenty-first birthday?.../Is it because you afraid to lose,/Or is yo 'hood full of niggas with something to prove?/Whatever it is, dog, you gotta stop/'Cos you're quick to kill yo boys, but you afraid of the cops...'

B-Red railed against the G-Code; to him, the 'G' stood for genocide. He preached the lessons he'd learned at Odyssey House: self-reliance, work, no excuses. Treme had become a prison to him. He was scared of getting shot, and slept in a different bed almost every night. Another family now shared Regina's home. They stole his money, destroyed his clothes, but he kept working, and at last he began to see some rewards. His live shows sold out, he was on the verge of a record deal. One last push and he'd be free, and he was driving home from work with his friend Dewitt, full of plans, when a cop car came speeding down the ramp from the freeway and rammed straight into them. Brandon Jones was twenty-three.

The T-shirts at Brandon's funeral, ignoring his true life, showed him in the camouflage gear of a Sixth Ward gangsta. B-RED, CERTIFIED HUSTLER, the inscription read. A COWARD DIES A THOUSAND DEATHS, A SOLDIER DIES BUT ONCE.

Bobby Murda also got a T-shirt that ignored his true life. When he went down on Orleans Avenue once too often, he had his head blown off. Melvin thought the T-shirt should say something about revenge, but Bobby's mother did not ask his opinion. Instead, she chose to use one of Bobby's baby pictures, captioned JESUS HAS A NEW FRIEND.

Melvin was at the burying. He even managed to drop a baggie of weed into the grave before they started shovelling. He wasn't invited to the food and drink after, but that was all right, he went anyway. He had some shrimps; nobody turned him away. But he started to have bad thoughts, he couldn't stay.

Truth? He was happy Bobby was gone. Not happy his head blew away, understand, but relieved he wasn't around. That first night they were on Orleans and those dudes tried to jack them, to Melvin that changed everything. When he felt that hand go in his pants and grab his money, he liked to snap. Baby's twenty was in there; he wasn't giving it up. They could kill his ass right there, he didn't give a fuck. But later, in lock-up, he saw the true facts. If he didn't cut loose from Bobby Murda, he'd be on a T-shirt himself or else in a wheelchair, either or.

Melvin was a person, he believed pretty much in signs. Uncle June had taught him that. June lived his whole life off of dream books and the stars. Well, you could take shit too far. But Baby's twenty, there was a meaning to it. Had to be.

When he left from the food and drink, it was coming on for evening. This hour of the day he liked to walk on Canal Street and watch the people come and go at the big hotels. Le Meridien was his first choice, it had the highest-class bitches.

He was standing outside the Burger King peeping when a sista with a gold dress and gold-steaked hair walked out, and Juvenile walked out right behind her. They got into Juvy's Bentley and drove away, and Melvin went in the Burger King. He ordered up a whopper, double fries and a large coke, then reached in his pocket and came up empty. Baby's twenty was all he owned.

He almost cancelled his order, but no, he had a better idea. He broke the twenty, let it go. Then he took a table by the window and sat down, Lil Mel, and started to write a rap. ☐

MEN, *Music*
MEMORY,

The Memory of Elephants
A Novel
Boman Desai

"[Written] with disarming unpretentiousness, humour and characterisation both warm and sharp. . . . This is an accomplished first novel, an ingenious approach to the family saga form. It is a fastidiously written experiment in time in which the author has brought off exactly what he set out to do—to bring everyone and everything . . . 'all together in one place and time.'"—Janice Elliott, *The Independent*
Paper $16.00

The Best of Jackson Payne
A Novel
Jack Fuller

"[O]ne of the few novels about jazz to recognize that language may never capture the magic of music but may just evoke the hell out of it." —Jonathan Levi, *Los Angeles Times*
Paper $15.00

A River Runs through It and Other Stories
Twenty-fifth Anniversary Edition
Norman Maclean
With a Foreword by Annie Proulx

"It is an enchanted tale. . . . I have read the story three times now, and each time it seems fuller."
—Roger Sale, *New York Review of Books*

"Altogether beautiful in the power of its feeling. . . . As beautiful as anything in Thoreau or Hemingway."
—Alfred Kazin, *Chicago Tribune Book World*
Paper $12.00 Cloth $22.00

Available in bookstores.
The University of Chicago Press
www.press.uchicago.edu

GRANTA

RESISTANCE
Richard Sennett

PHOTOGRAPHS BY
JILLIAN EDELSTEIN

For musicians, the sense of touch defines our physical experience of art: lips applied to reed, fingers pushing down keys or strings. It might seem that the more easily we touch, the better we play, but facility is only half the story. A pianist or a violinist has constantly to explore resistance, either in the instrument or in the musician's own body.

Like every cellist, I learned about touch through mastering movements like vibrato. Vibrato is the rocking motion of the left hand on a string which colours a note around its precise pitch; waves of sound spread out in vibrato like ripples from a pool into which one has thrown a stone. Vibrato does not start with the contact of the fingertip and the string; it begins further back at the elbow, the impulse to rock starting from that anchor, passing through the forearm into the palm of the hand and then through the finger.

There are many kinds of vibratos, some slow and liquid which colour long notes, some which last no more than an instant. These rocking movements of the left hand are also like fingerprints, giving every cellist his or her own distinctive sound. János Starker's vibrato is focused, the colouring of his notes is light, whereas Jacqueline du Pré often has a wide, wild vibrato. But even for her, vibrato is the result of discipline.

Freedom to rock requires that a cellist first master the capacity to play perfectly in tune. If a young cellist fails in that mastery, every time he or she vibrates the note will sound sour, accentuating the inaccuracy of pitch. At an advanced stage of our training, we use vibrato to gain entry to the contemporary world of semitones, the notes which lie between the normal divisions of the chromatic scale. But even playing the works of Boulez or Elliott Carter we must still aim at a precise tonal centre. There are acoustical reasons for this distinction between the sour and the vibrant, related to the overtones set going by a string. Still, the need for mastery of pitch in order to vibrate well tells a elementary truth: freedom depends on control, whereas purely impulsive expression produces just mess—a piece of folk wisdom as true of the hand as of the heart.

When I began studying the cello at the age of eight, vibrato came easily to me, in part because I was blessed with a sense of perfect pitch. The Garden of Eden in which a child prodigy dwells is indeed the sheer ease of making sound. Exit from that musical Garden began for me when I began to perform in public.

I have yet to meet the musician who walks on stage with the same insouciance he or she might feel in walking to the bank or in practising in private—though it has been said of the violinist Fritz Kreisler that he barely noticed that he played in front of thousands of people. Usually stage fright follows the outlines of a simple story.

Chapter one begins at the moment of anticipation: faced with performing, adrenalin flows, and the stomach tightens, which is why few musicians dare eat before performing. Chapter two is the withdrawal (before the event) into a concentrated silence—again, a 'natural' like Artur Rubinstein often entertained in his dressing room before a performance, but most musicians can barely manage to cope with the presence of their partners. Chapter three opens when we walk on stage, and is hard to describe; it's like a trance in which we become hyper-alert.

In this trance our bodies can betray us, and no more so than in the work of vibrato. The vibrating forearm suddenly promises to release the tensions built up in chapters one and two, but it can be a false promise. Energy can flow away from the elbow; often the wrist begins to flex, further cutting off the secure transmission of energy from elbow to finger. The result of this short circuit is that the weakened hand may then begin pushing too hard on the string in order to recover strength; the fingers may lock on to the fingerboard beneath the string; movement then will become jerky rather than fluid. These concrete events are what may make a musician sound 'nervous' to an audience, even when the cellist is in the midst of performing technical feats.

Nerves have cost us the loss of coherent vibrating touch, and so the problem may seem simply a matter of learning to relax. At least it seemed so to me, aged thirteen and fourteen, when I suddenly lost control of my vibrato in concerts. By fifteen, I had discovered one simple way to trick my nerves: reading non-stop during the hours before concerts; the murder mysteries of Agatha Christie were particularly calming, and usually, but not always, took me out of myself. Once I'd found a way to deal with my own stage fright, I became more attuned to other dimensions of

resistance, as part of the expressive process.

From its origins, the cello was not a perfect machine. For reasons we still don't fully understand, the cellos made by late seventeenth-century makers have remained the greatest examples of the luthier's art, but even these are physically imperfect in sounding the E and F notes on the G string; though powerful instruments, they have a tendency to fracture these two tones into a kind of bleating noise like a sheep singing. To vibrate under these conditions risks an even worse sound. Yet when the cellist faces the instrument's limitations on the G string, carrying on despite the bleating sound, the result can be an immense physical release and feeling of freedom.

When I once performed the Schubert Cello Quintet with Jacqueline du Pré—she was barely adolescent at the time—she was gripped by a crisis of nerves until the famous moment in the first movement when the second cello becomes mired in this danger zone. Her F bleated for a fraction of a second, but then she conquered it; she began making a richly vibrant, generous sound; her body relaxed.

In the performing trance, physical resistance often heightens the musician's awareness of the music itself. For instance, in the Adagio of Beethoven's Cello Sonata Op. 102 No. 1, the cellist is called on to play octaves in the zone of strings closest to the pegbox; it's a perilous procedure because the cut of the fingerboard does not easily accommodate the stretched hand pushing down two strings at once. To vibrate the strings under these conditions is a challenge, but rising to that challenge often gives these octaves the urgency the score requires, while simultaneously calming down the nervous player.

What I'm describing is not a Romantic struggle with wood and gut impeding the Soul, rather an experience of which musicians themselves are mostly unconscious. At best, we use the word 'focus' to describe it: loss of focus equals loss of touch. The sense of control we have on stage is nothing like the freedom of the rehearsal studio, no return to the Garden where we play unselfconsciously without worrying about mistakes. Now hundreds or thousands of people are listening. Indeed, making a mistake on stage can be a signal to us to pay more bodily attention. There is a kind of dialogue between courting danger and feeling physically free which, on stage, keeps us focused.

By the time I'd entered the conservatory, I'd learned one further and larger thing about what happens when resistance is not faced squarely. If the whole arm ceases to serve the cellist—breaking secure contact between flesh, string and wood—the cellist's perceptions of her or himself performing can split in two. In one domain there is the ideal of what the music should sound like; in the other, awareness of the music as it actually sounds, sounds which are insufficient, and from which the musician withdraws. This is just what Du Pré remarked to me a few years after our performance of the Schubert Quintet—she had heard two musics that evening, one in her head where everything is beautiful and just right, and the other in her ears, neither right nor beautiful. For her, the divide did not last long; in fact it can be only a matter of a few moments in which the artist is aware the music doesn't sound as it should; then this divide disappears as the body takes over, the artist's feeling that it should sound differently fades away, and he or she again converts to the immediate sound.

Romanticism provided a misleading vocabulary for this divide; musical notations like 'innerlich' or 'geistlich' ('inwardly' or 'with soulful feeling') suggest the musician's soul will at a particularly expressive moment withdraw to higher realm than the physical. The musician's fingers remain, unfortunately, on strings. It's not intentions, desires and longings which matter on stage; only the concrete and objective counts, because only sound sounds. I don't know if there's a German word like *outerlichkeit*—'outwardness' but there should be. Paradoxically, it's just the physical fusion between wood, string and body which courts danger, which is alive to resistance in performing, that rouses listeners to feel a musician to be 'in' the music, in contrast to the performer who seems disconnected, though he may have beautiful dreams.

When we are 'in touch', as American slang puts it, we do not dwell in the Garden, conflict and danger-free. But no more is the performing stage a scene of exile; in the heightened trance-like state in which performing occurs, danger and being in touch become expressively inseparable. The resistance of physical objects and their sounds can challenge the body yet, in the paradox I've described, relax it as well, as in a successful vibrato. When performing well, every musician feels the poet Wallace Stevens's famous declaration, 'no truth but in things'. □

With thanks to Adrian Brendel

FRANK'S PLACE
Richard Williams

THE CAL-NEVA LODGE

Marilyn Monroe, Wingy Grober and Frank Sinatra at the Cal-Neva Lodge (above)

The doors to the showroom are locked now, the music long since gone. Outside, the mountain air is as clear and sweet as it must have been forty years ago, when this place briefly felt like the centre of the world. Sunlight still sparkles on the lake, although on this afternoon a thin mist veils the far shore, drifting in from some distant forest fire. Mountain jays come and go between the tall pine trees with a flash of blue-green plumage while the dark lines left by speedboats stripe the lake and the unhurried drone of a piston-engined seaplane fills the sky.

This is where a certain idea of America began to come apart, although the young couples don't know that as they self-park their Chevy pickups and Japanese SUVs under the pines. Carrying their luggage to the entrance of the Cal-Neva Resort, checking in at the desk, their minds are on an act of union. These days, the Cal-Neva specializes in weddings and honeymoons. For their nuptial rites, the couples can choose between a broad terrace, with a white wrought-iron gazebo and a marquee holding about a hundred guests, and a smaller indoor parlour where the chairs are covered in white satin bound with gold sashes. Clustered on the slope beneath the main building, where the pine bluff descends sharply to the water, small wooden bungalows await the honeymooners.

Once this was the setting for a grander dream. It was here, in a location overlooking Lake Tahoe, 8,000 feet above sea level and ringed by the peaks of the High Sierra, that the most celebrated entertainer of his time had glimpsed an illusion. In this retreat, the most glamorous and notorious and powerful figures in America would come together—his friends, under his roof. And that was exactly how it seemed to be, until the autumn evening when he looked across the water at the lights on the southern shore, and knew that the world he had made was over.

Frank Sinatra sang his final encore in the showroom of the Cal-Neva Lodge, as it was then known, on the evening of September 5, 1963. It was the last night of the season, before the place closed up for the winter. Three years earlier he had bought a share of the hotel and its casino, and he had worked hard and put a great deal of money—some of it his own—into improving its features, trying to create an environment in which he could entertain his friends and attract customers who wanted to share a life in the upper atmosphere. The place had a history, even then. Jack Kennedy knew it well; his father had supplied liquor to a previous owner, and received hospitality for himself and his family in return. Marilyn Monroe had been there many times, and would later stay there the weekend before her death, when Sinatra gave her sanctuary while she avoided an ex-husband. Sam Giancana, the boss of the Chicago Mafia, who shared a girlfriend with Kennedy, was a silent partner in the syndicate which, with Sinatra as its front man, had taken control of the hotel in 1960.

Sinatra had performed there often. Each July, at the beginning of the three-month season, he would sing for the opening week, and as the summer went on he would drop in to make guest appearances. But he hadn't been expecting to appear there at all on this particular evening. It was Labor Day weekend and he had been in Las Vegas, showing up for Dean Martin's opening at the Sands, when he heard the news that inspectors from the Nevada Gaming Board had arrived at the Cal-Neva, looking for the evidence that would finally establish his links with organized crime, the culmination of a campaign stretching back to the opening of his FBI dossier in 1943.

When he arrived at the hotel from Reno airport, the first thing he did was to order the inspectors to get out. Then he elbowed aside Vic Damone, the scheduled attraction, and took the microphone. The audience was ecstatic, unaware of the anger that lay behind his sudden appearance. He already knew that when he checked out of his bungalow in the hotel grounds the following morning, he would be checking out of a project that he had believed would embody the finest things in his life, and his highest aspirations. That much was obvious to him. What he could not know, and probably did not even suspect, was that he was also saying goodbye to a whole world, one he had helped to create, one in which he had come to feel invulnerable.

Founded in 1927, the Cal-Neva took its name from the fact that it sits squarely on the border between California and Nevada. The state line bisects Lake Tahoe itself on a south-to-north axis before running up the hillside bordering the shoreline and through the hotel's old main lounge, where its existence is marked by a dark line painted across the wooden floor. In the old days it was said that guests could violate the Mann Act—which forbids a man from transporting an under-age girl across a state line for immoral purposes—without even leaving the premises. Nowadays its physical aspect is unchanged, from the striking porch, which echoes the steep-pitched roofs of A-frame barns, to the wooden bungalows set in the pines above a corner of the lake known as Crystal Bay.

Over the mountains and across the desert in Las Vegas, an eight-hour drive away, recent history has been erased. No trace remains of the Sands, the Dunes, the Desert Inn, the Flamingo, the Thunderbird and the other pioneering casino-hotels that made Las Vegas's name in the days when the gangland strategists could commission space-age architecture and pay the bills with money illegally borrowed from the pension fund of America's biggest labour organization, Jimmy Hoffa's Teamsters Union. Those places bit the dust when the big corporations moved into town, supplanting the old-time racketeers and taking the hookers off the street and turning the Strip into a series of giant theme parks—Paris, France; Venice, Italy; Luxor, Egypt; New York, New York—aimed at a family audience.

But Las Vegas hadn't really existed until the visionary mobster Benjamin 'Bugsy' Siegel built the lavishly appointed Flamingo hotel and casino in 1948. The result of Siegel's percipience was to raise the town's standing and render the early casinos obsolete almost overnight, but his overspending on the decor and the facilities upset his associates to such a degree that all his far-sightedness got him was shot dead one afternoon in his girlfriend's house in Los Angeles. There are no plaques in Vegas commemorating his contribution. The town that spread across the desert floor like a neon stain was always too busy making money to spare the time to develop a sense of its own history. The past was rolled up behind it in a process of continuous renewal. If it found itself in need of history, it borrowed and recreated it—a Sphinx, for example, standing outside the black glass pyramid of the Luxor, is twice the size of the original, which was not impressive enough for the Nevada desert. Only when the Sands itself, the last of the line, was demolished in 1997 to make way for a recreation of the Grand Canal and St Mark's Square did a few people begin to regret the disappearance of buildings that had also provided an accurate reflection of the time and the culture in which they had once prospered; an American, rather than Venetian, way of life.

Tahoe was a very different proposition. The summer home of the Washoe tribe, the lake was discovered by white men in 1844, when Kit Carson, the great Indian scout, led a group of pioneers through the mountains. Four years later the Comstock Lode was discovered in Virginia City, prompting the arrival of hordes of prospectors bent on mining the silver. Logging camps were set up around the lake, to strip the hills of pine for use in the mines and on the new railroad. Loggers liked to gamble their pay, and parlours were set up to accommodate their pastime. Over the course of a century and more, even after the ending of the silver standard had sent the prospectors elsewhere, Tahoe and the towns surrounding it developed a sense of historical continuity. And so the Cal-Neva, which would have been blown up years ago in Vegas, remains more or less unaltered today.

It was built in 1927 by Robert Sherman, a San Francisco real estate developer who wanted somewhere to entertain prospective clients. The original lodge was a sturdy rustic guest house built from split pine logs; at the rear, overlooking the lake, he placed a long sun deck and a swimming pool. When the hotel burned down one night in 1937 it was rebuilt in thirty days by 500 men, working round the clock. Its next owner, Norman Biltz, a well-connected developer who became known as the 'Duke of Nevada', added more guest bungalows between the granite outcrops below the main building and expanded the casino, encouraged by the state's decision in 1931 to remove almost all legal restraints on gambling. In its advertising, the hotel called itself 'The Lady of the Lake'. From Biltz it passed through other hands, including those of Elmer 'Bones' Remmer, a prominent San Francisco gangster, and eventually into the stewardship of Bert 'Wingy' Grober, a restaurateur with interests in Philadelphia and Miami, where the East Coast bootlegger Joe Kennedy had kept him supplied during the years of Prohibition.

Wingy Grober, whose withered left arm earned him his nickname during his New Jersey schooldays, liked entertaining his liquor supplier's large family at the Cal-Neva. By 1960, when Kennedy's eldest son was running for president of the United States, they had become regular guests. But Grober was already preparing to sell his interest, and documents submitted to the Nevada gaming control board on September 20 of that year revealed that a new group of investors had bought his fifty-seven per cent stake in the operation. The largest new holding, twenty-five per cent, was in Sinatra's name. The remainder was shared between Hank Sanicola, the singer's boyhood friend and his business manager since his days with the big bands; Dean Martin, a fellow member of the so-called Rat Pack, who took what seemed like a token slice, a mere three per cent; and Paul 'Skinny' D'Amato, who had run the 500 Club in Atlantic City, a favourite of Sinatra's, before moving west to take over the manager's role at the Cal-Neva. Later it became clear that part of Sinatra's share was really owned by Giancana, who had brokered the deal with Grober but, as an accredited gangster, was barred from casino ownership.

In one sense, it seemed a curious choice for Sinatra to make. His parallel but much smaller financial involvement in the Sands—he had bought a nine per cent stake in 1953—made sense because that was where he and Martin and Sammy Davis Jr and the other members of the Rat Pack, Joey Bishop and Peter Lawford (Jack Kennedy's brother-in-law), had set up their headquarters, attracting thousands of fans anxious to witness the joshing, boozing, backslapping spectacle of the show they called the Summit Conference. His memories of the Cal-Neva, by contrast, included the night nine years earlier when, driven to distraction by his affair with Ava Gardner, he had tried for the first time to commit suicide.

On August 30, 1951 he and Ava had gone to dinner with Sanicola and his wife at the Christmas Tree, a popular restaurant which still sits beside the state highway that crosses Mount Rose, a thirty-minute drive from the lake. Sinatra and Gardner both drank too much that night, and talked too much, too. When she said something about having had an affair with a bullfighter during a shoot in Spain the previous year—an affair of which Sinatra had suspected her at the time, but which she had never previously acknowledged—one of their regular screaming matches broke out. Gardner's response was to get into her car and head straight back to Los Angeles, a drive of ten or eleven hours. She had hardly opened the door of her house in Pacific

Palisades when the phone rang. It was Sanicola, telling her that Sinatra had taken an overdose of sleeping pills. She flew straight back and, with the doctors hovering around his bedside, they were reconciled.

Gardner eventually concluded that it had been less of a genuine suicide attempt than an unusually dramatic attempt to reawaken her affections. It came, after all, at a time in their professional lives when she was unquestionably the dominant partner. She had a big new contract with MGM and had successfully disentangled herself from marriages to Mickey Rooney and the bandleader Artie Shaw. By contrast, Sinatra had lost his bobby-soxer audience—when he played the Paramount Theatre in Times Square that year, the scene of his greatest early triumph exactly a decade earlier, his press agent found that he could no longer even bribe teenagers to mob the entrance for the benefit of news cameras—and he was still caught up in the wreck of his marriage to his childhood sweetheart, Nancy Barbato, the mother of his three children. If he was not the love of Ava's life, she was certainly that of his. The devasting version of 'I'm a Fool to Want You' that he recorded in March 1951 left no one in any doubt of it.

At the time he bought the Cal-Neva, Sinatra and his friends had been working hard for Jack Kennedy during the long and closely contested presidential campaign of 1960. Skinny D'Amato and Sam Giancana helped out by delivering votes that swung crucial wards in West Virginia and Chicago away from Kennedy's opponent, Richard Nixon. Their involvement was purely pragmatic, and they received their first repayment when the new president refused the early opportunity of a rapprochement with Fidel Castro, who had ejected Meyer Lansky and his casino-operating associates from their profitable operations in Havana the previous year. Sinatra's interest, on the other hand, was largely romantic. He had been a lifelong Democrat, thanks to his mother, a prominent activist in the New Jersey wards; in particular he had been an unflinching advocate of civil rights even when such a stance might have cost him popularity. And he had always loved proximity to real power, whether that of politicians or gangsters. In 1947, when he was thirty and just past the apex of his early success with the wartime teenage generation, he had accepted the offer of a trip to Havana. There, at the Hotel

Nacional, he socialized with the exiled Mafia boss Lucky Luciano and various figures from the FBI's most-wanted list: Santo Trafficante, Frank Costello, Albert Anastasia and others. When J. Edgar Hoover provided American newspapers with details of the trip gathered by his bureau's agents, the revelation precipitated Sinatra's decline in popularity. It was a swift and painful fall, from which the recovery was long and arduous. However successful he became, he had never quite succeeded in ridding himself of the taint. But the opportunity to pal around with a new president would certainly make a difference, and the chance to bring the two worlds together took the game to another level altogether.

After the 1960 election, Sinatra produced the pre-inaugural gala in Washington. Leonard Bernstein and Mahalia Jackson were among the performers, and Sinatra himself brought the house down with 'That Old Jack Magic'. By this time he had also introduced Kennedy to two women, Marilyn Monroe and Judith Campbell Exner, and had stood back to watch the sparks fly. After Monroe and JFK were both dead, their affair would take on a mythic dimension. But the president's liaison with Judy Exner, while more earthbound, was where the true danger turned out to reside. Exner was Giancana's girlfriend. Thanks to Sinatra's instincts as a procurer, the same woman was sleeping with the boss of the Chicago Mob and the president of the United States. Reading his agents' reports on the comings and goings at the White House, the Cal-Neva, and various residences in Chicago and California, Hoover could hardly fail to notice Sinatra's achievement.

At the end of the summer of 1961, as Kennedy's presidency approached its first anniversary, there were changes at the Cal-Neva. Dean Martin, who disliked Giancana's involvement, sold his shares. The new partnership in Park Lake Enterprises Inc. consisted of Sinatra (270 shares), Sanicola (180), and Sanford Waterman (ninety shares). A Miami casino manager, Waterman had worked for Meyer Lansky in Havana and had been one of Wingy Grober's original Cal-Neva partners. Sinatra was the company president, Sanicola the secretary, and Waterman the treasurer. Skinny D'Amato, who had acted as the hotel's manager, was under investigation by the FBI and had faded into the background. Giancana's sub rosa involvement was nevertheless undiminished, and it was he who tried to repeat the formula used so often in Vegas of funding Sinatra's proposed $2.2 million refit by borrowing the money from the Teamsters' pension fund. This time, however, Hoffa refused to play along, deterred by Giancana's notoriety and perhaps by the hot breath of the FBI, which within a few years would succeed in getting him sent to prison for pension fraud. Instead, $1.5 million was borrowed from the Bank of Nevada, most of which went on installing a new showroom, luxury shops, and a helicopter landing pad on the roof.

In March 1962, shortly before the refitted Cal-Neva was due to open, Sinatra prepared himself for the greatest moment of all: as part of a tour of the West Coast, the president was going to spend two nights at his home in Palm Springs. In a fever of anticipation, Sinatra built new guest houses for the secret service men who would be part of the presidential entourage. He had new phone lines installed. Here, too, he built a helicopter pad. He ordered a commemorative plaque for the bedroom in which the president would sleep. He was thrilled, and he didn't care who knew it. As Giancana once remarked, the only trouble with Sinatra was that he couldn't keep his mouth shut. And then came the news that signalled the beginning of the end.

Robert Kennedy, appointed US Attorney-General by his brother, had embarked on his campaign against organized crime and J. Edgar Hoover had made him aware of Sinatra's role as the link between the president, Judy Exner and Giancana. Bobby Kennedy told his brother that it would be inappropriate for him to be the house guest of a man known to consort with mobsters. Peter Lawford, the First Brother-in-Law, was chosen to break the news, in a conversation which threw Sinatra into such a rage that he ended their friendship on the spot. What made it worse was that the president was still going to sleep over in Palm Springs, but at the home of Bing Crosby.

Now, as far as Sinatra was concerned, the state line that ran across the floor of the Cal-Neva might as well have been the San Andreas Fault. On the surface, his career had reached a new peak of success and influence. He had started his own record company, with considerable success. His records were as well received as the great works he had produced in the Fifties, and he was making more money from them. He was appearing in worthwhile films, such as

John Frankenheimer's *The Manchurian Candidate*, in which Sinatra's character, an army intelligence officer, tried to save the president of the United States from an assassin's bullet. On July 5 he reopened the Cal-Neva, taking the stage in the new Celebrity Showroom, which was filled to its capacity of more than 600 guests hungry for his ring-a-ding versions of 'I Get A Kick Out of You' and 'The Lady Is a Tramp'. Beneath the exuberance, however, an unstoppable entropy was at work.

A week before her death in August 1962, Marilyn Monroe spent a couple of nights at the Cal-Neva. Sinatra knew she was in a bad way. He was fond of her and, wanting to help, he put her up at one of the best bungalows. But two bad things happened during her stay. Joe DiMaggio, the former New York Yankees baseball star who was her ex-husband, turned up. Once he and Sinatra had been friendly, but that was before his ex-wife and the singer had begun an on-and-off affair which lasted throughout the late 1950s. It had started after the collapse of the Monroe–DiMaggio marriage and continued even through the actress's subsequent marriage to the playwright Arthur Miller, but it was something that DiMaggio could not accept. Now he had come to believe there was a chance that Monroe might remarry him. When he was told that there was no room for him at the Cal-Neva, he checked in at a motel across the street. Monroe needed to have her stomach pumped during her stay, after taking too many pills, which may or may not have been an accident. An FBI agent claimed that Giancana slept with her during this visit; such reports, however, were often the work of fantasists anxious to impress Hoover.

There was also trouble between the hotel's owners, and Sinatra's obsession with ploughing money into upgrading the facilities had provoked a disagreement with Hank Sanicola. While driving across the desert from Palm Springs to Las Vegas, the two old friends had started an argument which ended when Sinatra agreed to swap a chunk of his lucrative music publishing interests for Sanicola's entire holding in Cal-Neva. Once they had reached an agreement, so the story goes, Sinatra stopped the car and Sanicola found his own way to their destination.

But it was when the gaming board heard about Sam Giancana's visit to the hotel by the lake that the real trouble began. Until ten years earlier Nevada hadn't even had a gaming board. The tax authorities made a vague show of keeping a eye on the industry, but in truth there was nothing to stop a generation of mobsters across America from building their casinos in Las Vegas with money borrowed from Jimmy Hoffa's unwitting members, after which they skimmed the profits and took the cash back home to Miami, Chicago or Philadelphia. As Vegas prospered, however, it became evident that some form of regulation was necessary. Now here was Ed Olsen, the board's chairman, informing Sinatra that he had been told by the FBI that Giancana, one of the country's most notorious racketeers, had recently visited the Cal-Neva as the guest of the owner. Giancana had been in the company of his girlfriend, Phyllis McGuire, of the singing McGuire Sisters, who were due to fulfil a week's engagement in the showroom. As Olsen pointed out, Giancana was one of eleven men named in Nevada's 'black book', a select group of known racketeers who were not allowed to set foot on premises the state had licensed for gambling. But then, to make matters worse, Giancana had intervened in a drunken dispute between Phyllis and the sisters' road manager, and a brawl had developed in one of the bungalows. According to Olsen's informant, Sinatra and his valet, George Jacobs, had helped Giancana give the road manager a severe beating. Giancana left the hotel the next morning, but the damage had been done. Eighteen months earlier, his closeness to the mobster had cost Sinatra his most valuable relationship, ending his access to the power vested in a president. Now it threatened to deprive him of the licence that had given him power in his own right.

He denied that Giancana had been his guest. He denied any knowledge of a fight. He told Olsen that if he persisted with the investigation, he had better watch out. But even before he reached Lake Tahoe that night, his mind was made up. Enough was enough. Before they could get him, he'd get out.

A few days later the board issued charges against him and gave him three months to sell his share in the operation. On October 9, however, he took pre-emptive action by announcing that he was divesting himself of all his holdings, not only in the Cal-Neva but also in the Sands, worth more than $3 million all told. That day, too, his operator's licence was revoked.

Warner Brothers purchased his holdings as part of a deal in which two thirds of his record company, Reprise Records, also changed hands. Jack Warner, it was said, had been the most influential voice in Sinatra's decision to get out of the casino business, warning him not to do any further damage to his public image. Sinatra made a million dollars' profit and was given a deal for his film production company. But the insult of having his right to operate a casino taken away was a wound that never healed. 'To say that he had worked hard to make the Cal-Neva a success would not begin to approximate his efforts,' his daughter Nancy said many years later. But the world of which his dreams were a part began to disintegrate the day he left, taking the high rollers and the big-name entertainers with him. A few months later the Beatles arrived in America, changing rather more than just the sound of popular music. For a while, no one would want the bel canto phrasing, the tailored witticisms of Broadway-trained lyricists, or the smooth, sophisticated mode of presentation that went with them. The era was over. Eventually it would mean that even he had to change his musical approach, in the process exchanging the civilized applause that once signalled the end of 'Violets for Your Furs' or 'Glad to Be Unhappy' for the raucous ovations that would greet the shamelessly importunate climax of 'My Way'. He changed his politics, too. His rejection by Kennedy sent him into the arms of the Republicans and when, in 1980, he produced another inaugural gala in Washington, it was for Ronald Reagan. Within weeks the new president had repaid the favour. When Sinatra applied to have his Nevada casino operator's licence returned, Reagan wrote a letter of warm recommendation to the state's gaming commission. It worked, but it was twenty years too late.

The effects were also felt locally. After Sinatra left the hotel in 1963, its fortunes tumbled. His departure depressed the economy of the whole of the lake's north shore; the golden aura had gone with him. Over the next two decades the Cal-Neva passed through many pairs of hands, some of them dirtied by allegations of financial improprieties related to gambling. Eventually the north shore's fortunes revived, but although plots that could have been had for $20,000 in Sinatra's day were going for $2 million a quarter of a century later, the Cal-Neva had been just about given up for dead. It was revived in 1985 when a developer from Southern California and his associates paid $10 million for the property, persuaded the state to give them a fresh gaming licence, and began a lengthy restoration of some of its oldest features.

The stretch of land down to the shore, where one previous owner built a steel jetty and lined up half a dozen speedboats for the use of guests, has been sold. The Joseph Magnin store and Sy Devore's menswear shop, brought in by Sinatra, are long gone, replaced by a beauty parlour and a florist serving the bridal trade on which the hotel now depends. In the showroom, where Ella Fitzgerald, Mickey Rooney, Keely Smith, Tommy Sands and Trini Lopez once performed, the stage provides a platform for the speeches of the bride's father and the best man. In the casino there are kidney-shaped blackjack tables and a single craps table and slot machines and video poker and, in the evenings, a real poker game in a downstairs room, but the ambience is hardly the one Sinatra had in mind in the days when a high-roller would drop a grand on a single hand and casually raise a finger to summon another complimentary cocktail. Today the tables are occupied by vacationers and honeymooners who don't bother changing out of the T-shirts, shorts and trainers in which they arrived. They wander along the corridors, pausing occasionally to glance at framed photographs of Sinatra, Monroe and JFK, each one also available in a small laminated print, with a magnetized strip on the back, for affixing to the refrigerator door back home. A rack in the gift shop contains second-hand copies of some of Sinatra's finest albums. *Frank Sinatra Sings for Only the Lonely*, his 1957 masterpiece, is priced at ten dollars, in the original mono and only slightly distressed. When the hotel's most famous proprietor died in May 1998, a day-long wake was held in the showroom. A single red rose was placed on the grand piano and his records were played while people from the surrounding hotels and casinos came by to reminisce and to drink a special blue cocktail— 'For his eyes,' a spokesman for the management said. ☐

BRANDY
Philip Hensher

The hotel room was dark and cool. The shutters were closed. Outside, in the warm garden, the early evening birdsong was carrying on; more distantly, the country town noise of hooters, klaxons, cars left idling in the main street. If you closed your eyes, and concentrated, you would probably be able to hear the siren of the town's only ambulance. You might even, if you listened hard, be able to tell it from the pitch of the police car.

I couldn't tell the difference, to be honest. Once, my mother told me that the *ni-naw* of the police, the ambulance, the fire engine were quite different. That was in England, of course. Each had its own pitch, its own note, and if you listened, and remembered the note, you could shut your eyes and hear what emergency was coming for you. For weeks afterwards, I listened in the streets, but could never tell, not reliably.

I tried again now.

Two, maybe three sirens. Not English noises, but a smooth upward glissando, crossing and recrossing. Two of them; that was right. Police; ambulance. They sounded the same to me. I shut my eyes. They still sounded the same. Far away, but not far enough.

The doors were shut, and the windows. Something was fleeing the room, flying from me as fast as it could run, running through walls, through glass, through shutters. I could feel it. I sat there on the edge of the bed with my eyes shut, listening, trembling. I waited for it—whatever it might be—to go. And it was as if something turned, just once, and said nothing, and looked at me, trembling, and left without saying goodbye.

Afterwards, when I understood that music had gone from my life, I had to think what, in all truth, my life consisted of. It was a serious question. Those sudden absences present the question, and, somehow, some answer must be produced. Something big disappears, and life goes on. What kind of life? Sometimes, half your life depends on an external fact, an external fact you thought would always be there; and sometimes, against your trust and expectations, the fact just goes, leaving you with half a life. Or, perhaps, with none.

In five minutes, half my life went from me; quite suddenly, there, in the South of France, in a summer in the middle of the 1990s. It took me a week to realize exactly what had happened; at the time, there was too much blood, too much *ni-naw* coming at me, too much to walk away from. Music went from me, in five minutes, never to return; five minutes, there, in the South of France, in the middle of the 1990s, when music was the last thing I was thinking of. It took me a week to realize that, from now on, music would always be the last thing I would think of. It had been half my life, and now it was gone.

The abrupt disappearance is something many people are familiar with. In my own way, I knew about it. That summer was two years after my lover left me. I met him when I was twenty-one; he left me when I was thirty. That was odd, and terrible, too; because for a decade, my concept of myself was as Philip-and-Maurizio. At thirty, you know you are not the same person you were when you were twenty. Your lover leaves, and you have two big wrong ideas of what sort of person you are now going to be; the person, the stranger, you were ten years ago, or the remnants of a man left when the pillar of your life announces, out of the blue, that he has met somebody else. Neither will quite do.

An ordinary story, but mine, I think, isn't an ordinary story. What left, there, in St-Rémy-de-Provence, wasn't a lover, but music. And when a lover leaves, you console yourself with the truth that these things happen; you were an adult before, and you are an adult now. Music left me, and that doesn't happen. It came to me before I could speak, and when it left me, I did not know if there was anything left, there in my head. It was all music; it had all been music; and I did not know if there was anything left there to put back together.

How did it start?
It is Bonfire Night, 1971, or perhaps 1972. I have just learned to tell the time. There is a clock over the piano, and I know what time it says. It says four o'clock. Outside, it is getting dark; there is a rich blue in the sky, and I connect the two facts. It is getting dark, and it is four o'clock in the afternoon.

This is not my house. It is the house of a girl I play with, who lives three streets away. There is a fire in the grate, dying down, purring away like a sleepy cat. The grown-ups come in and out, but they are leaving us alone, returning to their other world.

Philip Hensher

I have no real idea about the difference between one grown-up and another. Sometimes, walking to school with my mother, she meets someone she knows, and stops to talk. It always seems like a very long time. I don't listen. Afterwards, I don't remember anything she says. I stand there and look up at her, talking and talking. I have a blue duffel coat, which is tightly buttoned up. My mittens are attached to each other by a piece of elastic which runs up the sleeves and behind my neck. Sometimes the piece of elastic rides up, and presses against the back of my head.

The grown-ups are in another world. I don't know about them. A mother comes in and turns the light on. It is four o'clock. The world is getting dark. Out of the window, there is the same place we live; there is the same picture of gardens, running up and down against each other. I can see the high weather vane of the house four houses from my house. But it is a different picture, because this is a different house. Out there it is quiet. A bird flies through the gloom. You can't see anyone in any of the gardens. I stand there for a minute.

The other people in the room are people I go to school with. One is the girl whose house this is. Another is a boy called Robert, I do not know if he is my friend or not.

They are here, and two other girls. It occurs to me that it is now time for *Junior Showtime*. I don't know what to say if I want to watch it. And then I don't know if I want to watch it at all.

One of the girls goes to the piano, and very casually starts to play something on it. She plays for a minute, and then stops and gets down. Another of the girls goes over and plays something else. When she stops, she says to everyone, 'I don't like Miss Hartley. I don't like her at all.' The others all agree. I don't know what they are talking about. I've never heard of Miss Hartley. There isn't a teacher at school called that. 'She made me play this,' the first girl says, and goes back to the piano, and plays something. 'I played that,' Robert says. 'Years ago. Before Miss Hartley even.'

It seems like a secret they all have, that they all go to Miss Hartley. She teaches them the piano, it seems. After a while, they all stop playing what they can play, and come and sit down again. Perhaps they want to watch *Junior Showtime*, too. But nobody mentions it.

There is something I want to say. 'I can play the piano too,' I say. And I can. I go over to the piano and start to play the tune in my head, which is not a tune that anyone else has been playing. I play with my right hand and with my left. But something is not right. It does not sound like the music in my head. It sounds like a horrible noise, making no sense at all. I only play for a second, and then stop. Something is wrong. I don't know what. I stop.

No one says anything. They don't even seem surprised. Outside, there is a single huge explosion in the sky. I look at the clock, and see that now, it is five o'clock. Outside it is completely black. Soon it will be night, and tonight is fireworks night.

So there is music and music. It is not easy, after all.

In my room at home, there is a toy piano. It is made of plastic, and the keyboard is coloured ten different colours. You have to sit on the floor to play it, not on a chair. Inside the pink thing, there is something which chimes, bright chiming sounds. It's easy. I sit in my room, and concentrate, and think of a tune, and begin to play. The bells obey you. You think hard of a tune, and press down one bright finger after another, and the tune in your head is echoed, distantly, by the vague nice noise.

I know how to do that, but not, it seems, this. In someone else's house, I go over again and say, 'I can play the piano, too,' and begin to play, the music in my head as strong as I can make it. But the keys are only black and white. They make the noise they want to make. They don't make anything like the noise in my head, and soon you have to stop.

So there is music and music. It is not easy, after all. It is not a machine you press a button to make work. It is a big thing. Hard to know how big. You can't, it seems, just decide to do it. It is bigger than a pink plastic thing on the floor of your room, and bigger than your will. Perhaps it is like a person, who will do what he wants to do, and not, always, what you want him to do. Perhaps it is bigger even than this. I don't know yet. I don't know when I will know, just how big it is.

I don't know a great deal about my family. Most of what I know, I've discovered in the last year or two. Now and again, the telephone rings on a Sunday morning, often before ten. An unusual thing; most people assume that I'll be lying in, an assumption I don't correct. It is nice for a writer to have a few undisturbed hours in the morning, once a week. The only person who calls is a distant cousin in Australia, a gentleman also called Hensher, who is devoting his retirement to researching his family tree, and mine; the name is unusual, and his searches on the internet have directed him towards a Swedish furniture company; his brother, the Australian professor; and me. His diligent researches are all new to me; I always assumed that my name was German (Germans, on the other hand, often think, on the basis of my name, that I am probably Jewish). It turns out that we are descendants of French Huguenots called Hennechard, who came over after the Revocation of the Edict of Nantes.

I enjoy my distant cousin's phone calls, but he has quite failed to turn up anyone of any great interest in my ancestry, and my sense of my father's family is roughly as it was. My father, I always thought, was rescued by music, and the long transoceanic discussions of Huguenots and eighteenth-century manufacturers of clay pipes has little to contribute. What matters in my family is this: my father learned the piano. Self-improvement mattered then; and self-improvement meant culture. My grandmother acquired sets of novels; she encouraged my father to paint; she made him learn the piano, and later, the French horn. Music was good for you, because it was culture; and you needed to learn it, and not just learn to like it, because that was work, which was good for you too.

My father was born in 1934 in London. His parents were from London, too, and were born at the turn of the century. Their families always lived in the East End of London. Some of them were furniture makers. One distant grandfather was a waterboatman, who fell overboard and drowned. In the dense London particular, the other boatmen probably heard the splash, but could not see far enough to rescue him. He died at twenty-four, leaving a wife and a baby to shift as well they could. His patents were written on vellum, against precisely this accident, and they survived intact to identify the body. I have the patents, identifying everything that is left of my great-great-great-grandfather.

My grandmother had three brothers and sisters. One died as a baby, another died at twelve or thirteen. Her brother was a sickly baby, and went on to have poor health all his life. Princess Mary of Teck, later Queen, was visiting the hospital where he was born, and stopped at the end of the bed where my great-grandmother and my infant great-uncle were lying, and inspected the child. 'He won't live,' she said, and moved on. That was in 1909. My great-uncle was still telling the story at the turn of the next century.

I don't know anything about my grandfather's family, where my name comes from. He was called Sid. He married my grandmother in the 1920s, in the East End. They migrated some time in the 1920s to the healthier air of the South London municipal suburbs. They must have felt the urge to improve quite strongly. They had a piano for my father to learn on, and bought cheap, complete sets of the novels of H. G. Wells and Dickens. My grandmother is always said to have loved Dickens. I read the same set from beginning to end between the ages of twelve and seventeen. You could tell the books she had read, and the books she had not opened, by the crack as you turn back the cover. And by the smell. The ones she had not read had a quite different smell from those she had, and I guess she liked the early ones, the funny ones, and was quickly bored by *Our Mutual Friend*. It has been opened, but she didn't read it: didn't get much beyond the first chapter, the one about the waterboatman fishing things out of the river, talking of death. I suppose, reading in the late 1970s and early 1980s, that her enthusiasm for Dickens dried up roughly halfway through, but she did well. My father was born in 1934. He plays the piano and reads and goes to art galleries. And so do I.

My mother's family came from the North. Her mother had ten brothers and sisters in Carlisle. They were a Salvation Army family; my great-grandmother was blinded in a riot against General Booth's movement. A stone was thrown, and hit her, who never again found her faith seriously tested. My grandfather was an insurance agent when he married my grandmother. Afterwards, he decided to take his vocation to the Salvation Army and worked for them, for no money. They had three daughters. My mother was the middle of the three. They moved around the North of England as the Army required, never settling or owning anything much. Finally, they settled in Kingston on Thames, where my grandfather died. My grandfather died, I suppose, young. He was playing the organ in the Citadel, which is the term for the Salvation Army's place of worship.

My mother and father met at the Salvation Army. My mother was in it from birth. My father joined because he wanted to play a brass instrument, and the Salvation Army's bands were famously good. He played the euphonium, I think. My mother sang, or, as the Army's peculiar terminology had it, was a songstress. Music runs through my family, on both sides, and drowning, too.

I can do odd bits of the terminology now. Songstress; Citadel; promoted to Glory. That last one is what they say when somebody dies.

There are photographs of my parents' wedding, in 1959. My mother is wearing a knee-length wedding frock. My father is in Salvation Army uniform. He looks very much as I do now.

I go to piano lessons now that I am seven. My sister goes, too. She started first. Miss Stanton lives near the station, and she teaches first my sister, then me, in a room which is full of different instruments. There is a set of drums. There is a flute, which my sister has tried to play. I have tried, too, but I can't make a noise on it. 'It's just like blowing across the top of a bottle,' Miss Stanton says. I can't do it.

Mostly, we play the piano. Now, I can read music, and can't remember what it was like before I could. Every week we have a piece to learn, and some scales. I sit with Miss Stanton, and she says, 'Yes, yes, good, yes, slowly, yes, very good, yes, yes.' She says this even when I make mistakes. At the end of the piece, she takes out a sheet of paper with gold and silver stars on it, and sticks one into the book. The rest of the week, I play the piano at home, for half an hour before tea. I never want to practise, but my mother tells me to, and I do.

Sometimes at the weekend my father plays the piano. He has a big brown book with all Beethoven's piano sonatas in it, which he plays from. He plays Chopin, too. He goes upstairs, sometimes, and practises the French horn. It is like listening to someone singing on their own. The colour of the French horn and the golden noise it makes are the same thing but not the same thing. It is like hot meaning two different things without anyone noticing.

My father, I discover, plays in an orchestra. One day, we get in the car and go with him and my mother to the Fairfield Hall. He is wearing a black suit and a white shirt and a black bow tie, and has his French horn in its odd-shaped case. My mother and my sister and I sit in the audience and listen to the music they are playing. In the first half, there is the *Carnival of the Animals*. The lion, the donkey, the elephant, the birds, the fish. We sit and listen. The piece is turning notes into animals, and I forget that my father is up there somewhere, because it is turning people into music, too. Afterwards, there is Mozart. I know who Mozart is. It is not anywhere near as good— it is just notes, one after the other, for forty minutes—and I am glad when it is over.

After the concert, we are standing with my father and mother in the hall. My father is talking to someone, another grown-up. In his hand there is his French horn in its case, with its curious angles. Someone calls 'Ray' and he turns, too suddenly, and the thing swings right into someone's knee. It is sharply angled and hits them hard. My father thinks this is the funniest thing ever, and laughs even while he is apologizing.

In my parents' house, as far back as I can remember, there is a grand piano; above the keys, written in languid pressed gold *Jugendstil* lettering, is the legend *Gebr. Zimmermann Leipzig*. Underneath the Leipzig piano, in a weirdly shaped case, like a black drooping water lily, is my father's French horn. There is another memory of my childhood; the noise of my father in the dining room, warming up with arpeggios, C major, stretching up two octaves like a yawn and then closing again, C sharp, D, E flat… Opening up and then closing down, rising up the scale by degrees until it gets too high, the top note cracks with a pip and, warmed up, he settles down to Schumann, to Strauss, to Mozart. I am sitting, two rooms away, probably with a book and not really listening; only when he starts on the finale of a Mozart concerto, because two of them begin with the same seven notes, and, enchantingly, you never know until the eighth note which of the two concertos it is going to be.

One day, a dull afternoon, I wander over to the piano. I haven't touched it for two or three years now. This is a different house. When we moved, the piano lessons came to an end and have not been resumed. The house is empty. I open up the piano stool, not really knowing what I am looking for, but there, at the bottom of the pile is the old piano tutor I learned from. It's more to strike a funny pose than for anything else, but I put it grandly on the music stand and sit at the keyboard like a cartoon virtuoso. The book is open at a piece called 'The Waves'; I start to play, C, E, G, C, G, E... The left-hand part is harder; that clef, I can't remember so easily how to read it, but I stop and go back and work out what the first note is, then the second, then the third. I play, very slowly, picking out each note one by one, almost entranced, going back and starting again. Each time I go back it is a little better. The afternoon goes on, with me and 'The Waves', and after some time—I don't know how long—the door of the dining room opens, and my mother is standing there. I hadn't heard the front door opening. I am embarrassed, as if caught out doing something shameful, but she doesn't say anything; she just smiles, and goes out, shutting the door quietly. For a moment, I stop playing, and read the paragraph, the encouraging introduction written at the top of the piece. 'Have you ever seen the sea?' it says. 'Do you remember what it is like?' That is absurd, I think, not understanding that the book I am playing from is written for Americans.

I play the piece, again and again; at first only when no one else is in, but then not caring; and then wanting people to hear, hear this marvellous music under my hands. 'The Waves' is the only piece I want to play, and then it is not; then, there are other pieces, more music, more and more; volumes in the cupboard, all of Mozart, of Beethoven, of Schubert.

There is music, too, in the public library; shelves and shelves of it, and the long days stretch ahead of me. And then, suddenly, there are records too; records of music. That is all I want. There are books about music to be read: my aunt gives me a book called *The Lives of the Great Composers* by Harold C. Schonberg, and I read it, over and over again, reading about composers I haven't heard yet, learning what to think about pieces of music I haven't got out of the library yet.

Thinking about this time, now, I realize I have no sense of the passing of time: no idea whether this inward journey, this unexpected puberty lasted months or years. Some memories of the time are precise, but they are all memories of pieces of music, of the first time I heard something. Sometimes I preferred what my guide says about music to the music itself; I read, over and over again, a paragraph about Beethoven, a piece called the Grosse Fuge, a piece too difficult to play, and it was so clear in my head, huge and terrifying and echoing. After the Grosse Fuge I dreamed of, the real thing was a disappointment, scratchy, niggling, frantic. But sometimes the words and the music matched; sometimes, my guide told me that Schoenberg was terrifying; *The Rite of Spring* baffling and horrifying; and I listened, and it was exactly right. I discovered something all for myself, the magical day, the fifteenth time through, when the furious pace of battle and chaos, the whole great mass of *The Rite of Spring* suddenly changes: the day you are inexplicably lifted into the air, above the cavalry charge of the great orchestra, and see, all at once, the orders of battle, the dispositions, the controlling intelligence, and understand that here is something which will be there for the rest of your life.

I bought 'Pierrot Lunaire', and Webern's orchestral music, and Boulez's 'Le Marteau sans Maître' and listened to them, again and again and again, till, alone among the music lovers of the Western world, I could sing them from beginning to end. No one I knew would like this music; it made people leave the room; and that was good, because I wanted to be alone with music, more than anything.

B etween the ages of twelve and eighteen, I did nothing, it seems to me now, but write music. That must be an illusion; I must have gone to school and learned about the ordinary things; I had friends and learned about sex and boys, I had a religious phase lasting six months, I rode my bike and daringly got drunk on Guinness on my sixteenth birthday. I made desultory attempts to have sex with girls. There was a girl called Amanda and a girl called Susan, whom everyone called Crusher, and a girl called Margaret, who I think was properly in love with me—at any rate her attempts to console herself afterwards were energetic enough to land her with a baby at sixteen. I sat in the kitchen of a sympathetic girl called Miriam and told her that I was homosexual, and faked an anguish I didn't really feel. Several times, too, I hopefully said, late at night to a handsome boy, when we were alone, what everyone like me says and never really believes, that of course, everyone is basically bisexual, until one of them crossed the room and kissed me, and after that I never said anything so foolish ever again. All that faded, all that life, afterwards; it seemed, even at the time, like the sort of things that everyone does. What mattered was what I did, ceaselessly, in solitude; wrote music.

The creativity of children, how unstoppable it is, and how bad. I wrote and wrote, filling up books of manuscript paper with grandiose enterprises. A string quartet, strictly obeying Schoenberg's twelve-tone theory—or what I could gather of it from *The Lives of the Great Composers*. Then another, and a song cycle, *The Ship of Death*, for voice and five instruments, words by D. H. Lawrence; the beginnings of an opera, two movements of a symphony with voices (I planned five), a wind quintet, a solo cello piece called 'Le Visage Devenu Jeune'. It was something Proust says about the appearance of the grandmother after death: for a few dizzying days I had an idea of dozens of exquisite chamber pieces all based on Proust. There was so much more: a symphony for strings in twenty-three-part counterpoint, choral pieces, piano pieces ('Le Tombeau de Debussy'). I wrote and wrote, producing whole string quartets in a week, a symphonic movement in a month, entranced by the movement of the pen over the page, filled with amazement at the idea that if I wrote a B flat, just there, for the bassoon, and an A natural, just there, for alto flute, it would happen. You could make it happen. The notebooks filled, and I finished one piece and went on to the next thing; and all of it completely terrible.

It was only when I was seventeen that I discovered this. Before that, the ecstasy of creation obscured the simple question with the simple answer. Of course, no one had ever played anything that I had written. And this was odd, since many of my friends were musicians—I was playing double bass in a pretty good youth orchestra. Nothing, really, could have been easier than to have written a chamber piece for a few friends, and run through it; but I never suggested it. One day, my father said, quite abruptly, 'Wouldn't you like anyone to perform any of this stuff?' I thought; I couldn't see any argument against it, or one that could be brought out. I nodded. 'We could play one, I suppose,' he said, and drifted off cheerfully. He meant his orchestra, the local chamber orchestra. There was no reason why not. In the three weeks before this conversation, I'd been writing a piece for small orchestra; *Eventail*, on—'inspired by,' I would say, superciliously—a poem by Mallarmé. Why not? The title was from Mallarmé, after all.

There is nothing more awful than to sit in an audience and listen to a piece of music—your piece of music—and endure a countless series of realizations that what you have done is entirely without merit. The piece was ten minutes long, the hall was full. For ten minutes, to listen and think, 'Not that note: not that sound: not that tune: not that instrument,' and afterwards to have to endure kind reviews and the compliments of strangers and to say nothing in return, with no one to blame but yourself. In my head, I had been writing *Erwartung*; and now, as the orchestra did its patient best with my best efforts, I saw it for what it was. The audience applauded politely; the next day I got up, and the creative urge slowly trickled to a halt. After that evening I wrote a little more music, slowly, painfully, and kept seeing how dry and laboured it all was, how incompetent; and then, with relief, it was over. There is a tape of the piece, somewhere. I've never listened to it.

Perhaps then was the moment for music to come to an end for me, but it didn't; only the understanding, so strangely like relief, that it was not for me to create it. Looking back, the way my life would go was always evident; every piece I ever wrote was driven, in some way, by literature (pieces for cello trying to illustrate Proust! Orchestral pieces about Mallarmé!). I had a tendency, too, which only seems bizarre in retrospect, to sit down the second I'd written a piece and write the programme note for it; lavish with description, shameless with superlative, these accounts of what I wanted to do were driven by an urge almost stronger than the music itself, as if I only wrote the music in order to be able to describe it, as if what I most wanted to do was to descant on the fact of music, in prose.

Anyway, it finished; what was left was a view from the outside, the view of someone who loved and now, so strangely, understood music. That, too, could have proved an illusion, but I think it did not. I'd had to come to terms with the knowledge that I was not, as I had somehow always thought, remarkable; the evidence of *Eventail* (that title! those notes!) was so incontrovertible. But I only knew that with such certainty because, by now, I knew what music was. I understood it, somehow; it was simply that I could not do it myself. Music, kindly, benevolent, had shaken its head in sorrow and given me a consolation prize; a place in the audience.

The frustrated creativity of the audience: a powerful, embarrassing emotion. When I was a boy, I knew people who played imaginary guitars to heavy metal music; there are those who, alone, conduct their CD collection; I have sat next to people who have conducted the entire second act of *Tristan und Isolde* from the tenth row of the stalls. To listen is not always enough; and the act of applause is sometimes a display of the creative urge. When an opera-goer bellows *brava!* over the coda of Susanna's '*Deh vieni, non tardar*', that, too, is the creative urge; mine was to know, as a point of honour, the exact conclusion of the most advanced pieces of music, and be first to contribute appreciation, to feel a little glow of pride at knowing, unlike anyone else in the audience, the moment Stockhausen's *Gruppen* had come to an end.

An undignified, powerful urge. But if my direct creative involvement in music had come to an end, the creative desire had not gone away. I would never again produce a string quartet; I would never again know the direct ecstasy of manoeuvring through the double bass part of a Mahler symphony. Fragments of opportunity remained. I still played the piano, though I kept quiet about it; the pleasure of surprising friends with a late-night, thunderous rendition of 'L'Isle Joyeuse' all lay in the casual effrontery, and not in the accomplishment of the performance. But, overwhelmingly, my relationship with music had become one of thwarted creativity, my relations with it not far from the player of the air guitar. I could not make it happen, and in various ways, I could only make some mark on it. Cheering from the stalls, I was celebrating not what I had heard, but what I could myself once have done. There is no performance on earth as grand as the drawing-room performance of a frustrated conductor, swooning and beckoning over the record-player; and what I was discovering was that, if the splendour of that imagined music could not be conveyed through music, it could lead to other things. The music I had written as a boy, I had come to think, was not really music, but a prologue to a prose description. What had initially excited me about music had something, at least, to do with Harold C. Schonberg's rapturous descriptions. Music was closed to me; what began to open up was the imaginative recreation of its means.

For a while, I wrote music criticism, and discovered for myself how satisfying the rapturous recreation of the musical experience in prose could be. And then it went a little further, and I began a novel. Music is expressed in a series of formal structures—fugue, sonata form, rondo. Novels are not; their form is improvised, chaotic, loose. But even in fiction, there is form; and the only models I had were those of music. In my head, as I wrote, a chapter took the shape of a sonata form, the recapitulations and repetitions those of a Brahms symphony. A sequence fell naturally into the dominant key; a scene in the shape of the double exposition of a classical concerto. There were fugues, slow movements, modulations into the minor, codas, accelerandos and diminuendos. I was writing music again, and in the oddest of media, in prose. And that was enough.

It ended, like this.
In May 1997, I flew to Lyons, my bicycle stowed in the hold. I was between novels, as they say: I had been working too hard, and had taken two weeks off, to be on my own with my racing bicycle. In the panniers was a set of Chekhov's stories, and my oldest T-shirts. I would go southwards, hunting out satisfying mountains to climb, following the Rhône, discarding dirty clothes and finished volumes as I went, and in two weeks I would fly back, luggageless and tanned, with an arse like iron.

For a blissful week it went much like that, stopping each night at an expensive hotel, stuffing myself with foie gras, undoing, like Penelope, the good I had done during the day. In a week I reached St-Rémy-de-Provence, a town I had never been to, the perfect French town: the plane trees, the creamy baroque mansions, the pavement cafes. I unpacked in the beautiful hotel, and showered: it was five in the afternoon, the sun filtering through the deep green shutters. Somewhere there was the sound of a piano, a sound I always found happy: someone, somewhere, practising his scales. This was a good place.

I went down into the town to wander and find somewhere for dinner. There was a golden holiday atmosphere and I sat down on the terrace of a cafe. It was crowded. I ordered a brandy. Not my usual drink, but I felt like it: it was the sort of thing the *peloton* would drink at the end of a hard day in the *Tour de France*. Chekhov resting on my lap, I settled down to some agreeable eavesdropping. The couple next to me, late-middle-aged holidaymakers, were discussing the next day's outing with guide and maps; their accent was Swiss, a leisurely way of talking I always liked since, at seventeen, I went with an orchestra to Montreux. The brandy came, and, lost in naive pleasure, I watched the beginning of the town's evening parade.

In ten minutes, I finished my brandy and thought of ordering another. No: I felt like walking a little. I paid, affecting to have a little difficulty with the money for the purpose of flirting with the handsome waiter, and got up to leave. I put one foot in front of the other: another step, another, another: I took seven steps, away from the cafe, and then everything came to an end.

That noise I never want to hear again in my life, and in my head I hear it every day. Behind me, a sort of mechanical whinnying, and, as if in some kind of antiphonal response, the sound of forty human voices, rising in a glissando, and then—

That I cannot describe, cannot orchestrate, cannot recreate for you. The sound of metal on metal and engine grinding into flesh. How long it went on I do not know, and afterwards, a silence before the sound of running, towards me. I turned round, and in a pantomime transformation, the terrace of the cafe was not what it was. In the middle of it, planted, was a van: the sort of van French farmers drive, and everything else was still. There was blood. I made a step, irresolutely, in the direction I had been going, and then turned back, and with the same seven steps was where I had been sitting. There was a man lying there, thrown from the table, his broken face upwards. I knelt down by him. Don't move him. Don't leave him. I put my hands to his face and his eyes looked into mine. I saw them palpating, dilating, closing, his eyes fixed on mine. I put my knees around his face, and looked into his upside-down features, and began to talk. '*Ne bougez pas—je reste ici—c'est rien—*' I took his hand— '*les ambulances*'—Christ, was that the word, I could only think of

Krankenwagen—'seront ici—tout va bien—monsieur, je vous en prie—n'ayez pas peur—ne bougez pas—'

And then he died. I saw him die, like the smallest of movements. He was the Swiss man: I had listened to him, talking about the rest of his holiday, and he had died in my lap. I got up and tried to turn away without looking. I had already seen too much.

The next day I was in London. I left my bicycle and luggage where they were, in St Remy—that, I can't explain, but there was no argument to be had—and took four trains, and in fifteen hours I was back in London. I felt nothing: no, that's not right. In the days immediately afterwards I was seized with an inexplicable and frightening exhilaration, a frantic energy. I telephoned everyone I knew and told them the story, unable to stop talking. It was probably a week before things started to go wrong.

For a couple of months, I had had tickets for the Vienna Philharmonic at the Royal Festival Hall. I took the tube to Embankment and got out. It was a pleasant evening and I walked over Hungerford footbridge. Halfway across, I suddenly stopped, and looked down at the river, and a thought, an alien evil thought came to me: *You could throw yourself into the river, now.* It stopped me in my tracks. I am not suicidal by temperament, and I was not—I did not feel—depressed at that moment. It felt like a thought from outside. I walked on, confused.

The Vienna Philharmonic is my favourite orchestra, and I settled down in my seat and prepared for a favourite piece, Stravinsky's *Le Baiser de la Fée*. The musicians filed on, the first violin, the conductor. I have the programme somewhere. The piece began, with that familiar sinuous tune, and I started to listen. It went on, but I couldn't hear it. I was in the middle of a row, and suddenly I was sweating. The tutti began. Something was wrong here. I tried again, and for a while the feeling went, as if I had pushed a buoyant object beneath the surface of a black lake. Next to me, my friend was looking at me oddly. I looked down, and my hands were white, gripping my knees. There was something terrible here. I tried once more, and then, like nausea, a wave of terror came over me, and, having no alternative, I stood up and stumbled the long puzzled journey through the concert-goers, clattering down the stairs, and out.

It took me a while to understand that that was the end of it. Three more concerts, all brought to a premature end in much the same way. My record collection, too, was suddenly worthless. To put on a record was torture. It felt like submitting to bullying. Other things went: I could not, I found, sit in the audience in the theatre; I could not endure to sit in a traffic jam. But music was what most conspicuously went. It had been my life, and I had to discover what remained of my life without it.

It is easier, now, to think about music whole and entire, now that it is outside me. It is outside me, but I understand it, as well as possess the memory of understanding it. It has substance, and sometimes fills a room; and at the same time, it has none, displacing no physical substance, leaving no trace of its stormy passage when it is done. Each piece of music tells a story, but it is not a human story, as these insubstantial presences exit, return, insist on themselves, fall into silence, and no moral is drawn. A single fact can be the same and utterly changed: a chord, a note, a tune, an entire sequence of sounds can be repeated, unchanged, in different places, at different times, by different people, and with no explicable difference, are changed beyond recognition. The first E flat chord of the 'Eroica' Symphony is not the same as the last: an E flat chord by Beethoven is not the same as an E flat chord by Brahms, and no one knows how, or why.

I have a party trick, an abstruse one: I can identify pieces of music. Once, a sceptical friend played the game with me, with single chords. A chord. 'The "Eroica".' Another chord. 'The "Emperor" Concerto.' Another chord. 'The Liszt First Piano Concerto, the end.' Another chord. 'The "Rhine" Symphony. I love Schumann's symphonies.' My friend looked at me and I shrugged. They are different chords, and they are unmistakable if these are pieces you know; but they are the same chord. An E flat chord: another E flat chord: a third: a fourth. All the same, all different. Now, I understand music, and feel I understand it for the first time, because for the first time, I understand how strange it is. When I was inside it, or it was inside me, I never wondered about these questions. I know, now, it has substance, because I can feel the emptiness it left, but I never knew that before. I know its stories are not my stories, and not human stories, but its own stories, enacted in great halls between vast reaches of the city's silence. I know, too, how strange it is that a single note, on a single instrument, can be played, and it means one thing; and when, an hour, a month, a lifetime, a century later, the same note is played on the same instrument in the same way, it means something different. It can mean so many things I wonder if it ever meant anything at all. And, last of all, for the first time, I now understand what Shaw meant when he said that music was the brandy of the damned.

There is one last thing, a memory of my adolescence. I think we are having dinner, my family and me. Vaguely, I seem to think there was someone else there as well: perhaps an aunt or some friend of my sister's. For some reason, the question of sport came up. It might have been that I was complaining about compulsory team sports at school, or perhaps the phantom visitor had brought it up. My mother said something meant for me, and she aimed it well, because it stayed with me; two decades later, I remember what she said. 'People say that you need sport, or you won't get a sense of team spirit,' she said. 'But it's not true, is it?' She looked at me, a little nervously, with a tinge of assessment. 'You can develop team spirit in lots of ways. If you play in an orchestra, for instance...' She trailed off. I was glad of what she said, but she was wrong, and I knew she was wrong. I played in orchestras, all the time, and I knew what no one ever said: that everyone, even the sixth double bass in a provincial youth orchestra, is always alone with music, and music is always a way to be alone.

Now, it all seems so long ago, and as little worth arguing over as the general election of 1951; it all mattered so much, once, and now the story has come to an end. Some sort of end. Things have improved, slowly. My feelings towards music, now, much resemble my feelings towards old lovers. Maurizio, who I spent a decade with, turned up in London six months ago, and my feelings towards him were what you might expect: I knew him intimately, could still guess at what he was thinking: from time to time, I had flashes of great fondness, and flashes, too, of more recent rage and loathing. But for the most part, I felt nothing very much—perhaps, most of all, the boredom which sometimes accompanies complete and long-held understanding. I was, to be honest, looking forward to his going home, in the end. And music feels like that. I can reconstruct the old passionate enthusiasm, and have flashes of violent dislike and revulsion. I understand it, and am polite and patient with it. But mostly, I feel weary with familiarity, as if there were nothing more to discover about it. I have heard all the notes; every single one; and there is nothing more for me to find in an E flat major chord.

Now and again, I go to a concert, and don't mind it that much, if I sit at the end of a row, and can see the exit from where I sit. Once, music would have sent me out speechless with joy; more recently, I could have endured only ten minutes before fleeing, sick with terror. Now, I can listen with interest and admiration; no more.

There is one consolation: I can still play, and with something like pleasure. That is not the same. That is like a conversation between equals. Sometimes, late at night, I fetch down a volume of Schumann, and play the piece of his I always loved best, the *Davidsbundlertanze*, and it is not like being lectured, or shouted at, or bullied, but like an act of creation. But that is all. To be a member of an audience, to return to the pact I once made with music, is a possibility which is returning slowly, but will never return fully. To play, to inhabit the music is different, and for a moment Schumann, and music, is all mine, and possesses all the freedom it ever did.

I always put it like this; music left me. It felt like that. But now I start to wonder whether we prefer to think of these catastrophes as a desertion when it is more truthful to think of them as a dismissal. It took me years to understand the real ways in which relationship ends. I always thought that I was innocent, mistreated, passive. But that was not so. At some level, I had understood that the relationship had run its course, and, with some subconscious ingenuity, engineered situations which would demonstrate this truth to my partner. And perhaps music left me because I dismissed it, too. By 1997, in the South of France, I had taken what I could from it, and had no further use for it. I left it as I left the empty glass of brandy, sitting on the table as I walked away. Perhaps, there, in a moment, my psyche saw the excuse it was waiting for. Liberation is painful, and takes time to see it for what it is. Some abandonment took place there: but who abandoned what, I don't know any more. □

BAHT 'AT

Blake Morrison

ON ILKLA' MOOR BAHT 'AT

Wheer wor' ta bahn w'en Ah saw thee,
On Ilkla' Moor baht 'at ?
Wheer wor' ta bahn w'en Ah saw thee ?
Wheer wor' ta bahn w'en Ah saw thee ?
On Ilkla' Moor baht 'at, On Ilkla' Moor baht 'at,
On Ilkla' Moor baht 'at.

2
Tha's bin a-courtin' Mary Jane,
On Ilkla' Moor baht 'at
Tha's bin… (same ageean, twice) On Ilkla'… (3 times)
3
Tha's bahn to get thi deeath o' cowd,
(folla' on as afore)
4
Then we shall ha' to bury thee,
(as ta getten t'heng of it, nah ?)
5
Then t'wurms 'll come an' ate thee up
6
Then t'ducks 'll come an ate up t'wurms
7
Then we shall go an' ate up t'ducks
8
Then we shall all 'ave etten thee
9
That's wheer we get us oahn back
(If tha wants ony moor tha mun
sing it thisen)

I say ! What's it all about ?

Tha's nooan baht 'at a' ta ?

Translations can be obtained
from any Genuine Tyke !

X 17

JOHN HINDE UK LTD

Wheer wor' ta bahn w'en Ah saw thee,
On Ilkla Moor baht 'at?
Wheer wor' ta bahn w'en Ah saw thee?
Wheer wor' ta bahn w'en Ah saw thee?

People sang it in a jaunty fashion, with a knowing wink, but the
song unnerved me. The tune itself was banal, but the verses went
on and on, just as the moors themselves did. The bleakness made me
feel claustrophobic and agoraphobic simultaneously—as though
trapped in infinite space. If someone had told me there were only eight
verses, I'd not have believed them. Eighty seemed nearer the mark.

I felt excluded by the dialect, too. 'Bahn' I could just about make
sense of but 'baht' meant nothing at all—I sang it as a rumpety-ti-
tump nonsense ending, 'bah-tat'. (Others often amend the opening
line, I notice, so that it goes, Rambo-istically: 'Where hasta bin sin
I sore thee?') The song was popular in the playground and on the
radio. And the place it commemorates, Ilkley, was just a dozen miles
from my home: Skipton, where I went to school, is a not dissimilar
West Yorkshire town, dominated by sheep farming rather than
industry and set in a valley overshadowed by moors. But we were
outsiders (my father came from Lancashire, my mother from Ireland),
and the dialect of Skipton was different from that of Ilkley. In the
end the opening lines had to be translated for me: 'Where were you
going when I saw you/On Ilkley Moor, without a hat?'

Later I got the point, that the song was a dire warning about
what could happen to someone if he didn't look after himself and
keep warm while out on the hills—first a cold, then death, then
burial, then his corpse being eaten by worms, and the worms being
eaten by ducks, and the ducks being eaten by people, till the hapless
(hatless) victim had in effect been swallowed and digested by his own
tribe. It seemed an odd subject for a song. But adults were always
urging us to 'wrap up properly', and one of the strictest rules at
Skipton Grammar concerned the wearing of caps to and from
school. 'The sun has got his hat on,' went another song, 'hip-hip-hip
hooray.' Put your hat on, and all would be well. Leave it off and
you'd end up dead or in detention.

Hats seemed a big thing, in the grown-up world: people were

accused of talking out of them or asked to pass them round. At Turf Moor, where we went to watch Burnley play football, the older men wore flat checked caps, the younger knitted claret-and-blue bobble hats. My father's was a peaked RAF hat and kept in a cupboard: he'd not worn it since 1946. My mother wore hers—which was small and black and had a visor of mesh that could be lowered over the eyes—only at funerals. Hats had two uses: keeping your head warm and showing respect. Only a fool or heathen would attempt to survive without.

> *On Ilkla Moor baht 'at.*
> *On Ilkla Moor baht 'at.*
> *On Ilkla Moor baht 'at.*

The refrain is all that non-residents tend to know about Ilkley. And these days the town is happy to exploit the association. If you call up its website (www.ilkley.org), a tinny version of the tune starts to play as the front page downloads. Now that Ilkley has stopped being grand, a spa town for rich mill-owners, the song is on every mug and T-shirt; there's even a bistro in town called Bar T'ats. But this rapprochement is comparatively recent. Earlier guides and gazetteers don't allude to the song. (Oddly, Tim Binding's recent *On Ilkley Moor: The Story of an English Town* makes no mention of it either, despite borrowing the title.) Nor does it appear on the list of 300 Yorkshire ballads and songs compiled by Abraham Holroyd of Shipley in the 1880s. Studies of folk music or popular song are similarly tight-lipped: a passing reference to it being performed by Muriel George and Ernest Butcher (music-hall artists of the 1920s and '30s) is all I've come across. There's a simple explanation for this silence. Although the words of 'On Ilkla Moor' have a ballad-like, seemingly ancient lineage, and the tune, 'Cranbrook' by Thomas Clark, was composed (as a Wesleyan hymn) in 1815, it wasn't until the early twentieth century that the song became popular. But embarrassment may be a factor, too. I feel embarrassed whenever I hear it myself. There's neither the sonority of a good hymn nor the resonance of a good folk-song. The dittiness of the ditty makes me squirm.

The music teachers I had as a child disowned it. When my sister and I, along with the other children in the village, were dragooned into putting on a Christmas show, the songs chosen for us were strictly American: 'My Darling Clementine', 'Camptown Races', etc. Mrs Brown, my piano teacher, would have no truck with it, either. And such was the missionary zeal of Mr Brown (no relation), head of music at the grammar school, in raising our appreciation of classical music, that he tried to lead us from the temptation of popular song altogether: 'Little Brown Jug', 'On Ilkla Moor', 'Rock around the Clock, 'I Wanna Hold Your Hand'—it was all, we understood, 'sentimental rubbish'. Mr Brown, whose first name was John, played long, whirling organ solos at the annual Founders' Day Service. He was also, the older boys said, a pooftah, and if you boarded at School House, which he had charge of, you had to watch out. I doubted this was true, but in any case I wasn't a boarder, and Mr Brown soon went on to be head of music at a proper boarding school, Repton. Within a year or two of his moving, word came back that he'd dropped dead, though barely forty. I thought of a song—'John Brown's body lies a-mouldering in the grave'—and then of the songs about which he'd been sniffy. 'On Ilkla Moor' had taken its revenge.

Tha's bin a-courtin', [?] Mary Jane,
On Ilkla Moor baht 'at.

Was there a comma? Had Mary Jane been courting? Or was she the one being courted? I wasn't sure. Nor was it clear who led the way in any courting we did: lads were meant to take the initiative, but lasses had the power to say no. My fantasy was to make love in a grassy hollow hidden by ferns, while hikers or grouse-shooters unknowingly passed by. But it was always raining up on the moors. And few of us had the legs. Most courting took place in cinemas or bus shelters.

On Ilkley Moor there is a pair of large rocks known as the Cow and Calf, a popular haunt for summer tourists and novice climbers. Below them sat a pub of the same name. The pub served a trendy southern keg beer, Watney's Red Barrel, and boasted a discotheque ('Discotek' it said on the tickets). 'Come on,' my friend Brian Hartley said, after passing his driving test, 'let's go looking for little duckies.' We could hear the bass pounding before we got there: the hills were alive with the sound of Hendrix. At the door, we lied about our age. Once in, we felt lost among student types from Leeds, with their knotted silk scarfs and orange flares. Get off with someone? We'd not a chance. But every other sod seemed to be doing all right: there was snogging under strobe lights on the dance floor and snogging in the shadows by the Gents. Afterwards, leaving the car park, Brian's headlights caught a flash of whiteness on the moor beyond. 'Look,' he laughed, 'a bloke shagging his bird,' and drove off before I could see.

'Make sure to have a hat on,' went the advice we were given in our one and only sex lesson at school, 'or that she's wearing a cap.' Had the couple on the moor thought of precautions, I wondered? There was only one greater fear than a bun in the oven: the fear of death.

> Tha's bahn to get thi deeath o' cowd,
> On Ilkla Moor baht 'at.

'Ilkley has always been famous for its delightful situation, the picturesque beauty of its surroundings, its health-restoring springs of pure water, and the cheerful, invigorating effects of its atmosphere.' So the Reverend Robert Collyer and J. Horsfall Turner write in their *Ilkley: Ancient and Modern* (1885). In the nineteenth century, the town was famous for its hydropathy—Charles Darwin was among those who came for a cure—and as children we went there for the open-air swimming baths. But the song speaks of death rather than health. And that's how it always seemed to me. At a certain point of the moor, you'd reach a cattle grid—a bed of iron bars set in the road, separating civilization from the wilds. Below lay home and warmth. Beyond the wind sang of endless vacancy and cold. Crossing that grid sent a shudder through the car. I came to dread its metallic roll and to think of it as the death rattle.

One night in 1969, three girls from Skipton High School were killed in a car crash just outside Ilkley, on their way back from the Cow and Calf pub. One of them was Barbara McGuinn, the girlfriend of my best friend Steve. (He'd been going out with her since a last-minute change of plan some months before had meant him sharing a tent with her, and me with Isabel MacSween, not vice versa.) I remember Barbara's face still; Steve's, too, when he told me the news.

Not long before there'd been another death. A girl's body was found, by a wood up on the moor above Carleton. It appeared she'd been suffocated or strangled, and a murder hunt began. A suspect was named, the man who'd been out with her that night, and the police interviewed him at length. Then all went quiet. The man had been released, we learned; the girl, so it was whispered, had died 'naturally', during 'an intimate act'. Some said the man had got off too lightly; my brother-in-law recalls taking a knife from a lodger of his, who had plans to settle the score. The rest of us were simply baffled. Could a girl really die in that way? We were still only half convinced that oral sex carried no risk of pregnancy—and now this. Had they been drunk? Had he broken her neck, in extremis? Was it some freakishly vast ejaculation? We didn't know and the local newspapers were too decorous to say. 'That's done it,' a friend complained, 'no chance of getting blow job round here for ten year at least.' I'd already begun to suspect that sex brought misery or death, and now I knew.

> *Then we shall ha' to bury thee,*
> *On Ilkla Moor baht 'at.*

> *Then t'wurms'll come an' ate thee up,*
> *On Ilkla Moor baht 'at.*

The macabre is a distinguished literary tradition. The authorship of 'On Ilkla Moor' is distinguished, too: the multiply talented Anon. In his anthology *Yorkshire in Verse*, Ian Hamilton prints the song alongside two other pieces of Anonymous macabre, 'The Twa Corbies' (a pair of crows relish feasting on the white bones of a slain knight) and the 'Cleveland Lyke-Wake Dirge' ('if milk or drink thou never gave nean,/Every night and awle:/The fire shall burn thee to the bare beane,/And Christ receive thy Sawle'). An earlier anthology, the *White Rose Garland* (1949), offers an even creepier example of Yorkshire Gothic, 'A Dree Neet', which gleefully imparts what we've all got coming to us:

When t'een grows dim, an' fau'k draw nigh,
Fra t'other sahde o' t'graave,
It's laate ti square up au'd accoonts,
A gannin' sowl ti save.

(In rough translation: 'When the evening grows dim, and folk draw nigh/From the other side of the grave,/It's [too] late to square up old accounts/A departing soul to save.') The departing soul can be saved by good deeds performed earlier in life. But nothing can save the body. All flesh is grass, says the Bible. Yorkshire texts put it less gently: all flesh is food for worms.

Is taking sadistic pleasure in putrefaction quintessentially northern? I suspect so. But there may be something more to the frisson of 'On Ilkla Moor'. In 1934, Wm. Walker & Sons of Otley published a thirty-six-page pamphlet called 'The Haunted Moor', by a man called Nicholas Size, who claimed to have seen ghosts up there—no ordinary spirits but victims of Druidic sacrifice and cannibalism. At the time, Size was 'a fairly successful' and 'reasonably courageous' businessman in his forties, somewhat solitary, it's true ('Having long ago married an impossible wife, I was more alone in the world than other men'), and a touch short-sighted, but not prone to wild or fearful imaginings. The book's meanderings in history and topography, and its earnest black-and-white photographs, establish the author's credentials as an honest soul; he reads a bit like W. G. Sebald. But then come the experiences at the Place of Horror, up on the moor: strange fires, eerie visions, terrible groans and sobbings, and a climactic episode in which a crate of screaming children is about to be cremated, till the author intervenes and is set upon by Druids before passing out—a hallucination, or maybe not, 'since dead bodies have been found here and elsewhere in curious circumstances', says Size, who swears he's telling the truth about the violence and cannibalism he saw.

All moors are spooky. Even sheep can look like ghosts, in the mist. But Ilkley Moor is spookier than most. In recent years there have been numerous UFO sightings and claims that three ramblers from Leeds were abducted by aliens. 'No wonder everybody has an instinctive feeling of dread when they see the place,' writes Size.

'Never again would I go near to it. Never again would I trust myself on Ilkley Moor.'

> *Then t'ducks'll come an ate up t'wurms,*
> *On Ilkla Moor baht 'at.*

Did ducks eat worms? I had my doubts. But the entry for 'Mallard, or Wild Duck' on page 134 of the *Observer's Book of Birds* (one of the colour plates, not the disappointing black and white spreads with which they alternated) said ducks would eat 'almost anything: insects, worms, slugs, snails, shellfish, frogs, grain and berries'. On the other hand, their usual haunt was marshland and estuary—I'd seen grouse, lapwings and curlews high up among heather and gorse, but never a duck. Was the song playing loose with the facts, then? It seemed so. Those ducks it described weren't common or garden, the sort that sat on ponds in parks. They were like the birds seen in nature documentaries, perching on the backs of bison or wildebeest and snaffling their tics: eco-ducks, recyclers, garbage-collectors, friends of the earth.

The worms are part of the recycling process too, of course. In the only book written about 'On Ilkla Moor', the Methodist preacher and local historian Arnold Kellett rehearses the popular theory of how the song came into existence, when a Halifax chapel choir, on an outing to the moor in the mid-nineteenth century, set about teasing two lovelorn younger members. But Kellett throws in a theory of his own: mightn't the worms in the song be an allusion to Ilkley's most famous Victorian visitor, Charles Darwin, who believed that 'worms have played a more important part in the history of the world than most persons would first suppose' and whose *Origin of Species* ends by inviting the reader to contemplate 'worms crawling through the damp earth' as an example of the interdependency of all creation?

> *Then we shall go an' ate up t'ducks,*
> *On Ilka Moor baht 'at.*

Most people I've talked to dislike the song. They remember singing it at church camps. They recall killing time with it on long car journeys, in preference to 'Ten Green Bottles'. They recount annoying Scots or baffling Japanese with it, when forced to do their bit at karaoke evenings. But they hold it in little affection, those from Yorkshire least of all.

Children used to make merry with 'On Ilkla Moor' by singing 'with-aht thee trousers on' after 'tha's been a courtin' Mary Jane'. But the trouserless version of the song is no more appealing than the hatless original. 'Grim' and 'curmudgeonly' are the words that most often come up.

Then we shall all 'ave etten thee,
On Ilkla Moor baht 'at.

The circularity is the song's raison d'être. The repetitions test our patience, and we finish back where we started, little the wiser. 'There's a Hole in My Bucket' works a similar trick, but for comic purposes— performers of it pause before the last verse, to get the maximum gotcha effect. The gotcha of 'On Ilkla Moor' is different: it creeps up by surprise and with grisly pleasure. And it's not a character in the song who's outwitted, a Lisa ensnared by a Henry; it's ourselves. The song of life is a bleak rondelet: that's the message. Don't get your hopes up. And don't imagine that pleasure will go unpunished. Death will get you in the end.

In music, repetition needn't mean monotony. The Yorkshire composer Gavin Bryars had a surprise hit a few years ago with *Jesus' Blood Never Failed Me Yet*, a seventy-four-minute CD featuring the voice of a tramp singing the same few words of a hymn over and over. Most listeners find themselves curiously moved by it, and the gradually increased orchestral accompaniment makes them forget they're in a loop. 'On Ilkla Moor' is less forgiving. The refrains come round like nails in a coffin. Can it be a coincidence that Gavin Bryars's birthplace is Goole, in the East Riding? The landscapes there are very different from those of West Yorkshire—big skies, broad acres, bright horizons—which must be what gives his music its sense of freedom. Whereas whoever wrote 'On Ilkla Moor' grew up, as I did, hemmed in by darkness and wet hills.

Perhaps that's why 'On Ilka Moor' unnerved me when I first

heard it: because I knew one day I'd want to leave home, and the song said I never could. Beyond the universal themes, timor mortis and memento mori, that's its Yorkshire subtext: no one from God's country gets away. A jollier version of the song, which eventually merges into a chorus of 'Auld Lang Syne', casts it as a dialogue between a mother and son: she asks him where he has been, he replies 'courting Mary Jane', she threatens 'I'll tell thi father when he comes home', he says 'don't take on so', and then they swap lines about death and worms and ducks, till he ends up:

> An' yo can gobble oop t'ducks
> An' so get back yor awn;
> An' appen they will pizen [poison] ye,
> An' then yo'll keep me company
> On Ilkla Moor baht 'at.

This idea of the land, or community, reclaiming its dead—getting back its own—also appears in an optional extra verse to the better-known version:

> That's wheer we get us oahn back,
> On Ilkla Moor baht 'at.

Looking after your own is nice and protective; getting back your own is possessive, tight-fisted, nasty, even vengeful. Or so it seemed to me forty years ago. Which is why 'On Ilkla Moor' used to fill me not just with boredom but with fear.

I'm making a meal of it. It's only a song. But the song said Yorkshire would make a meal of me. □

Actus Tragicus   John Eliot Gardiner

Even to his most ardent admirers Bach can sometimes seem remote: his genius as a musician is too far out of reach for most of us to comprehend. But that he was a very human genius comes across in all sorts of ways: not so much via the bric-a-brac of personal evidence like family letters and anecdotes, because these are few and far between, but through the chinks in his musical armour-plating, moments when we glimpse the vulnerability of an ordinary person struggling with an ordinary person's doubts, worries and perplexities. Such a chink is the 'Actus Tragicus'—a funerary piece written when he was twenty-two.

No one has so far been able to pinpoint the exact occasion for which it was composed. There has been conjecture that it was written either for his uncle Tobias, who died in August 1707, or possibly for Susanne Tilesius, the sister of Bach's friend and ally Pastor Eilmar of Mühlhausen. Susanne was thirty-four when she died, leaving a husband and four children, just as Bach's own mother had done fourteen years before. Might the 'Actus Tragicus' in some way be a cathartic musical outpouring of his own unresolved grief?

Bach had frequent and painful brushes with death throughout his lifetime, starting from an early age. Within the space of nine months, just before his tenth birthday, first his mother and then his father died; the family home in Eisenach was disbanded and he went to live with his much older brother. As soon as he began to compose he discovered ways of converting that early pain of grieving into consoling music of extraordinary profundity. Impressively it is never saccharine, self-indulgent, or morbid: on the contrary, though deeply serious, it is full of optimism. Many of his mature works, including the two great *Passion* settings, deal with the same subject and the characteristic conflict between a world of tribulation and the hope of redemption, but none more poignantly or serenely than the 'Actus Tragicus'. I wonder whether Bach himself, at the end of a life spent amid 'continual vexation, envy and persecution' (his own words to an old school friend), was able to face his own death with the calm strong faith he expressed in the 'Actus Tragicus'.

If the 'Actus Tragicus' represents the Lutheran ideal of the 'good death', it's also the kind of piece that can be enjoyed at any level. Unlike some of Bach's busier contrapuntal inventions, this work has good 'surface' attraction, no doubt as a result of its unusual soft-toned instrumentation: just two recorders, an organ and a pair of violas da gamba. The opening Sonatina comprises twenty of the most heart-rending bars in all of Bach's concerted music. From the yearning dissonances given to the two gambas to the ravishing way the recorders entwine and exchange adjacent notes, slipping in and out of unison, we are being offered music to soothe the battered spirit. Though it brims over with variety and invention the whole work lasts less than twenty minutes, flowing seamlessly through several switches of mood and metre. As with much of the best music, there is a brilliant use of silence. At the moment when the soprano sings repeated pleas of 'Come, Lord Jesus!', all the other voices and instruments drop out leaving her unsupported voice to trail away in a fragile arabesque. Bach notates a blank bar with a pause over it: this mystical silence turns out to be the exact mid-point of the work.

This is just one example of deliberate and effective planning, for the 'Actus Tragicus' turns out to be increasingly complex the more you peer below the surface. Through the particular disposition of seven biblical quotations, interleaved with Lutheran chorales, we are presented with a clear juxtaposition of Old Testament Law and New Testament Gospel. Where the Law insists that 'in the midst of life we are in death', in essence the Gospel (according to Martin Luther) replies 'in the midst of death we are in life'. The underlying purpose is clear: to comfort the bereaved with the notion that life is essentially a preparation for death and that it is God who sets the clock of human life and orders matters according to his own timetable.

Bach devises an ingenious symmetrical structure to underpin in music the theological division between Law and Gospel. Individual movements are organized in such a way that we can trace in music the journey of the believer as he progresses via Old Testament scripture (with its bald statements about the inevitability of death) downwards to his lowest ebb, and then moves upwards again, through prayer, to a more spiritual outlook. The solo arias on both sides of the divide are arranged in contrasted pairs so, for example, the first authoritative Old Testament injunction to 'set thy house in order, for thou shalt die, and not live' is answered by Christ's words from the cross to the malefactor: 'today shalt thou be with me in paradise'.

To mirror scripture with music Bach goes a step further by

arranging a progression of keys—an example of that tonal allegory that Eric Chafe has identified in Bach's *Passion*s and *Cantata*s. Again we have a symmetrical design: a descent from E flat via C minor and F minor, for those grim Old Testament injunctions, to that nadir of silence and finally to the remote key of B flat minor—one that he reserves for the depths of spiritual torment in the *St Matthew Passion*—then rising, through the comfort of the Gospel texts, via A flat and C minor back to E flat.

But the most brilliant feature of Bach's fusion of music and theology occurs around that central blank, silent bar. To illustrate the overwhelming need of divine help at the point of death, he leaves the soprano's final invocation tonally ambiguous. It is up to us how we interpret it in the silence that follows. If we hear her last notes as a perfect cadence (albeit a weak one) in F minor, that would indicate her expiry—death as a kind of full stop. But we are also being gently encouraged to hear her final oscillation between A and B flat as the leading note and tonic respectively in the key of the movement which follows—B flat minor. Christ's presence in answer to those insistent appeals is then clearly implied in the mystical silent bar. Bach's message is now unequivocally one of hope indicating physical death to be only a midway point on our journey and—with that tonal upswing—just the beginning of what comes after.

Bach's 'Actus Tragicus' comes as close as any piece of music I know towards piercing the membrane that separates the material world from whatever lies beyond it. Of course one can no more describe this phenomenon, or define the emotional charge generated by Bach's music, than a neuro-scientist can measure what is real and what is fantasy. The presence of so many layers of meaning may seem baffling to us, but in Bach's time, when music was ranked as a mathematical science and the borders between different disciplines were far less defined than they are now, such an approach would have been accepted as normal practice. It is of course perfectly possible to enjoy Bach's music for its purely musical and sensory pleasures. But is it just a coincidence that his work should appeal so strongly to scientists and mathematicians, or is it possible that—beyond the sheer beauty of the music—we are all capable of recognizing, if only unconsciously, the underlying symmetry of such a piece as the 'Actus Tragicus'? □

KLEVER KAFF
Ian Jack

Kathleen Ferrier by Cecil Beaton, 1951

BY COURTESY OF SOTHEBY'S, LONDON

1. A voice is a person

Blackburn in the northern county of Lancashire is a town built in a trough in the moors, with streets which pour down from all sides into its centre. Some noble reminders of its golden century still remain: the town hall, the concert hall, the library, the railway station, the cathedral, the museum, all of them except the cathedral Victorian or Edwardian and now stranded among the slap-dash new primitivism of shopping malls and car parks thrown up in Blackburn, and many other northern manufacturing towns, during the 1960s and 1970s. The good end of town—the best end, the West End, the Mayfair of Blackburn—lies on the north-western slope, along and above Preston New Road, probably because (a common theory about the layout of Victorian towns and cities) richer people took care to live up-wind of the mill smoke, and the prevailing wind in Britain is from the south-west. Lynwood Road is one of these streets which run steeply down the hill from the moorland. At the top of the street is the Dog Inn and, beyond that, the crest of the hill and fine views stretching north across the green valley of the Ribble to the Bowland Fells. Lynwood Road itself faces south; not a poor street—the terraced houses have bay windows; but not a rich one either—two rooms upstairs and two down, the kind of place that a mill foreman or a shopkeeper or a schoolmaster might have paid rent on a hundred years ago. Migrant families from the Indian subcontinent, mainly Muslims from Pakistan, their children and grandchildren, live here now. On this September evening, they come and go from each other's houses, women in loose folds of white, small boys in prayer caps carrying green velvet cases which contain the Koran. '*Salaam alaikum*', one bearded man says to another, as they pass on the slope.

Number 57 is on the steepest stretch, an end-of-terrace with a satellite dish fixed to its gable wall. The curtains are drawn in the bay. A pennant for the town's football team, Blackburn Rovers, hangs in one window. Beside the door there is a plaque which says that from 1913 to 1933 this was 'the home of Kathleen Ferrier, contralto singer'; a small plaque, modestly phrased—a Mr Mujib-Ur-Rehman has a larger and shinier nameplate just across the street, and he is not yet among the dead and great. Standing on the pavement, I looked at the view Kathleen Ferrier would have had, from age one to age twenty-one, as she was jiggled on her father's shoulder, or ran to school, or set off every morning to work as a switchboard girl at the Blackburn telephone exchange. A view of a street, then a town in a valley, both under drizzle and dark now, and on the horizon, standing out sharp and patched with wet sunlight, the southern moors.

This would have been her view, and yet not quite her view: she would have been lucky to see the hills. Blackburn in the years she lived there was a different place, more sharply defined in character and more blurred atmospherically. A cotton-weaving town—J. B. Priestley wrote that it once wove 'every dhoti in India'—with many mill chimneys between Lynwood Road and the southern horizon, and an atmosphere that cleared of smoke only one week in the year when the mills closed for the summer holiday—'wakes week'—and their workers went to the seaside.

Standing there, I remembered that I had first come to Blackburn when it was such a place. We took the train a few miles from Bolton, where our home then was, came through the cuttings in the hills that can be seen from Lynwood Road and at Blackburn changed to a different train that took us up into the Yorkshire Dales. Blackburn's station, I remember, was filled with crowds hurrying up and down the subways between platforms, rather like the opening scene in *Mr Hulot's Holiday*, and on our platform there was a model of a two-funnelled steamer inside a glass case, placed there by the shipping company that took holidaymakers from Fleetwood and Liverpool to the Isle of Man. That was the summer of 1951. I was six. Kathleen Ferrier had her first operation for cancer that spring, though very few people knew that then. She was a voice on the radio, singing British folk songs ('Blow the Wind Southerly') or the aria in English translation from Gluck's *Orfeo ed Euridice* ('What Is Life to Me Without Thee?'). Four years later, my elder brother brought home our first gramophone—or rather that new thing, a record player, portable, with three speeds—and two 78rpm records which had to be slipped carefully from their paper sleeves. They had these two Ferrier songs on their A-sides. My brother, who had charge of this delicate machinery, would wait for the deck to stop spinning, turn the discs over with his fingertips, and we would hear 'Weel May the

Keel Row' and Handel's 'Art Thou Troubled?' on their reverse. Now, to hear Ferrier, the family need no longer wait on the caprice of the BBC Light Programme's record selection.

'She has such a lovely voice,' my mother said in the present tense, though by then Kathleen Ferrier was two years dead. We agreed—it was deep, it was thrilling, it was singular. But there were also two things which then I would have found hard to put into words (and it may be no easier now). First, I think we felt that Ferrier's was the opposite of a disembodied 'voice'; a personality housed in flesh and blood was singing, and directly, it seemed, to us. Second, the voice made us respectful and contemplative—even to a ten-year-old it could do this. I suppose we were in the presence of beauty—often a grave beauty; even the jauntiest folksong, 'The Keel Row', had something sad inside it. Well, it made you want to cry. But was that the composer's notes, and the way they were sung, or the words in the lyrics and the way they were sung, or something you knew or sensed about the history of the person who sang them?

The answer to the last question, should it have been asked in our house in 1955, would have become almost immediately complicated. That same year, a few months after the record player arrived, my brother gave our mother as a Christmas present a newly published biography of Ferrier by her sister, Winifred. It had (still has—though often read, it has been carefully preserved) a pink dust-jacket with a Cecil Beaton portrait on the front showing Ferrier apparently in mid-song: erect, strong-necked, hair glinting in the photographer's lights, teeth shining, eyes resolute, her wide mouth open (a mouth, as the critic Neville Cardus wrote, that 'you could dive into'). This was the singer at her zenith in 1951, a lovely and celebrated woman who had sung at Glyndebourne and the Edinburgh Festival and at the Carnegie Hall in New York; in Salzburg, Chicago, Paris, Amsterdam, Montreal. But inside the book was a different kind of picture; snapshots of a girl who, in her clothes, her hair, her smile, her locations on municipal park benches and cold northern beaches, was as ordinary (and by extension as interesting) as ourselves. For us, and many people like us, it may have been the first moment of appeal in the Ferrier story—that such a voice could come from such a place: 57 Lynwood Road, Blackburn, Lancashire.

Kathleen on her twenty-first birthday, 1933

What this provenance implied—an implication the biography reinforced—was that Kathleen was a 'Lancashire lass' and therefore ungrand and unsnobbish, a 'good sort' and true to her origins, with 'never a trace of swank'. People knew her by affectionate nicknames: to the conductor Sir John Barbirolli she was 'Katie'; to Gerald Moore, her frequent accompanist on the piano, she was 'Kath'; and to herself she was 'Klever Kaff' or 'Klever Question Mark Kaff' or 'Not-so-Klever Kaff', and sometimes, at the end of her letters, simply 'KK'.

The biography by her sister told the story of this last name. In her pre-war obscurity as a young housewife—Mrs Kathleen Wilson, wife to Mr Bert Wilson, bank manager—she had once sewn a button on to a coat as a favour to a friend. The friend was Wyn Hetherington. The coat belonged to her husband, Jack Hetherington, who needed it in a hurry; the Wilsons and the Hetheringtons were about to set out for a picnic, which Mrs Hetherington was preparing in the kitchen. So, watched by the Hetheringtons' three-year-old son, Kathleen sewed quickly and with a nice final flourish, at which point the boy remarked ('with respect and surprise in his voice' writes Winifred Ferrier): 'Clever Kaff!' Perhaps because this is a childish story, it appealed to me as a child when I first skipped through the book. What the book did not disclose, however, was the fate of Mr Hetherington or Mrs Hetherington or Kathleen's husband, Mr Wilson. Jack Hetherington died a few years later. Kathleen divorced Bert Wilson, who eventually married Wyn Hetherington. His first marriage produced no children. His second one did.

All of this took place in Silloth, a small and declining port town on the Cumberland coast, and all of it is interesting, and some of it may even be pertinent to the question of Ferrier's voice and career. But when she was alive, her audience knew very little about her life, even when she was losing it ('arthritis' was the public explanation for her absences from the opera stage and concert platform). During the years she sang, the fully-fledged notion of 'celebrity' had still to be invented. She gave very few newspaper interviews. She never appeared on television or in cinema newsreels. There is, so far as I can tell, no film footage of her outside a few silent and fleeting seconds, which are now in the hands of a devout enthusiast. As for her speaking voice, it can be heard only briefly and only twice, on a tape made at a post-concert New York party, and in a short speech she made for the BBC at an Edinburgh Festival (and a wonderfully modulated and enunciated voice it is too, without a trace of Lancashire; as a young woman in Blackburn, she had elocution lessons). In any case, who among the crowd that filled the Carnegie Hall in 1948 to hear her sing Mahler's *Das Lied von der Erde*, Bruno Walter conducting, could have cared about her original place in the echelons of British social class and geography? They had come to hear her sing. Already in Britain she had achieved a remarkable and—a safe prediction—unrepeatable thing. For a few months in 1946–47, her recording of the aria 'What Is Life?' (Christoph Willibald Gluck, 1714–87) outsold any other record in any musical category. Well, it made you want to cry, or at least think a bit. As an anonymous listener is quoted as saying in another biography, by Charles Rigby, her singing 'made you wish you had led a better life'.

Whether or not Ferrier was the finest singer of serious music to come out of Britain in the twentieth century is a futile discussion; some would question if she was even the best contralto. Her vocal range and interpretation were limited, and not every critic cared for her ('this goitrous singer with the contralto hoot'—*New Statesman*). Neville Cardus, the *Manchester Guardian*'s music writer, a fellow Lancastrian and a great supporter, conceded, for example, that it was no accident that her only two attempts at opera, the title roles in *Orfeo* and Benjamin Britten's *Rape of Lucretia*, were parts that required statuesque nobility and no flirtatious movement: 'There was no surface glamour in her art and little exhibition of sex.' Then again, how wide a repertoire does a singer need to have? Ferrier knew what suited, and what didn't suit, her self-conscious body and voice. Verdi was out, even the *Requiem*—her voice wasn't hard enough. Wagner was a temptation resisted, even when the invitation came ultimately from Herbert von Karajan and Bayreuth, though by then she was also too ill to accept. She sang mainly Handel, Bach, Schubert, Schumann, Brahms, Elgar and Mahler—God, love, and death—plus a selection of plainly arranged British folk songs which brought her a popular audience. On the one hand, 'Ye Banks and Braes'; on the other, Mahler's *Kindertotenlieder*, his 'Songs for Dead Children'. She and her greatest mentor, Bruno Walter, established Mahler's vocal music in the British repertoire with a performance of *Das Lied* at the first Edinburgh Festival in 1947. Walter had been Mahler's pupil and friend, had in fact conducted the first performance of *Das Lied* in 1911 in Vienna in the year of the composer's death (he didn't live to hear it). After Ferrier died, Walter said that the two greatest musical experiences of his life had been knowing Ferrier and Mahler, 'in that order'.

He loved her, and, according to the suggestion of Ferrier's third and most recent biographer, Maurice Leonard, for more than her voice. Most of her mentors did. Sir John Barbirolli, conductor of the Hallé in Manchester, and previously, like Walter, of the New York Philharmonic; Sir Malcolm Sargent, of the London Symphony; Walter Legge, the artistic director of Columbia Gramophone Company and the soprano Elisabeth Schwarzkopf's husband: all loved her in one way or another. For Barbirolli, it was a matter of deep and familial friendship, playing and singing for fun, cooking and eating together, his wife and his mother usually present as well. But Legge tried it on in a taxi—Ferrier moved to the Decca company soon after—and Sargent is said to have gone further. Both were rebuffed.

Gerald Moore, her accompanist, wrote that one of her friends had told him: 'Any man who does not acknowledge that Kathleen Ferrier is the most wonderful woman in the world has something wrong with him.' Moore added that it was 'not a case of a hundred men and a girl, for though we men loved her, our wives loved her themselves'. And they did. Women who were not always wives began to follow her from concert to concert during her second North American tour in 1949. From Chicago, she wrote to her sister Winifred: 'I've made some wonderful friends here—all women o'course. I've had women following me from one concert to the next 200 miles apart—and they are the nicest pets...I could ever wish to meet.' Three years on, there were groupies in the modern and less engaging sense. On October 28, 1952, the *Daily Mail* reported that, on the same evening that Ferrier was to perform Handel's *Messiah* in the Albert Hall, eight chauffeur-driven cars had arrived outside her Hampstead flat. They had not been ordered. There had also been anonymous telephone calls and other japes; Gerald Moore later wrote that he had arrived home with her after a concert one night to find her door barricaded with dustbins.

Ferrier told the *Daily Mail*: 'A number of young girls have been following me around concerts in London and the provinces—they have even been present when I sang in Edinburgh, Newcastle, and Dublin. They sit up all night in the queue and then get rather noisy, screaming at the ends of performances. I can only assume that the people who perpetrate the hoaxes belong to the same group.' Then a typical Ferrier touch: 'I do not mind so much for myself, but I am sorry for the firms who suffer the expense and inconvenience.' Though her fans were not to know this, she was gravely ill.

So the finest British singer of the century? Who can say. But best-loved is beyond doubt. Who else could make a girl scream at the end of Handel? By the time she died in Coronation year, 1953, she was probably the most celebrated woman in Britain after the Queen. To most of her audience, who heard her on the radio and on records and who never set foot in a concert hall, she was also an invisible one. But then, though the voice is an instrument, it is not a thing of brass or wood like a trumpet or a violin. As the tenor Peter Pears once said, referring to Ferrier, with whom he had often sung: 'A voice is a person.' What kind of person did we at home detect? Somebody sympathetic and simple and direct—all three words occur often in her friends' descriptions—but also someone who had grieved, or who knew what grieving was, our time here being short and not always a bowl of cherries. Bruno Walter wrote: 'She was very simple and natural; one could seem to read her mind like an open book, but only her singing revealed the abundant wealth of her inner life...to hear her meant to feel her innermost affectionate, rich and lofty self. She was not enigmatic, not problematic, but a rare combination of profundity and clarity, of abundance and simplicity.'

Reading her letters in the Kathleen Ferrier archive at Blackburn's museum, I began to fall in love with her myself.

2. Accidents

It is a cold-blooded observation, but Ferrier's life was made to be filmed. The arc and incident of it are dramatically perfect. Since 1953, several people have had the idea, including Lewis Gilbert, who directed *Reach For the Sky*, the story of the Second World War pilot, Douglas Bader, and his tin-legged triumph over adversity. But their

Mrs Alice Ferrier with Kathleen, possibly on her Christening day in 1912, and Winifred and George

projects always fell on the stony ground of Winifred Ferrier, who refused to cooperate because she feared that her sister's life would be turned into a weepie. Triumph was fine; adversity, and particularly the final adversity, not. By the account of everyone who knew her, Winifred was, right up until her death in 1995, a formidable woman and a most jealous keeper of the Ferrier flame, and her fingerprints are all over most of what has so far been published about Kathleen's private history. In life, Winifred and Kathleen were close.

The singer was born on April 22, 1912, in the Lancashire mill village of Higher Walton, near Preston, where her father, William Ferrier, was the headmaster of the primary school. The next year the family moved to Blackburn where he was given charge of a larger school. Kathleen was the youngest of three children, and a late child—her mother was forty and her father forty-five when she was born. The family were on the lower rungs of middle-class respectability, but only a generation away from a harder way of living: clogs and shawls, and steam whistles rather than school bells announcing the start of the working day. Her father's father was a guard on the railways, her mother's father went to work in a mill at the age of nine. Winifred was the eldest child, and then came brother George, who vanishes from the story at an early stage. He had, in Winifred's words, 'always caused the family anxiety' and ran away from home three times. Eventually, showing no inclination to work and earn in Blackburn, he was packed off to Canada under an emigrant scheme funded by the Salvation Army. According to Maurice Leonard, who was a friend of Winifred's, in later life Kathleen was always 'terrified that he would turn up out of the blue and touch her for money'. All the Ferrier children were large; at fourteen George stood 6ft 8in. They were 'big-boned', as people used to say. Kathleen herself grew to 5ft 9½ in and, in the years of her success, often weighed more than twelve stone. Neither she nor her siblings were particularly handsome children, and Kathleen's later beauty came unexpectedly. Her mother used to tease her for her plain looks, a cruel habit on the face of it, though as Neville Cardus observed: 'It is a Lancashire custom to lock endearment up in the heart except at weddings, Christmas, and at funerals.'

Music was then one of the main recreations of northern

England. People sang for pleasure, in front parlours, at concert parties, and in churches, with the *Messiah* every Christmas at the town hall. The Ferriers were no exception to this tradition, though Kathleen's particular skill was at the piano. At school, as at the keyboard, she was an able student and her teachers expected her to stay on for the examinations that would get her into university; her sister was already at college and training to be a teacher. Then the Ferrier family hit a money crisis. Her father was about to retire, George continued to be a worry, her sister had still to earn. At fourteen, Kathleen left school and went to work on the switchboard at the Blackburn telephone exchange for eight shillings and threepence (41p) a week. For the next nine years she answered callers and put them through. In 1933, she entered a contest to find the recorded voice which would automatically announce the time to anyone who dialled the letters T.I.M.—a new device called the 'speaking clock'. Along with hundreds of other young women entrants, she had to say 'At the third stroke it will be ten forty-five and thirty seconds', but she failed to get past the local heats. Her voice remained untrained—her first serious singing lessons began only in 1939, when she was twenty-seven. Musically, she confined herself to the piano. She won competitions and accompanied prominent local and visiting singers. When she got married in 1935, the *Blackburn Times* felt able to announce MISS K. FERRIER MARRIED: BRILLIANT BLACKBURN MUSICIAN.

Her husband, Albert Wilson, came from over the hill in Chorley and worked at a bank on the outskirts of Blackpool. His family was well-to-do and—in Chorley—prominent; his father, a businessman, chaired the local council and sat on the magistrate's bench. The wedding, therefore, took place at a Methodist church in the bridegroom's parish rather than the bride's and, by the standards of the time, was quite grand. The *Blackburn Times* recorded the details under a photograph four columns wide. The presents included an oak standard lamp from Kathleen's fellow telephonists and a walnut clock from the bridegroom's colleagues at the bank. After the reception, Mr and Mrs Wilson left 'for a touring honeymoon in the South'.

Kathleen had to give up her job; in 1935, married women could not be employed in telephone exchanges or any other department of the Post Office. The Wilsons first set up house in Wharton, just east of Preston at the beginnings of the Lancashire holiday coast, and then, when Bert was promoted to the rank of manager the following year, moved a hundred miles north to Silloth in Cumberland. There Kathleen lived the life of a bank-manager's wife in a small town. She learned to play golf well and tennis well enough, she swam, she gallantly got up on stage in amateur theatricals, she gave piano lessons, she shopped, she cooked. It began to be noticed that the Wilsons produced no children, though Kathleen was by now in her mid-twenties and in ruddy health. It was also noticed, by her friends the Hetheringtons among others, that she could sing. There were musical evenings at the flat over the bank. In 1937, her husband bet her a shilling that she wouldn't dare compete at the annual music festival in Carlisle, the nearest large town, as a singer as well as a pianist. Kathleen took on the bet and won the silver rose bowl for the festival's best singer, a judge recording that 'Mrs Wilson, of Silloth, had a very, very beautiful voice indeed'. For the next two years, she sang at local concerts, sometimes for nothing and sometimes for trivial fees, and often with crowd-pleasers such as 'The End of a Perfect Day' and 'Curly Headed Babby'. In 1938, she appeared with acrobats and comics at the Workington Opera House in a variety show called *Artists You Might Never Have Heard*. The next year she sang a couple of songs ('The End of a Perfect Day' again) on a regional radio show from Newcastle. She was becoming known—'Mrs Kathleen Wilson, the Silloth contralto'—but it would be hard to detect from her engagement book any sign of onwards-and-upwards progress, any suggestion that her future lay anywhere other than in being a woman with a 'natural' but untrained voice, who, because she was a childless wife-at-home supported by her husband, could afford the time to sing. Professional classical singers need seven or eight years' coaching—breathing, vocal technique, lyric interpretation, musicianship, foreign languages—which, ideally, they should start in their teens.

And then the war happened and everything changed. Her husband was called up to the army, her father, now a widower, came to live with her (as it turned out permanently, until his death in 1951). She turned her back on her marriage, hired one of the best teachers

Winifred and Kathleen, 1928

in northern England (Dr J. E. Hutchinson, of Newcastle), and relaunched herself as Miss Kathleen Ferrier. The war unleashed a new supply of work in the form of uplifting entertainment—this at a time when 'uplifting' and 'entertainment' were less divisible—which was brought direct to the factory floor in lunchtime concerts, or in the evenings to country barns and working men's clubs. Kathleen got a contract from a government body called the Council for the Encouragement of Music and the Arts, CEMA, and took Handel and Bach and Purcell to men and women who had just finished a morning shift making rubber dinghies for the Royal Air Force or a day digging coal. By the end of 1942, she had a comprehensive knowledge of the geography of industrial England, its railway junctions, cold lodging-houses, sparse food, tinny upright pianos, and blacked-out streets. She sang for CEMA in places that are difficult to find on a medium-scale map—between November 25 and December 12, 1942, for example, in Stanley, Holmes Chapel, Winsfold, Great Sanghall, Runswick Bay, Crook, and Hackness, as well as in Cockermouth, Crewe, Chester, Newcastle, Durham and Sunderland. But by then she knew her destination was London. Earlier that year, Malcolm Sargent had met her in Manchester and encouraged her to move south, and there had been an enthusiastic notice of one of her lunchtime performances in the *Manchester Guardian*, her first review in a national newspaper, which began with the words 'Miss Kathleen Ferrier, a new singer of remarkable talent...'

She was now earning eighteen guineas a week. She was determined to rise to a new level as performer. On Christmas Eve 1942 she and Winifred and their father moved into a rented, £150-a-year flat in Hampstead, 2 Frognal Mansions. She acquired an influential agent, John Tillett, of the Ibbs and Tillett concert agency, and a new teacher, Professor Roy Henderson, who taught at the Royal Academy of Music. Kathleen was thirty; Henderson thought she had come to him ten years too late, but what lay inside her mouth amazed him— a 'wonderful cavity at the back of her throat'. Later he wrote: 'In the course of my teaching I have looked into hundreds of throats, but with the exception of a coloured bass with a rich voice, I have seen nothing to equal it...one could have shot a fair-sized apple right to the back of her throat without meeting obstruction. This space gave her that depth and roundness of tone which were distinctive. The voice rolled out because there was nothing to stop it.'

Henderson worked with her for the rest of her career. This wasn't easy. Ferrier grew to be in such demand—seventeen *Messiahs* in seventeen different towns, for example, in the month of December 1945—that the time for private coaching had always to be fitted around her public performances. Musicianship was not a problem; Ferrier was an excellent pianist and understood scores. But she and Henderson had to work hard on her unreliable top notes, her interpretation, her memory, her awkward platform stance, and her breathing. He would make her lean with her back against a wall and kick hard with her diaphragm against the force of his fist (Enrico Caruso could kick his diaphragm against a grand piano and move it several inches). In the end, Henderson wrote, 'she played her voice as she willed'.

Her career at this national and international level—finally, a diva—lasted barely ten years. She first entered the musical consciousness of London—as opposed to Silloth or Workington—in May 1943, when she sang the *Messiah* at Westminster Abbey. After that, the milestones came regularly: 1944, Elgar's *Dream of Gerontius* in Leeds, and her first recordings; 1946, the first *Lucretia* in Benjamin Britten's new opera at Glyndebourne, and her first overseas performances, in Holland; 1947, the first of her six Edinburgh Festivals and her first Mahler; 1948, the first of her three North American tours, and at the Edinburgh Festival of that year a programme which gave her equal prominence with Yehudi Menuhin, Jean-Louis Barrault, Artur Schnabel, Margot Fonteyn, Andres Segovia and John Gielgud; 1949, New York again, Havana, Holland for the premier of Britten's 'Spring' Symphony, Salzburg, Copenhagen, Oslo; 1950, New York for the last time, Nebraska, Wisconsin, Illinois, Missouri, New Mexico, California, Montreal, and Bach's B Minor Mass with von Karjan and Schwarzkopf at La Scala, Milan; 1952, in Vienna to record *Das Lied* with Walter, in England a private recital for the new Queen; 1953, February 6, at Covent Garden as Orpheus, in a new English translation of Gluck, her last public appearance.

Accidents. What if her marriage had been happy? If her

KATHLEEN FERRIER
Contralto

A new singer of remarkable talent.
Manchester Guardian

Her first publicity leaflet, 1942

marriage, unhappy or happy, had led to children? If there had been no war? Wonderful throat cavity or not, it seems unlikely that those ten years would have unfolded for her in the way they did. Cardus, her admirer, wrote that he doubted that she would have turned away from a more loving and rewarding domesticity 'to embark on the wandering life of a concert singer'; that 'disappointment in marriage probably canalized her emotional impulses...and [her] aim and purpose were consciously or sub-consciously crystallized'.

Still, there was a price. In November 1952, Cardus heard her sing Schumann's *Frauenliebe und Leben* cycle—'A woman's life and love'—at the Royal Festival Hall. He thought she had made too many gestures, that she'd overstressed the lyrics with too much theatrical 'business' with her face and hands. After the concert, he walked up and down the Embankment 'battling with his conscience' over the duties of friendship and honest criticism, and then, criticism winning, committed his thoughts to the pages of the *Manchester Guardian*. He wrote to Ferrier explaining his reasons, and Ferrier replied graciously. The fact was, she wrote, that she hadn't been consciously 'acting'—she couldn't help singing these songs about love, marriage and children this way: 'If someone I adored had just proposed to me, I should be breathless with excitement and unable to keep still; and if I had a child, I should hug it till it yelled...'

3. Tears

She liked to laugh. All her friends attest to that. She liked to laugh, and cook, and paint, and garden. Also, she liked to smoke. Passing Cloud was her favourite brand; expensive, oval cigarettes with a King Charles cavalier on the packet lying back and smoking with his boots on. Untipped, of course. During her tours, she would ration herself to one after each concert, but when she was ill and at home in bed she could smoke to her heart's content: a silver lining—she never neglected those. Neither was she averse to a drink. The phrase 'a dirty big pint' appears in one of her letters, and when Barbirolli brought good vintage wine and port to her flat for celebrations, the bottles were emptied. Above all, perhaps, she liked to eat. After seven years of British rationing, she found a cornucopia in North America, and on the way there. Her letters delight in the details of ship's menus, and never mind

At Glyndebourne in 1946 and 1947. Top left, with contralto Nancy Evans
Top right, with soprano Zoë Vlachopoulos

the swell. Rarely can the food of Cunard liners have slipped down a more appreciative throat, or one so wide and free of obstruction.

A woman of hearty appetites, then, a good woman for men to be with. She liked their company. Sex? We may never know. Romantic love? We'll come to that.

There are apparent paradoxes, but only to those of us who expect other people to be all of a piece, and chained to their upbringing. For a woman who left school at fourteen, she showed fine instincts for eighteenth-century furniture and glass. For a woman of great and almost Victorian personal probity—incontestable on the evidence—she took enormous pleasure, again incontestably, from what was then known as filth. She loved double entendres, limericks, swearing, all kinds of bawdiness and ribaldry. Barbirolli, Benjamin Britten and Peter Pears called her 'Rabelaisian'. Cardus said that she could 'lend to a sequence of swear-words the rhythm of hexameters'. One of her more harmless favourites is quoted in Maurice Leonard's biography. She liked to recite:

> I wish I were a fascinating bitch
> I'd never be poor, I'd always be rich.
> I'd live in a house with a little red light,
> And sleep all day, and work all night.

Probity and ribaldry may be the complementary sides of the same old northern English coin. The paradox which is harder to reconcile is her determination to make zestful light of everything—even her music, even (and especially) her illness—with her musical ability to move an audience to the point of tears. In her letters, almost to the end, Ferrier is a writer marked by the multiple exclamation mark: whoopee!!! Life is a great adventure for 'lucky, lucky Kaff' this 'lucky old twerp' who is 'tickled pink' and sometimes 'pickled tink': nothing is sacred, and nothing numinous. Brahms's Alto Rhapsody becomes his Alto Raspberry. Saint-Saëns has composed 'Softly Awakes My Tart'. Purcell didn't write 'Mad Bess of Bedlam' but Bad Mess of the same.

Her mastectomy means removing 'a bump on mi busto'.

You have to smile. Listen to Brahms's Raspberry on a CD, however, to the point where the previously-silent chorus joins Ferrier

At the Edinburgh Festival, 1947

HULTON DEUTSCH

in the final stanza, the one that asks God to save Goethe's bereft young wanderer: and is that or is it not a pricking behind the eyes? No cause for shame. Hardened conductors and orchestral players have also cried. According to Elizabeth Schwarzkopf, Herbert von Karajan burst into tears when Ferrier began to sing the 'Agnus Dei' in Bach's B Minor Mass at La Scala, though he had heard it often enough before and he was conducting her (and Schwarzkopf) at the time. The following year, 1952, she did *Das Lied* with Josef Krips conducting the London Symphony at the Festival Hall, and at the end, according to Krips, 'we all, the orchestra and myself, were in tears'.

Only when she was singing did Ferrier herself cry in front of other people. It often gave her difficulty. As Peter Pears told a BBC programme in 1978: 'If anything, Kath felt things almost too strongly. She often had to fight to control her tears.' In 1944 Winifred watched her practising Brahms's *Four Serious Songs*, which are set to verses from the Biblical books of Ecclesiastes and Corinthians, and noticed how one of them, 'Oh Death, How Bitter Art Thou', regularly made her cry. But Mahler, after she was introduced to his music by Bruno Walter, gave her the fiercest struggle. There had been a lot of death in Gustav Mahler's life—his siblings, his four-year-old daughter—and when he sat down to compose *Das Lied von der Erde*, 'The Song of the Earth', a heart ailment was already giving him intimations of his own. The music has parts for a tenor and a contralto, who sing alternately, with lyrics which are translated from a collection of Chinese poetry. The last song, the 'Abschied', or 'Farewell', is given to the contralto and lasts, with orchestral punctuation, for twenty-eight minutes. The message is: our lives are brief, but the beauties of the world go on.

Allüberall und ewig blauen licht die Fernen!
Ewig...ewig...ewig...ewig

Everywhere and forever, the blue distance shines!
Forever...(and) ever...(and) ever...(and) ever

Rehearsing these final lines with Walter before her first performance of *Das Lied* in Edinburgh in September, 1947, Ferrier sometimes choked and could not finish. At the performance itself, she could barely get the final two *'ewigs'* out. Her face was running with tears. Nobody complained. In Britain, nobody had heard Mahler so brilliantly sung before. The critic in *Punch* wrote: 'Days afterwards I still seem to hear that haunting heartbreaking farewell and Kathleen Ferrier's glorious voice singing *"Ewig...ewig...ewig"* across time and space.' Cardus wrote: 'Such experiences cannot be written of in terms of musical criticism.' Afterwards, he went round to the artists' room to congratulate her—they had never met before. She greeted him 'as though she had known me for a lifetime' and said: 'What a fool I've made of myself. And what will Dr Walter think of me?' Cardus told her that she shouldn't worry, for he was sure that Walter would take both her hands in his and reply: 'My dear child, if we had all been artists as great as you we should all have wept—myself, orchestra, audience, everybody.'

What was it in her that responded so fully, so rawly, to music which, as Walter later said, 'men wrote in moments of solemnity and devotion'? A few people, though not her intimates, saw her jollity as a disguise. Ronald Duncan, who wrote the libretto for Britten's *Lucretia*, met her several times during production meetings in 1946 and said that he thought tears were never far from her eyes, caused 'not only by her unfortunate marriage but a need for love which life itself could not fulfil.' But there was also a more general morbidity. According to Winifred, both in her book and in conversations with Maurice Leonard, Kathleen had feared cancer ever since childhood, when she witnessed the slow death of a woman neighbour in Blackburn. An underlying reason for the move to London in 1942 had been access to better doctors and hospitals. Though her cancer wasn't diagnosed until 1951, she had gone through the 1940s worrying intermittently about pains in her breast. According to Winifred, the soreness had started soon after she was married in 1935, when someone had 'accidently caught her a blow with his elbow'. According to Winifred, the someone was Kathleen's husband, Bert Wilson.

4. Winifred

A modern question, which nobody would have asked in 1953: was Ferrier a lesbian? A few women, too young to have known her or that time, like to think so. A lesbian colleague of a friend of mine, hearing that I was interested in the singer, said: 'She spent only one night with a man, and that put her off it for life.' But we know that, or think we know it, because of Winifred's opinion, as it is indirectly quoted in Leonard's biography: 'Years later Kathleen confessed to Winifred that she had dreaded every night of her honeymoon.' In Winifred's own biography, there is a passage which, considering the period and the fact that Bert Wilson was still alive (he died in 1966), is remarkable for its intimacy and implication. During the rehearsals for *Lucretia*, Ferrier found that she could not reach the climactic top A which she had to ring out while stabbing herself. Britten rescored the piece to replace the A with an F sharp. Then, at one of the last Glyndebourne performances, Britten was startled to hear her hit the original higher note—'the first she had ever sung in public, I think I remember her saying'. Winifred Ferrier makes a great deal of the event. She reproduces Ronald Duncan's libretto and Britten's music—the only place that musical notation occurs in her narrative.

> Last night Tarquinius ravished me
> And took his peace from me...
> Even love's too frail to bear the weight of shadows,
> Now [*she stabs herself*] I'll be forever chaste,
> With only death to ravish me.

Winifred's commentary runs underneath: 'In this opera to sing these words demands a high order of emotional control, but when their meaning has personal significance, the strain can be almost intolerable. Perhaps the real explanation of that "Top A" lies in its symbolic revelation of how she dealt with the deep problems of her life.'

It is hard to be completely certain where Winifred is pointing her readers with these words: rape seems the likeliest destination, on the other hand it could be the line about a life of chastity, with or without rape to set it off. But if rape was in Winifred's mind, then the consequence of her vindictiveness towards another Ferrier biography which was published in the same year suggests otherwise. While Winifred was writing her book for the publisher Hamish Hamilton (who was a friend of Kathleen's), a journalist called

Charles Rigby was finishing a rival biography for the publisher
Robert Hale. Rigby's book appeared first, though the author died
before its publication. Winifred read it and insisted—she was indeed
a formidable woman—that it was republished to include a page that
would correct, in the publisher's words, 'errors of fact and
expressions of opinion which are clearly wrong'. There were nine of
them, none of them serious apart from the marriage question. Rigby
had dealt with it as a private matter. Kathleen and her husband had
'just gone their separate ways'; the divorce had not been reported in
the press, and Kathleen never talked of it. Winifred, however, wanted
things more public and more plain. The note published at her request
reads: 'The author has clearly formed a misleading impression of one
important aspect of Kathleen Ferrier's marriage. This was dissolved
by reason of her husband's incapacity to consummate it.'

Not rape then, but the opposite of rape, or rape successfully
thwarted, or—the common thing—some want of desire in the
chemistry between two people. But Winifred always remained keen
on the idea of non-consummation as the husband's fault. Among
Kathleen's papers in the archive at Blackburn's museum, there is one
of Winifred's own: a typewritten sheet which reads like a memo to
herself, reminding her of the facts she would disclose to any future
biographer or inquiring journalist:

KATHLEEN FERRIER'S MARRIAGE

While she was married to Albert Wilson, Kathleen never talked
about it. I did not question her although I was surprised that they
had no children.

After the Annulment she told me that, even before the wedding
she realized that it was a mistake but she had got so involved with
his family and with the people in the village that she could not face
the prospect of upsetting them all by breaking it off. She said that
her future father-in-law would have had a stroke if she had!

She tried to be a good wife to Albert and said to him once, 'I do
wish that you would make a bit of a fuss of me' and he replied,
'You don't run after a bus when you have caught it.'

In the War it was Albert's call-up and Kathleen's growing
reputation as a singer which set her free. Eventually she applied for
an Annulment of the marriage and this is an extract from the

As Orfeo, with Ann Ayars as Euridice: a break in rehearsals, Glyndebourne, 1947

MARIA AUSTRIA

Divorce Registry in the High Court of Justice. [March 31, 1947]
  Kathleen Mary Wilson Ferrier, Petitioner
  Albert Wilson, Respondent.
The marriage at Brinscoll Methodist Chapel, Chorley, to be
pronounced and declared to be absolutely null and void to all
intents and purposes in the law by reason of the incapacity of the
Respondent to consummate the marriage.

According to Maurice Leonard, Winifred was simply so peeved
at the idea of anyone other than her writing a book about her sister
that she would have done anything to spoil its chance of success, even
to the extent of breaching Bert Wilson's privacy in her need to correct
its 'mistakes'. But there may be more to it—resentment towards the
man who had taken Kathleen from her. Winifred was, even for a big
sister, unusually devoted to Kathleen. The 'touring honeymoon in the
South' reported in the *Blackburn Times* was in fact spent with
Winifred at her flat in Edgware, north London, where she had a job
as a teacher. When Bert was called up in 1940, Winifred took another
teaching job in Carlisle, so that she could live again with her sister
and her father. And in London the same ménage à trois continued
for several years. She never married. She was her sister's biggest
supporter. She became headmistress of a school in Chiswick, west
London, and then, thanks to a connection made through Kathleen,
went to work as a fashion buyer for Marks & Spencer. For the forty-
two years she lived after 1953, her emotional life was gathered
around her sister's memory, and the medical charities and musical
scholarships which served it.

The obvious explanation for the speculation about Kathleen's
sexuality is that she seemed to fit a certain lesbian stereotype. She was
a tall, beautiful woman with a deep voice and no apparent ties to men.
Very few people knew she had been married. Several of the songs she
sang were originally written for the male voice. Her most famous
dramatic role, as Orfeo, required her to act as a man (the part was
written by Gluck for a castrato). The private truth, however, is that
she loved men and was involved with them. One of the boxes in the
museum at Blackburn contains her pocket diaries, which start early
in the war, after Bert had left for the army. They are touching in the

brevity and simplicity of their entries, and by what they show of her ability to pick herself up and get on with life. A man called John appears in 1942.

May 16	Sunderland. Up at 5am!! John met me in Newcastle. Had breakfast in station. Went to Station Hotel to pass the time till lunch and train for Sunderland. Concert went off very well. Tea in Station Hotel all together. Home at 8.20 after salmon mayonnaise in Eldon Grill! Walked home. Two heart-to-heart talks today. What a strain.
June 8	Letter from John.
June 10	Bert coming home.
July 7	London. Met John. Went to [unclear] and punted.
July 11	John rang up from Bedford.
July 23	Telegram from John.
August 4	Letters from John and Bert.
August 13	Gateshead Miners' Welfare Hall Whickham. Stay at Mrs Cookes [in ink—then in pencil:] Letter from John. Rang him up. Final break. Concert not bad.
August 14	Came home. Depressed. Went to flix [the cinema] with Mrs Simpson. Shopped.

So much for John. Rick arrived in 1944.

May 4	L'pool. Dinner dance with Rick Davies. Gorgeous time.
February 15 (1945)	Rick rang from Liverpool!!

Rick Davies, who was a Liverpool antique dealer, appears regularly in her diaries until December 1951. He wanted to marry her, but by that stage Ferrier had decided she was 'a lone she-wolf' whose dedication to singing was absolute. In June 1950, Davies had flown to Zurich to spend some time with her. Kathleen wrote to Winifred: 'I don't mind him for a buddy for two days, then I've had enough and want to retire behind an iron curtain and not have to listen and make conversation. Fickle, that's me.'

Winifred and Kathleen outside Notre Dame, 1951

5. A lucky ole twerp

How else did Ferrier see herself? If private correspondence is any key to a person's character, then as blessed and stoic and lucky, oh so very lucky. In 1978, Tennessee Williams heard a recording of Ferrier for the first time and was so moved by her voice that he immediately wrote a mournful and not very good poem about her ('the string of the violins/Are a thousand knives in her breast'). But there is no self-mourning in Ferrier, or none that she wants to let on about. Alan Bennett might have invented her, or indeed she, and other north country women like her, might have invented *him*. The letters at the Blackburn archive almost dance out of their cardboard boxes with good humour.

America was her great discovery. On her way there for the first time, on the *Mauretania*, she wrote to her sister.

January 6, 1948

Dearest Win,

Hello love! Here I am, propped up in bed, having had a gorgeous breakfast & feeling the complete diva!

Heavens! I never expected to enjoy this trip so much. We've had sunshine, gales—heavy swells and I've never turned a hair—even when I've seen other folk in distress! Bless Dr Morton for his littul pills.

I don't know where to start, but our main conversation is the food! I have never ever seen such dishes, and we are being very spoiled by the chief steward who thinks up meals for us, so that we start with tomato juice, caviar with all the trimmings, soup, fish, lobster or salmon, beef, steaks, joints of all descriptions, and the most amazing sweets ever. Baked ice-cream—that is ice cream with cherries in brandy & the brandy lit with a match till there are blue flames all over it. Mr Tillett [her agent] has a liver, but if he will have two eggs for breakfast—! True he only asked for one, but they always double the order!

I have a cabin to myself with my own shower & lav, and everything is sheer luxury. We have deck chairs on the Promenade deck, and as soon as we arrive in the morning our feet are tucked up in warm rugs & we get chicken soup & a dry biscuit!

We share a dining table with James Mason's mother-in-law, and an Australian lady,—Mrs Stilwell, whom I always have to arrive at her name by steps—such as 'Quite good' 'Getting better' and 'Very well'!! Also on ship are Zoltan Korda (film man who made Sanders of the River) Viscountess Rothermere and Ernest Ansermet [her conductor at Glyndebourne in 1946] and wife! But otherwise nobody startling. We have been invited to cocktails with the Chief Steward & the Captain, and altogether have had a wonderful time & a grand rest. I won 10/- on the horseracing & lost it all the next night!!

There are people on board who haven't had more than a couple of meals the whole trip they have been so ill, so I'm feeling elated at my seaworthiness! Mr Tillett's a good sailor—it's just his liver wot gets him down! He's grand and good company and very anxious as to my welfare, and we're getting on fine.

Have seen about four films & the time has just flown! My earrings are lovely & I'm taking great care of them—will write again after we arrive tomorrow.

Loads of love to you both and I hope all's well with you.

Klever Kaff!

In New York, she wrote to her father and her personal assistant and secretary, Paddy Jewett. In conversation, she always used 'me' for 'my'—'me face, me breakfast'—which in her letters becomes 'mi'.

> Hotel Weylin, New York City
> Sunday 20th March

Dearest Pop & Paddy,

...I now have six concerts off mi chest, and they have all gone very well. Pittsburg was a huge success, thank goodness!

Sandor [Arpad Sandor, her accompanist] continues to annoy me almost more than I can bear—he played so softly in the Ash Grove the other night I could hardly hear him, & I had to say 'LOUDER' out of the corner of my mouth in between verses, but of course he didn't hear me! He's the only thing that makes me nervous for my recital here—I never know what he'll do next. At Pittsburg we did Heidenröslein as an encore, unrehearsed, and he put in trills where there weren't any—I stood with my mouth open—the audience would think it was peculiar interpretation!! Twice, he's put in a major chord where there's only an octave in the Erl King & when

I asked him to play it & Röslein again at a rehearsal the other day, he played them both just as written! I think he'll go ga-ga one day very soon!

I think mi pitcher's good in the Evening News—it flatters me. I can hardly wear that hat now cos Ann chopped mi hair off the other day & now I'm like this—s'rather fetching!!

Yesterday I bought myself a girdle for mi spare tyre—it's a beauty & comes right above mi waist line. Instead of oozing at mi waistline I just ooze top & bottom—it's beautiful! I also got a brassière-top petticoat—no bra needed—in nylon & 3 prs of pants—all needing no ironing!! And it works too, cos I've washed a pair of pants to make sure! I think even John would be proud of my waist now.

Bruno Walter is going to play for me in a New York recital next year as well as Edinburgh & London (Sep 28th) Isn't that marvellous? He's given me 8 new songs to learn, but I do it gladly for him!...Loads of love to you all... Kaff

She went alone on her second tour of North America. Her agent, John Tillett, had died. For sixteen weeks she criss-crossed the USA and Canada by train. She wrote to her father that at Granville, Ohio, 'the concert was about a quarter filled, and some of them knitting!! I could have spat at them'. From Saint John, New Brunswick, she wrote to Tillett's widow, Emmie, who now ran the agency.

March 12, 1949

My dear Emmie,

I am enclosing a few criticisms I have collected on my travels, Los Angeles San Francisco, New York and Montreal, and I would like— if you agree—to have an insertion in the Times and Telegraph with a few quotations just to let people know I've been working hard— and not disappeared for three months! Aren't they lovely ones? I'm being very spoiled and just lapping it up!

...All goes well here—it's been a lovely tour—and I still haven't signed owt! Klever Kaff!

...Tell Miss Lereculey [in Paris] my French grows apace—I'm learning some Chausson—and she'll have to look for competition! I can say 'Darling, je vous aime beaucoup—passepartout—cul-de-

I never know what he'll do next. At Pittsburg we did Haiden Röslein as an encore, unrehearsed. He put in trills where there weren't any — I stood with my mouth open — the audience would think it was peculiar interpretation!! Twice, he's put in a major chord where there's only an octave in the "Erl King" & when I asked him to play it & Röslein again at a rehearsal the other day, he played them both just as written!! I think he'll go gaga one day very soon!

I think mi pitcher's good in the Evening News — it flatters me. I can hardly wear that hat now cos Ann chopped mi hair off the other day & now I'm like this — s'rather fetching!!

Yesterday I bought myself a girdle for mi spare tyre — it's a beauty & comes right above mi waist line. Instead of oozing at mi waistline I just ooze top & bottom — it's beautiful! I also got a brassiere-top petticoat — no bra needed — in nylon & 3 prs of pants — all needing no ironing!! And it works too, cos I've washed a pair of pants to make sure! I think even John would be proud of mi waist now.

Bruno Walter is going to play for me in a New York recital next year as wellas Edinburgh & London (Sep 28th) Isn't that marvellous? He's given me 8 new songs to learn, but I do it gladly for him. We've also (Ann & I) been booked for two repeats of Orfeo in N.Y. Kleve Us! Will write again soon. At this address until the 29th. Loads of love to you all, not forgetting Closet!
Katt

sac—Vouley vous coucher avec—oh no! that's the rude one!
Heigh ho quelle vie! Ain't I a lucky ole budder!
Much love to you all
KATHLEEN

Later the same month, after a concert in New York, she wrote
to her sister from the Hotel Weylin.

Dearest Win,
Well, that's over, thank goodness! It was a complete sell-out with
about 100 people sitting on the platform!!

I've never known such applause—I couldn't start for about 5
mins! Must have been mi red frock. Bruno Walter and Eliz
Schumann were in the audience and the clapping became almost a
nuisance. I was a bit dry about my throat, and so wet about my
torso, I had to keep my frock from sticking to my legs by holding
it out in the front of me when I walked. People shouted and
stamped, but the critics this morning are only luke-warm. I can't
get away with the budders here, but it's the audience that are the
final judges, and they couldn't have been more marvellous.
Whattastrain.

...Well, poppet mine, look after yourself—love to Pop and
Paddy... Loads of love.
Klever Question Mark Kaff

In 1950, she was in the USA for what turned out to be her last
tour there. Bruno Walter gave her the use of his house in Beverly
Hills—the Walters were away—and from there she used his
typewriter to write to Emmie Tillett.

February 3, 1950
My dear Emmie,
Thank you so much for your letters love...I am so glad your back
is better again, and your Momma well—much love to her, and I
am looking forward to seeing her when I get back. I heard Dame
Myra [Hess] is ill and has cancelled her tour here—I do hope it isn't
serious??

Ooooooooooo, boy...Orpheus with Dr Bruno?????? YES PLEASE—would forgo all my holiday for that.

The Halle and Orpheus? I think as it was my suggestion that they do it, I must do the Sheffield date, tho I feel rather sadly about the Passion if Dr Jacques has asked for me—but I couldn't travel overnight to do it, as you say.

Gee whiz///// all this work// aren't I a lucky ole twerp/ (I have no exclam. marks on this machine—it does limit me)

Yes, I can do the Apostles for Hanley—it is the Music Makers that gets me doon. Lovely to do Gerontius for the Royal Choral on May 24th—whooppee...

All is going so well here. The concerts have been a great success—we've been to some lovely places—and now I am installed here, and have the house to myself with man and wife [servants] to look after me...The sun is shining—this place is just amazing—the palms and the houses and the glamour pussies, and the luxury of it all. I am being ruined here—I have the use of two superb cars at any time—my bathroom plumbing is an hourly—well nearly—delight, and, oh, it's so warm...I have so many dates with new found friends that it is almost embarrassing, but today I have started on my real holiday—ten days before going to North Calif,. so I am as happy as a lark, and feel very grateful for this wonderful opportunity to see so much...

...Much love to you and thank you for all your endeavours on my behalf—I am a lucky twerp.

Look after yourself,

love Kathleen

During her first American tour, Kathleen had sung at La Crosse, Wisconsin, and made friends with one of the concert's organisers, Benita (aka Bonnie) Cress, and her husband Bill. When she went back to La Crosse in 1950, she stayed with them. The Cresses became two of her closest friends. Ferrier wrote to them regularly until she was too ill to write.

April 8, 1950

Dearest Bill and Benita,

Well, loves, home at last, and the Spring is here to welcome me with blossom, bulbs and sticky horsechestnut buds. It all looks green and lovely.

...The flat looked lovely—Paddy's mother had colour-washed the walls of all the rooms & I had new curtains & carpet in my room—very swish! And everybody was well & happy, so it was a good home-coming after the most wonderful time & tour ever. Lucky Kaff!

Eggs are off the ration too & somebody brought us a pound of real farm butter this morning so we're in clover.

I'm seeing Mr Mertens [André Mertens, her US agent] next week & if I ask him to send you a cheque for $100 could you send us a few things occasionally? Our greatest miss at the moment is sugar—not cubes—and soap—toilet and flakes—& if it were possible to pack some white flour for baking cakes I should be top of the class with my manager here! The grocery stores—I think—will do it all for you, rather than you having the bother of finding boxes, paper & string. I hope this isn't asking too much of you love. Don't trouble for one minute if it is.

Mr Anderson in Chicago sends us Peacock Sliced Dried Beef (Cudahy? Wisconsin) & Paddy & her mother have thought of every way of cooking, steaming, baking & grilling it—with no success. Do you know anything about it—it comes from your part of the world. They've even tried soaking it overnight, but it still baffles.

...Much love to you both & thank you again for all you wonderful & many kindnesses.

God bless you & keep you,

Yours till hell freezes

Love, Kathleen

Three weeks later, on May 1, 1950, she wrote again with 'a naughty limerick'.

There was a young lady of Nantes
Tres chic, jolie et elegante,
Her hole was so small
She was no good at all
Except for la plume de ma tante!

Ian Jack

In July, Ferrier went to see a doctor about pains in her breast. Her teacher, Roy Henderson, went with her and waited outside the surgery. 'Look, Prof!' she said when she came out, 'he's given me a clean bill of health!'

The Cresses, meanwhile, sent two food parcels. Kathleen replied on August 10.

Dearest Bill and Benita,

A wondrous parcel arrived yesterday, full of just all the right things!! Bless you for a 1000 times—we haven't seen such salmon for 10 years so we're going to have a feast one of these days. Thankyou so very much for all your trouble. It couldn't be lovelier. Yes love the 2nd June box arrived safely and in wonderful order—food seems to get here without difficulty—fingers Xd!—we are getting a good store now—but as you say it's a jolly good idea with the world situation looking menacing! Isn't it a bluidy shame for young boys and their parents to be suffering five years after the last holocaust! Whattaworld!

...Going back to your letter. Coffee has always been easy here, because we are tea drinking nation—so there is no difficulty there. Paddy still gloating over the cake mixtures—they really are a blessing in a hurry particularly! We can get Fab here now too and soon soap should be off the ration altogether so we shan't need any more—it will be gorgeous to go in a shop and buy soap without coughing up a niggly bit of printed paper!

Schwarzkopf is a fine musician and she does a terrific amount of work—some things absolutely superb and others, I think, Unsuitable—but all the Viennese singers work themselves to a standstill—I just daudle in comparison! Klever me—I've been home nearly two months—having sometimes two lessons a day and a real rest from concert giving—and I think it has done me a world of good. I've been going a bit gay too, and going to theatres and dinners. Tonight I am going to the Promenade concert—a Beethoven night—and dining afterwards with Malcom Sargent and a friend—M.S. is conducting. I've been spending a lot of money too—bought a fur coat—dyed Russian ermine (very unpatriotic!) but very beautiful—ordered three cupboards to fit in my room for all my odds and sods—and ordered a Beau Decca—longplaying, shortplaying and radio—so now I'm broke, but tickled pink, so what the heck!!!!

My first concert is Aug 28th at Edinburgh with the Brahms Alto Rhap, with Fritz Busch—and it will be lovely when that is over, because I shall be able to relax and enjoy the rest of the festival.

Now I must get ready to go to a lesson before my night out, so thankyou again for everything and God bless.

Much love to you both,
Kaff

She was working hard, she was tired.

November 13, 1950

Dearest Bonnie,

I am 'all behind' mit my letters to you, but have been dashing madly round, now that the season is in full swing again.

The records should really be out now in the States—if they're not soon, I really will get a hat pin to Decca—they said Sept...the bar stewards!

The boxes you sent sound just wonderful... The canned chicken was gorgeous and fell to bits with tenderness, the pore littul budder! The cookies were a treat too—but they are off for me now, cos I'm getting too fat—so I'm cutting all starches (when I'm strong enough) and trying to get my bulges a bit less rotund. I had some new photies taken the other day, and I look like the bull at the other end of the Toreador!!—fraightful!! ...But, otherwise, all is well, and we're all full of beans—and hope you are too.

Dashing off to the north tomorrow—Manchester, Bolton, Huddersfield and Grimsby. Thankyou for everything, bless you, and look after yourselves.

Much love from us all,
Kaff

Early in 1951, her assistant, Paddy Jewett, left to get married. Ferrier hired as her replacement a young New Zealand woman, Bernie Hammond, who also happened to be a trained nurse. In

Ian Jack

March, Ferrier asked her: 'Have a look at this lump will you?'

28 March, 1951

Dearest Benita,

I have neglected you I fear—but things have been happening with such rapidity, I haven't written any personal letters for ages.

First I have got a 'jewel' to look after me & to keep Paddy company until the latter marries. She's a New Zealand girl called Bernie and a trained nurse—but wanting a job where she can be independent. She nursed my manager's mother when she died—and I knew her well, but never thought she'd consider such a mundane job. But she seems in her element, has a wonderful sense of humour & is altogether a pearl. She hasn't got out of her nursing as she thought, as I have to go into hospital any day now for a rather formidable op for a 'bump on mi busto'. But having Bernie here has lightened the load enormously & I am in the finest radiologists & surgeons hands in the country. I have had to cancel a month's tour in Scandinavia & everything until the middle of May—but I am glad of a rest—I feel better now that everything is getting done. I should have gone earlier but haven't been home for months. The X-ray yesterday was better than they thought.

So don't worry, love, & I'll ask Paddy to send you a line. We are fine for everything in the food line and don't want for <u>anything</u>— thanks to you. And I'm smoking with abandon being as 'ow I've not to sing for 6 weeks!

I hope you & Bill are both flourishing & much, much love to you—

Yours till hell freezes,

Kaff

April 18, 1951

Dearest Bonnie,

Bless you for my lovely birthday present—they arrived yesterday— and are so lovely—thank you very, very much.

I am writing my first letters for a bit & feeling real cocky—just waiting for the doctor to come—and being glad it isn't this time last week—when I threw up four times all down Bernie's front—

poor, sweet Bernie—she's been an absolutely bluidy marvel—and I just don't know what I should have done without her.

I don't know about my itinerary yet love—it's at home & I'm not even thinking about singing yet—but I'll let you know in a bit. I shall be here another week or ten days yet—then have to have some rays [radium treatment] for a few weeks—then a holiday— so I'm really enjoying a rest—& gee! I was ready for it. I seem to have startled all the staff here with quick recovery, and I'm being spoiled to death and thoroughly enjoying myself!!

I hope your arm is much better love—you just be a good honey-chile now and have a good rest—and thankyou again for the gorgeous present and lovely card. I am not telling any of my buddies in N.Y. about my op. as such exaggerated rumours get round— you'se the only one wot knows! Much love to you both, Kaff

May 17, 1951

Dearest Benita,

Thank you so much for all your letters—I am so sorry we have neglected you lately... I'm feeling better each day & my anaemia which was rather low, is almost normal again. I have been going each morning to the hospital for rays, and should have only another two weeks to do—perhaps even less. The budder of it is, I haven't to wash my neck and it's about an inch deep in dust—but, I suppose, one of these days, I'll be a clean girl again!

I haven't had a bath for over six weeks!—I don't 'arf pong!

The doctors are enormously pleased with me—and I'm in wonderful hands—I couldn't have been better cared for—and I've loved the rest, and don't ever want to start again!! My dr. says I have to go easy for 2 yrs that is why I have had to cancel the first month of America—but I shall be doing Chicago so hope to see you there. Bernie is coming with me & is pickled tink!

Between you and me, I'm very lop-sided at the top but am camouflaging with great taste & delicacy!! And what the heck, as long as I feel well & can sing a bit, eh?

...We're all right for parcels for the moment, love—and I'm not short of a single thing—I'm just spoiled to death!

Much love to you both—will write again, Kaff

She began to sing again. She toured Holland and appeared at the Edinburgh Festival in September. But she cancelled her American tour which was scheduled for later that year. Her disease and her frequent radium therapy were exhausting her.

August 7, 1951

Dearest Bonnie,

...I have been dashing about a bit since Holland, and have just been hibernating on my bed in between concerts to be ready for the next one. Bernie has been doing everything!! Keeping me in control, the housework, shopping (quite a long job here with queues!) endless letters and the cooking—and she's still bright and cheerful. You'll have to see her—she's every jewel rolled in one. Lucky Kaff!

Here it comes love! I have to cancel my American trip—not because I'm any worse—I hasten to tell you—but because Holland took it our of me a bit, and the doctor feels that so heavy a tour would be asking for trouble so soon. If I needed treatment it can really only be given here, as it is such an intricate business that only a doctor who knows the case could cope. HELL! HELL! HELL! My tour started off with a recital every other day and travelling in between, and it just makes me tired to think of it, but I am grieved to the core to miss my buddies there, and especially LaCrosse, but I think it is wise, and it will be the first long rest I have had in ten years! I know you will understand and try not to be too disappointed, because by this time next year I hope to be bouncing with health.

...I do hope you are well and happy and forgive me for not writing sooner—the days go so quickly!

God bless and look after yourselves and much love from
Kaff

24th September 24, 1951

Dearest Bonnie,

...Edinburgh went well—Bruno was 'pickled tink' and said it was a privilege to work with me, which made music in my heart! The hall was full and sitting on the platform and it was broadcast all over the place so it was quite a strain—and I've felt better ever since!

Had another X-ray last week and the doctor is very pleased and I have finished my treatment at the hospital which is a lovely thought—pets though they are! I hope it's for good. I'm putting on weight and getting so perky there's no holding me—but it's a lovely thought that I can have a complete rest until the New Year, even though it means not seeing my buddies in LaCrosse. I'm even catching up on letters as you can see—have tidied my drawers—the first time in ten years!!! and have even had a bit of decorating done to cheer up the place. We're looking fraightfully posh now old girl!

...Much love to you and Bill and God bless, and thankyou for everything

Kathleen

October 27, 1951

Dearest Bonnie,

Just a word in your ear of real thanks for the heavenly soap which arrived this morning—bless you—it's a very special treat and a real luxury. You are a poppet of the first rank!

...All's well here—I'm having a complete rest from singing and going gay a bit—to Covent Garden & theatres—first time in 10 yrs!

I hear there are all sorts of rumours [about her illness] about me there—originated from Edinburgh—Mr Mertens says. Between you & me, love, I think some it comes from Ethel Bartlett—I may be wrong—but will you keep your pretty pink ears open—or perhaps just ask for news of me if given the chance—& tell me what she says? I'd like to be proved wrong, but have mi suspicions! There are malicious rumours going around—so don't let on you know me. Okeydoke. And don't believe any of the rumours—I'll let you know the truth, first thing—and at this moment—I'm jes full o' beans! God bless, darlings—

I'll write again soon.

Much love to you both

Kaff

She spent 1952 in pain—backache, referred to publicly as 'mi rheutamics' or 'screwmatics'. Often she was cold. Hotels in provincial Britain had to be told to bank up the coal fires in her bedrooms. Recording *Das Lied* with Walter in Vienna, she at one point collapsed. Her itinerary that year included Aldeburgh and Edinburgh. She consulted a leading oncologist, Sir Stanford Cade, who suggested a 'bilateral adrenalectomy', though this was not at the time pursued. Radium therapy was renewed. After Ferrier had performed for the Queen at a country house party that summer, the monarch sat with her and asked how she was. Her reply, as given in Leonard's biography: 'Just the odd ache, Ma'am. You have to expect these things.'

In February 1953, she was scheduled to sing four performances of the new *Orpheus* with John Barbirolli at Covent Garden. That was thought to be the most she could manage. During the second performance, on February 6, the femur in her left leg snapped and partly disintegrated. She vomited through pain—but in the wings— and continued to sing till the close. After a morphine injection, she took several curtain calls and received well-wishers in her dressing room. She never sang in public again.

February 27, 1953

Dearest Benita,

I am so sorry I have not written for such an age, but I have been terribly busy rehearsing 'Orpheus', and then at the second performance I snipped a bit of bone off in my leg, so here I am once again, reposing in University College Hospital! I am having treatment every day and it is already much better, but I shall probably be here for another month at least. I don't feel a bit poorly, but am not allowed as yet to stand up on my legs, but hope I'll be all right for some more performances of 'Orpheus' in May.

Your wonderful, amazing, delicious, heavenly, gorgeous chocolates arrived a couple of days ago, and I haven't tasted anything like them for ages. They are so pretty, too. Thank you so very much—you do spoil me terribly... and how I lap it up!!

I had to miss going to Buckingham Palace [she had been awarded the CBE], but have heard a whisper that I may be pushed in to one of the summer Investitures. I do hope so, because I've got a new hat and coat!

The first night of 'Orpheus' was absolutely thrilling, with a very distinguished audience shouting their heads off at the end. Everyone was thrilled and the notices were all splendid, which makes it all the more disappointing that I could not carry on.

I have your face towels here with me—that you sent for Christmas—so have a constant reminder of you both. Bernie is here nursing me most of the day, not that I need it much, so that makes it very pleasant.

I do hope you are both full of beans and thank you again with all my heart for innumerable kindnesses. Much love to you both and God bless, Kathleen

April 3, 1953

Dearest Benita,

Thankyou so much for your sweet Easter card & handkerchief— it brightened my day considerably, and it's such a lovely hanky. I'm still in hospital, but leaving in the morning—whoopee, whoopee— & going to a new home at 40 Hamilton Terrace, which Bernie tells me is looking lovely. I should have gone three days ago but caught a bug from somewhere & a temperature & a very queasy stomach, so had to stay—I was furious! But I'm quite all right now & looking forward to the morning. My legs are much better & I can take a few steps, but not too many & for the moment will be whizzing round in a wheel chair.

We had 48 steps to my old flat & it meant that once up them and I should be a prisoner there, so Bernie & Win had to rush round & find something else. We've been very fortunate and got a maisonette (half an old house) with a bedroom & bathroom downstairs for me & a lovely garden, which is something I have always yearned for. We've had the house papered & painted (to hell with the expense!) so I can hardly wait to see it.

I am going to have a complete rest this summer & work quietly for Edinburgh. Will write again when I'm home & tell you all about it.

Much love to you both from Kathleen

On May 3 a profile of Ferrier in the *Sunday Times* said that during the Covent Garden *Orpheus* she had concealed from the audience 'the fact she was suffering most painfully from arthritis', and that 'we must possess our souls in patience and wish her well'. On May 22, Ferrier wrote in her pocket diary: 'Dr Eccles—must have

After her first operation, University College Hospital, 1951

mi ovaries removed'. All later entries have been crossed out.

Her ovaries were removed in June. On July 27, she had Sir Stanford's double adrenalectomy. Earlier, she had worried about the operation's effect on her voice. There was no point worrying about that now.

October 15, 1953

Dear Mrs Cress,

I am so sorry that I did not send you a cable or let you know about Kath, it must have been an awful shock to you—we were just snowed under with the Press and millions of other things and I just did not manage to do it. But I would like you to know that Kath was perfect to the end, the last few days she had injections and slept most of the time and just went very quietly in her sleep as I had hoped and prayed she would.

If this had to be in the first place, one just must accept it and make the necessary adjustments, Kath would expect that of us. She had so much to bear these last few months, if she was not going to get out of bed then it is much better thus and I am convinced that the essential part of Kath is never very far from those who loved her—so don't grieve too much sweetie, be thankful that now nothing can hurt her or cause her pain and <u>know</u> that she is happy somewhere. Do keep on writing to me.

All my love

Bernie [Hammond]

Kathleen Ferrier died on the morning of October 8, 1953. She was forty-one. Barbirolli said that it was 'one of the great tragedies of our time'. Bruno Walter wrote that 'whoever listened to her or met her personally felt enriched and uplifted'. But her nurse, Bernie Hammond, said the simplest thing: 'She was an extraordinary person, and an ordinary one.' □

If you were twenty in the summer of 1967, San Francisco was the only place to be. The number one song told us all to wear flowers in our hair, as we were going to meet some gentle people there.

But I was ten in the summer of 1967, and boarding two miles from Basingstoke, in a Roman Catholic prep school. My friend Miller tried wearing a flower in his hair, only to be told by Major Watt to take it out at once. Major Watt was rumoured to be a Nazi spy. Someone had seen him in the school grounds late at night flashing secret messages to the Germans with a torch.

Gentle people were few and far between. Our new history master, Mr Wall, who wore pink socks, had a slapdash, Bohemian air about him, but he left under a cloud, after dropping his trousers when someone enquired as to what colour his pants were. Gentleness, flowers, and even hair were in short supply.

I was studying hard for my confirmation. Why did God make me? God made me to know him love him and serve him in this world and be happy with him forever in the next. In our confirmation classes, we took a peculiar delight in cross-questioning Mr Callaghan on the fine points of Roman Catholic theology. It always came back to the same old desert island. Sir, sir, sir! But what if you were stuck on a desert island, and there was a baby who was dying, and the baby hadn't been christened, sir, and there was no water about, sir. Would you be allowed to use your spit, sir? Would you be allowed to use your *pee*, sir?

We had two Masses a week, on Wednesdays and Sundays, and two Benedictions, on Tuesdays and Fridays. Every Benediction, we would sing a hymn called 'Tantum Ergo'. '*Tantum ergo/Sacramentum/ Veneremur cernui/Et antiquum/Documentum...*' We sang it twice a week for five years. We never asked what it meant, and I still don't know. Sacraments, venerate, antique, documents...but its meaning didn't matter. Its sound was its meaning; its absence of meaning was its meaning. Latin was God's first language, and its meaning floated direct to heaven on a cloud of incense pouring out of a thurible swung with such vigour by the seniors that the new boys in the front row would often disappear, coughing and spluttering, in an unholy fog.

'Lady Madonna' came out halfway through the next spring term. I have a vivid memory of hearing it coming from a radio belonging to builders who were patching up the school swimming pool. Its title represented the perfect amalgam of the two essentials of a private Catholic education, suggesting that the Virgin herself was an aristocrat.

But what did it all mean? Why would Lady Madonna have to worry about making ends meet?

'Lady Madonna' was followed by 'Hey Jude' and 'Instant Karma'. Pop music was moving away from meaning, and closer to the language of 'Tantum Ergo', forcing sense to make way for something more mysterious.

At Scout camp we sang, 'Gin gan gooly-gooly-gooly-gooly watch-a, gin gan goo, gin gan goo'. In Maths, we drew Venn diagrams. The Beatles sang, 'I Am the Walrus' ('goo-goo-ga joo'). On Ash Wednesday, we heard the priest repeat, 'Remember man that thou art dust and unto dust thou shalt return,' over and over again as he rubbed ash on to our foreheads. On holy days of obligation, we all went to visit priest's hidey-holes in Catholic stately homes. I often wondered whether groups with Latin names like Procul Harum and Status Quo were Catholic too. And, behind it all, 'Tantum Ergo' was our soundtrack.

My reverence for the faraway heaven of San Francisco was never at odds with my reverence for what in another hymn we called the 'Faith of Our Fathers'. I remember feeling a sharp sense of shock on first glimpsing the heading at the top of the music master's sheet music for 'While Shepherds Watched'. It simply said 'Sox'.

Thirty or more years on, I make my living from parody, nudging sense into nonsense, translating the words of others back into their original gibberish. I find 'Tantum Ergo' has lodged in my head, a dissident group of my brain cells forming a chapel choir, singing it at full blast in impromptu moments. And my imagination keeps returning to Farleigh House, Farleigh Wallop, Basingstoke, Hants. Or perhaps it has always been stranded there, the boarder that never came home. □

The New Grove Dictionary of Music and Musicians, second edition

Edited by Stanley Sadie and John Tyrrell

The New Grove II is the world's premier authority on all aspects of music. Over 20,000 biographies. Over 10,000 cross-references. Over 5,000 illustrations. Over 6,000 of the world's leading scholars. Available in print in 29 volumes and online at www.grovemusic.com. A subscription to grovemusic.com will give you full access to an integrated music resource including *The New Grove II*, *Grove Opera*, and coming in early 2002, *Jazz Grove II*.

"I have already read enough to know that I shall go on reading and needing this latest revision for many years; *Grove* remains indispensable."
Michael Oliver, Gramophone

"*Grove*...may now be the most comprehensive musical dictionary in any language."
Allan Kozinn, The New York Times

Contact

USA and Canada
Grove's Dictionaries Inc.
345 Park Avenue South
New York, NY 10010, USA
tel: 800 221 2123 ext. 204
groves@mopna.com

Grove's Dictionaries of Music
The Macmillan Building
Crinan Street
London N1 9XW, UK
tel: +44 (0)20 7843 4612
email: grove@macmillan.co.uk

Free trial available at www.grovemusic.com

Available in Print and Online

THE SILENCE
Julian Barnes

LEBRECHT MUSIC COLLECTION

One feeling at least grows stronger in me with each year that passes—a longing to see the cranes. At this time of the year I stand on the hill and watch the sky. Today they did not come. There were only wild geese. Geese would be beautiful if cranes did not exist.

A young man from a newspaper helped me pass the time. We talked of Homer, we talked of jazz. He was unaware that my music had been used in *The Jazz Singer*. At times, the ignorance of the young excites me. Such ignorance is a kind of silence.

Slyly, after two hours, he asked about new compositions. I smiled. He asked about the Eighth Symphony. I compared music to the wings of a butterfly. He said that critics had complained that I was 'written out'. I smiled. He said that some—not himself, of course—had accused me of shirking my duties while in receipt of a government pension. He asked when exactly would my new symphony be finished? I smiled no more. 'It is you who are keeping me from finishing it,' I replied, and rang the bell to have him shown out.

I wanted to tell him that when I was a young composer I had once scored a piece for two clarinets and two bassoons. This represented an act of considerable optimism on my part, since at the time there were only two bassoonists in the country, and one of them was consumptive.

The young are on the way up. My natural enemies! You want to be a father figure to them and they don't give a damn. Perhaps with reason.

Naturally the artist is misunderstood. That is normal, and after a while becomes familiar. I merely repeat, and insist: misunderstand me correctly.

A letter from K. in Paris. He is worried about tempo markings. He must have my confirmation. He must have a metronome marking for the Allegro. He wants to know if *doppo piu lento* at letter K in the second movement applies only for three bars. I reply, Maestro K., I do not wish to oppose your intentions. In the end—forgive me if I sound confident—one may express the truth in more than one way.

Julian Barnes

I remember my talk with N. about Beethoven. N. was of the opinion that when the wheels of time have made a further turn, the best symphonies of Mozart will still be there, whereas those of Beethoven will have fallen by the wayside. This is typical of the differences between us. I do not have the same feelings for N. as I have for Busoni and Stenhammar.

It is reported that Mr Stravinsky considers my craftsmanship to be poor. I take this to be the greatest compliment I have received in the whole of my long life! Mr Stravinsky is one of those composers who swings back and forth between Bach and the latest modern fashions. But technique in music is not learned at school with blackboards and easels. In that respect Mr I. S. is at the top of the class. But when one compares my symphonies with his stillborn affectations...

A French critic, seeking to loathe my Third Symphony, quoted Gounod: 'Only God composes in C major.' Precisely.

Mahler and I once discussed composition. For him, the symphony must be like the world and contain everything. I replied that the essence of a symphony is form; it is the severity of style and the profound logic that creates the inner connection between motifs.

When music is literature, it is bad literature. Music begins where words cease. What happens when music ceases? Silence. All the other arts aspire to the condition of music. What does music aspire to? Silence. In that case, I have succeeded. I am now as famous for my long silence as I have been for my music.

Of course, I could still compose trifles. A birthday intermezzo for the new wife of cousin S., whose pedalling is not as secure as she imagines. I could answer the call of the state, the petitions of a dozen villages with a flag to hang out. But that would be pretence. My journey is nearly complete. Even my enemies, who loathe my music, admit that it has logic to it. The logic of music leads eventually to silence.

A. has the strength of character which is lacking in me. She is not a general's daughter for nothing. Others see me as a famous man with a wife and five daughters, a cock of the walk. They say that A. has sacrificed herself on the altar of my life. Yet I have sacrificed my life on the altar of my art. I am a very good composer, but as a human being—hmm, that's another matter. Yet I have loved her, and we have shared some happiness. When I met her she was for me Josephsson's mermaid, cushioning her knight among the violets. Only, things get harder. The demons manifest themselves. My sister in the mental hospital. Alcohol. Neurosis. Melancholy.

Cheer up! Death is round the corner.

Otto Andersson has worked out my family tree so thoroughly that it makes me ill.

Some consider me a tyrant because my five daughters have always been forbidden to sing or play music in the house. No cheerful screeches from an incompetent violin, no anxious flute running out of breath. What—no music in the great composer's own home! But A. understands. She understands that music must come from silence. Come from it and return to it.

A. herself also operates with silence. There is—God knows—much to rebuke me for. I have never claimed to be the sort of husband who is praised in churches. After Gothenburg she wrote me a letter which will be found when they check my pockets as rigor mortis is setting in. But on normal days she offers no rebuke. And unlike everyone else she never asks when my Eighth will be ready. She merely acts around me. At nights I compose. No, at nights I sit at my desk with a bottle of whiskey and try to work. Later, I wake, my head upon the score and my hand clasped round empty air. A. has removed the whiskey while I sleep. We do not speak of this.

Alcohol, which I once gave up, is now my most faithful companion. And the most understanding!

I go out by myself to dine alone and reflect upon mortality. Or I go to the Kämp, the Societetshuset, the König to discuss the subject with others. The strange business of *Man lebt nur einmal*. I join the lemon table at the Kämp. A. does not approve.

Among the Chinese, the lemon is the symbol of death. That poem by Anna Maria Lenngren—'Buried with a lemon in his hand'. Exactly. A. would try to forbid it on grounds of morbidity. But who is allowed to be morbid, if not a corpse?

I heard the cranes today but did not see them. The clouds were too low. But as I stood on that hill, I heard, coming towards me from above, the full-throated cry they give as they head south for the summer. Invisible, they were even more beautiful, more mysterious. They teach me about sonority all over again. Their music, my music, music. This is what it is. You stand on a hill and from beyond the clouds hear sounds that pierce the heart. Music—even my music— is always heading south, invisibly.

Nowadays, when friends desert me, I can no longer tell whether it is because of my success or because of my failure. Such is old age.

Perhaps I am a difficult man, but not that difficult. All my life, when I have gone missing, they have known where to find me—at the best restaurant serving oysters and champagne.

When I visited the United States, they were surprised that I had never shaved myself in my entire life. As if I were some kind of aristocrat. But I am not, nor even pretending to be. I am merely someone who has chosen never to waste his time by shaving himself. Let others do that for me.

No, that is not true. I am a difficult man, like my father and grandfather. Made worse in my case by being an artist. Also made worse by my most faithful and most understanding companion. There are few days to which I can append the note *sine alc*. It is hard to write music when your hands shake. It is hard also to conduct. In many ways A.'s life with me has become a martyrdom. I acknowledge that.

Gothenburg. I went missing before the concert. I was not to be found in the usual place. A.'s nerves were shredded. She went to the hall nonetheless, praying for the best. To her surprise, I made my entrance at the appointed time, took my bow, raised my baton. A few bars into the overture, she told me, I broke off, as if it were a rehearsal. The audience was puzzled, the orchestra more so. Then I gave a new upbeat and went back to the beginning. What followed, she assured me, was chaos. The audience was enthusiastic, the subsequent press respectful. But I believe A. After the concert, standing among friends outside the hall, I took a whiskey bottle from my pocket and smashed it on the steps. I have no memory of any of this.

When we returned home, and I was quietly drinking my morning coffee, she gave me a letter. After thirty years of marriage, she wrote to me in my own home. Her words have been with me ever since. She told me I was a useless weakling who took refuge from problems in alcohol; one who imagined drinking would help him create new masterpieces, but was grievously mistaken. In any event, she would not expose herself ever again to the public indignity of watching me conduct in an inebriated condition.

I offered no word of reply, written or spoken. I tried to respond by deed. She was true to her letter, and did not accompany me to Stockholm, nor to Copenhagen, nor to Malmö. I carry her letter with me all the time. I have written our eldest daughter's name on the envelope, so she will know, after my death, what was said.

How dreadful old age is for a composer! Things don't go as quickly as they used to, and self-criticism grows to impossible proportions. Others see only fame, applause, official dinners, a state pension, a devoted family, supporters across the oceans. They note that my shoes and shirts are made for me in Berlin. *Homo diurnalis* respects these trappings of success. But I regard *Homo diurnalis* as the lowest form of human life.

I remember the day my friend Toivo Kuula was laid to rest in the cold earth. He was shot in the head by Jaeger soldiers and died a few weeks later. At the funeral, I reflected upon the infinite wretchedness of the artist's lot. So much work, talent and courage, and then everything is over. To be misunderstood, and then to be forgotten, such is the artist's fate. My friend Lagerborg champions the views of Freud, according to whom the artist uses art as a means to escape from neurosis. Creativity provides a compensation for the artist's inability to live life to the full. Well, this is merely a development of Wagner's opinion. Wagner contended that if we enjoyed life fully we would have no need of art. To my mind, they have it back to front. Of course I do not deny that the artist has many neurotic aspects. How could I, of all people, deny that? Certainly I am neurotic and frequently unhappy, but that is largely the consequence of being an artist rather than the cause. When we aim so high and fall short so frequently, how can that not induce neurosis? We are not tram conductors who seek only to punch holes in tickets and call out the stops correctly. Besides, my reply to Wagner is simple: how can a fully lived life fail to include one of its noblest pleasures, which is the appreciation of art?

Freud's theories do not encompass the possibility that the symphonist's conflict—which is to divine laws for the movement of notes which will be applicable for all time—is a somewhat greater achievement than to die for king and country. Many can do that, while planting potatoes and punching tickets and other similarly useful things can be done by many more.

Wagner! His gods and heroes have made my flesh crawl for fifty years now.

In Germany, they took me to hear some new music. I said, 'You are manufacturing cocktails of all colours. And here I come with pure cold water.' My music is molten ice. In its movement you may detect its frozen beginnings, in its sonorities you may detect its initial silence.

I was asked which foreign country has shown the greatest sympathy for my work. I replied England. It is the land without chauvinism. On one visit, I was recognized by the immigration officer. I met Mr Vaughan Williams; we talked in French, our only common language apart from music. After a concert, I gave a speech. I said, I have plenty of friends here, and, naturally, I hope, enemies. In Bournemouth a music student paid his respects and mentioned, in all simplicity, that he could not afford to come to London to hear my Fourth. I put my hand in my pocket and said, 'I will give you *ein Pfund Sterling.'*

My orchestration is better than Beethoven's, and my themes are better. But he was born in a wine country, I in a land where yogurt rules the roost. A talent like mine, not to say genius, cannot be nourished on yogurt.

During the war the architect Nordman sent me a parcel shaped like a violin case. It was indeed a violin case, but inside was a leg of smoked lamb. I composed 'Fridolin's Folly' in gratitude and sent it to Nordman. I knew him for a keen *a cappella* singer. I thanked him for *le délicieux violon.* Later, someone sent me a case of lampreys. I responded with a choral piece. I reflected to myself that things had turned inside out. When artists had patrons, they would produce music, and as long as they continued to do so, they would be fed. Now, I am sent food, and respond by producing music. It is a more haphazard system.

Diktonius called my Fourth a 'bark bread symphony', referring to the old days when the poor used to adulterate flour with finely ground bark. The loaves that resulted were not of the finest quality, but starvation was usually kept at bay. Kalisch said that the Fourth expressed a sullen and unpleasant view of life in general.

When I was a young man, I was hurt by criticism. Now, when I am melancholy, I reread unpleasant words written about my work and am immensely cheered up. I tell my colleagues, 'Always remember, there is no city in the world which has erected a statue to a critic.'

The slow movement of the Fourth will be played at my funeral. And I wish to be buried with a lemon clasped in the hand which wrote those notes.

No, A. would take the lemon from my dead hand as she takes the whiskey bottle from my living one. But she will not countermand my instruction about the 'bark bread symphony'.

My Eighth, that is all they ask about. When, Maestro, will it be finished? When may we publish it? Perhaps just the opening movement? Will you offer it to K. to conduct? Why has it taken you so long? Why has the goose ceased to lay golden eggs for us?

Gentlemen, there may be a new symphony, or there may not. It has taken me ten, twenty years, nearly thirty. Perhaps it will take more than thirty. Perhaps there will be nothing there even at the end of thirty years. Perhaps it will end in fire. Fire, then silence. That is how everything ends, after all. But misunderstand me correctly, gentlemen. I do not choose silence. Silence chooses me.

A.'s name day. She wishes me to go mushrooming. The morels are ripening in the woods. Well, that is not my forte. However, by dint of work, and talent and courage, I found a morel. I picked it, put it to my nose and sniffed, laid it reverently in A.'s little basket. Then I dusted the pine needles from my cuffs and, having done my duty, went home. Later, we played duets. *Sine alc.*

A great auto-da-fé of manuscripts. I collected them in a laundry basket and in A.'s presence burned them in the open fire in the dining room. After a while she could stand it no longer and left. I continued the good work. By the end I was calmer and lighter in mood. It was a happy day.

Things don't go as quickly as they used to... True. But why should we expect life's final movement to be a *rondo allegro*? How should we best mark it? *Maestoso*? Few are so lucky. *Largo*—still a little too dignified. *Largamente e appassionato*? A final movement might begin like that—my own First did so. But in life it does not lead to an *allegro molto* with the conductor flaying the orchestra to greater speed and noise. No, life has a drunkard on the podium, an old man who does not recognize his own music, a fool who cannot tell rehearsal from performance. Mark it *tempo buffo*? No, I have it. Mark it merely *sostenuto*, and let the conductor make the decision. After all, one may express the truth in more than one way.

Today I went for my customary morning walk. I stood on the hill looking north. 'Birds of my youth!' I cried to the sky, 'Birds of my youth!' I waited. The day was heavy with clouds, but for once the cranes were flying beneath them. As they approached, one broke from the flock and flew directly towards me. I raised my arms in acclamation as it made a slow circle around me, trumpeting its cry, then headed back to rejoin its flock for the long journey south. I watched until my eyes blurred, I listened until my ears could hear nothing more, and silence resumed.

I walked slowly back to the house. I stood in the doorway, calling for a lemon. □

Granta

"A TOUR DE FORCE"
—The Times

BLOOD-DARK TRACK

A Family History

In this beautifully written memoir, Joseph O'Neill reconstructs the fate of two men he never met, and who never met each other, but who have had a profound effect on his life. His Turkish and Irish grandfathers were vigorous and strong-willed men, patriarchs and visionaries, and each was imprisoned, one in Palestine, the other in Ireland, during the Second World War. O'Neill retraces these extraordinary lives, and the secrets that he uncovers are both haunting and tragic.

"The progress of his investigations is imbued with all the darkening excitement of a novel by Le Carré or Greene." —Times Literary Supplement

HARDCOVER • 338 PAGES • 1-86207-288-4 • $27.95
www.granta.com/blood

JOSEPH O'NEILL

TRANSLATING CAETANO

John Ryle

John Ryle

In 1986 I was living in Salvador da Bahia, the old capital of Brazil, learning Portuguese. I spent little time in the classroom. There was a beach at the end of the street. And scattered all round the city and in the shanty-towns beyond were the temples of Candomblé, the Afro-Brazilian religion of which Salvador, an old slave port, is the heartland. At weekends I frequented a Candomblé temple beyond the airport, in a grove of trees in the lee of a sand dune. It was called Ilê Axé Opô Aganjú, the House of the Power of Xangó, the name of the Yoruba god to whom it was dedicated. The sound of drums summoning African divinities merged with the roar of planes and the murmur of surf. The Saturday-night trance-dance rituals in this poor, black rural suburb, where the devotees, dressed in eighteenth-century ritual costume, chanted Yoruba canticles over the drums, were a distraction from the study of Portuguese grammar, but they expanded my vocabulary, and my mind.

Weekdays I stayed at the Anglo-Americano, a five-dollar-a-night hotel overlooking the Bay of All Saints, the expanse of water where the city of Salvador lies. São Salvador da Bahia de Todos os Santos, with its sheltered anchorage and fertile hinterland, was the centre of the colonial state of Brazil from the sixteenth to the eighteenth century, staging post for the slave trade that fuelled the sugar industry in the interior, and paid for the baroque churches that cluster in the city centre. The Anglo-Americano dated from a later, less vainglorious era. A yellowing, tumble-down, turn-of-the-century edifice, it stood out like a broken tooth in the line of sleek, white high-rises on the bluff above the harbour.

I liked staying there. The coffee at breakfast was weak, the milk reconstituted from powder, but the view across the bay was mesmerizing. Changes in the light transformed the surface of the water from zinc to hammered bronze, rust-flecked where oil-tankers lay at anchor. Here—at my most besotted—I felt I was living in a *terra em transe*, the alternative universe I had come to Brazil to find. And here, in the City of Saints, I yearned for the miracle of Pentecost, for the gift of tongues, so I could merge into the language that was being sung and spoken all around me.

The radio played all day at the Anglo-Americano, a cascade of sambas, pagodes, frevos, afoxés, choros, bossas and jazz—music that seemed to be one with the sunlight that streamed into the room. It was here that I discovered Caetano Veloso. The word 'discovered' will seem odd to Brazilian readers. Caetano is Brazil's most celebrated musician and among its most famous citizens. The thirty or so albums he has released since 1966 define the musical era that follows bossa nova, spanning the radical innovations of *Tropicália* (the Sixties artistic and cultural movement in which he was a prime mover), the military dictatorship that suppressed it (and forced him and his fellow-tropicalista Gilberto Gil into exile in England from 1969 to 1972), and the three decades of productivity in music and film that he has enjoyed since his return. If anyone personifies the spirit of Brazilian music, with its rhythmic eclecticism, instrumental complexity and lyrical sophistication, it is Caetano. But I knew none of this in 1986. All I knew was on the sleeve of a record, in a language I was hardly beginning to understand.

The Portuguese I learned before I came to Brazil was gleaned this way, from albums bought in street markets, compilations of hits by the stars of MPB—*em-i-peh-beh*—Musica Popular Brasileira. Without the printed lyrics I could barely separate one word from another. So I scanned the hieroglyphs on *Os Grandes Compositores do Brasil* for clues to the new country, openings into the lusotropical world. It was the right place to start. If there is a body of music and song to set against the global hegemony of anglophone pop, it must be MPB, with its precursors in Brazilian regional folk music, and descendants today in the urban dance sounds of the clubs and concert halls of Salvador and São Paulo. Most of this music is only now beginning to be heard by audiences outside the Portuguese-speaking world. My nascent record collection back then featured Dorival Caymmi, Tom Jobim, Gilberto Gil, Chico Buarque, Elis Regina—names redolent of this parallel universe of sound. Now Caetano was added to the list.

The song playing on the radio when I came down to breakfast my first or second day at the Anglo-Americano was called 'Milagres do Povo' (Miracles of the People).

'*Quem é ateu,*' the song began, '*e viu milagres como eu...*'

I could barely parse the words, but the tenor had a clarity and authority that stood out from the ubiquitous sweetness of the playlist of the local FM station:

John Ryle

Atheists who've seen miracles, as I have done
Know that where God is not, the gods
Don't disappear; they multiply.
The gods don't give up,
For the sovereign heart, the Lord of all,
Cannot be confined by slavery,
Cannot be confined by No.
So much Yes can never be confined:
The dancing Yes, the Yes of sex—the glorious Yes
That arches across our history.

The refrain was an exercise in vowel sounds. '*Ojuobá ia,*' it
went, '*lá e via...*'

Ojuobá came here
And saw this clearly.
Ojuobahia.

The bridge—the midpoint of the song—consisted of a string of
names and attributes of Candomblé deities:

Xangó sends for him,
Obatalá becomes his guide,
Mama Oxum weeps
Tears of happiness,
Petals fall from Iemanjá,
Laughter from Iãnsa-Oiá.

It took me a long time to grasp the full meaning of 'Milagres
do Povo', which celebrates the reinvention of African belief systems
by descendants of slaves in the new world. Each month I spent in
Salvador I came to understand more about the influence of the
Candomblé pantheon on the poets and artists of the city. Xangó,
Obatalá, Oxum and Iemanjá ruled over Bahian popular music as
Greek and Roman deities did over the art and literature of
Renaissance Europe. At the same time, for practioners of Candomblé

and other African-derived religions, they were not literary symbols but living gods. The beat of the city was shot through with drumming patterns used to invoke them in the Saturday night ceremonies. It was a source of depth and vitality in Bahian music, a well of culture shared by black Bahians with their fellow inhabitants. Like most Bahian artists and writers Caetano was an aficionado of Candomblé; this cultural hybridity was something he personified, describing himself in another song as a *mulato nato:*

> I'm a native-born mulato
> In the widest sense,
> A democratic mulato from the coastal zone.

The most striking thing to me about 'Miracles of the People' was that it mentioned someone I knew, a French photographer and ethnologist, Pierre Verger, who had been living in Salvador for many decades, in a low-income *bairro* called Vila América. Verger was deeply involved in Afro-Brazilian religion, both as a chronicler and as a practitioner. He held ritual office in a long-established house of Candomblé, where he had been given one of the grandiloquent titles bestowed on people of influence, 'Ojuobá'—'Eye of the King' in Yoruba. Hence Caetano's punning reference to him in the song.

Verger was also a patron of the temple beyond the airport; the priest of the temple, Balbino Daniel de Paula, was a friend and erstwhile protégé of his. Later I spent some time as Verger's guest in Salvador, staying in a small house behind his own, studying the African heritage of the city. And listening to the radio. The neighbours there played music all the time. Often I would hear songs from Caetano's back catalogue, about places near where I was living, *bairros* with African names like Calabar and Curuzu. One of these songs was called 'Beleza Pura' (Pure Loveliness)

> It's not money I go for—
> It's good looks
> Not money, but
> A dark-skinned girl
> Not cash,

John Ryle

But flesh and blood
No, not money.

Around that time I met Caetano himself. I was introduced to him by Paulo Cesar de Souza, a young Bahian intellectual, translator of Freud and Nietzsche. Caetano had a serious interest in ideas, unlike any rock musician I had met in England or America. The memoir he published a few years ago, *Verdade Tropical* ('Tropical Truth'), due to appear in English in 2002, is full of references to European philosophy and modernist poetry. Although popular culture and high culture in Brazil are more closely linked than in the English-speaking world—a modernist poet, Vinicius de Moraes, wrote the original lyrics to 'The Girl from Ipanema' and Caetano's contemporary, Chico Buarque, has written two novels—Caetano is unique in his combination of literary and demotic, lyrical and metaphysical, and in the degree of cultural self-awareness he brings to the pop idiom.

One of his recent albums is called *Livro* ('Book'). The title track of this album, 'Livros' refers to his childhood in the 1940s and 1950s in the small town of Santo Amaro, an hour from Salvador, where books were rare objects, signs of the world beyond:

Books transcend time and place,
Yet the love we give them is the love of hands,
Such as we give to a pack of cigarettes.
We tame them, nurture them behind glass,
On shelves, in cages, lay them on fires
Or throw them from windows
(So as not to hurl ourselves out).
Or else, to show we hate them—this is worse—
We write more of them.
We fill pages with vain words,
Bookcases with confusion.

Caetano's songs guided my understanding of Brazil. Salvador, Rio de Janeiro, São Paolo—his songs about these places were part of the collective memory of the country. Back in Britain, I found that the memory of Brazilian music did not fade, nor that of the mysteries of Afro-Brazilian religion. In the 1980s I returned several times to Bahia. In 1990, though, these visits came to an end. I wrote a critical profile for the *Sunday Times* of the newly elected President, Fernando Collor de Mello. The article caused a furore. I was denounced in Brazilian newspapers; President Collor sued the *Sunday Times* and the paper hastily settled out of court.

My Brazilian friends were amused—it was not news to them that their politicians were corrupt. They suggested, though, that it might not be wise to return to the country straight away. Eighteen months passed. And then President Collor's misdeeds—greater than I or anyone had imagined—were confirmed by testimony from his own brother. Even for Brazilians, long accustomed to the rapacity of their political class, it was too much; Collor was removed from the presidency and I was free to return to Brazil. But it was seven years before I went back to Bahia. When I did I was gratified to see a recent paragraph in *A Tarde*, the city's leading newspaper, which ran as follows:

> Who still remembers John Ryle? Let us refresh your memory: he was the first journalist to make concrete accusations against ex-President Collor de Mello. The British newspaper that published the article had to pay a heavy fine. Would it not now be just for the Brazilian government to return the money?

As far as I know, the *Sunday Times* never asked for its money back. Nor did they ask me to write for them again.

Before I had a chance to go back to Brazil, Pierre Verger died. At home in London I sat down to write a piece about him. This was how I came to start translating Caetano. With a blank screen before me, I imagined myself in Salvador in the 1940s, when Verger first arrived there from France and Caetano was growing up in Santo Amaro. I downloaded the Portuguese lyrics of 'Milagres do Povo' from one of the multitudinous websites featuring Caetano's songs. '*Quem é ateu?*' The last line of Caetano's song echoes the first, but this time it's a question. In what sense can you be an atheist, he asks, when you draw your inspiration from a culture of faith? The suppleness of Caetano's thinking, where pantheism performs a *pas de deux* with reason, was evident in the song. To understand it properly, I had to translate it.

Not long after, at a party given by a neighbour in London, I met Caetano again. The same slight and elegant figure, dapper in a high-buttoned black suit, he was with his wife, Paula Lavigne, who, it transpired, had just completed a documentary about Pierre Verger. I mentioned that I had translated Caetano's song; I emailed it a few days later. Towards the end of the year Caetano wrote to ask if I would translate the lyrics for the sleeve-notes of the US version of his album, *Noites do Norte* ('Northern Nights').

This album is vintage Caetano, several of the songs are about the heritage of the slave trade and the distinctive Eurafrican culture of Bahia. The title comes from Joaquim Nabuco, a leading nineteenth-century Brazilian abolitionist. On one track, over an orchestral backing, Caetano recites a striking passage from Nabuco's work:

> For a long time slavery will remain the national characteristic of Brazil. It spread a great smoothness across these vast solitudes of ours; it left the first imprint on our virgin soil, an imprint that was retained; it expanded here as though it were a natural, living religion with its own myths and legends and marvels; it breathed into the land its childish spirit, its sadness without substance, its tears without bitterness, its unfocused silence, its random joy and inconsequential happiness... It is the indefinable sigh half-heard in our moonlit northern nights.

Like 'Milagres do Povo' the passage has a subtle balance of sentiment in it, acknowledging the profound effects of slavery without endorsing them. Caetano, who has written songs in English, was exercised over the precise translation of the passage, even more so than over the translations of his own lyrics. During the winter months in London I got up each morning in the dark and worked on this and the other songs on the album, emailing them to him five thousand miles away in the height of the Bahian summer. Swiftly he would write back, questioning some points, accepting others. I was struck by his diligence, and at my own.

The new album was not all about the past. There were songs
in a purely lyrical mode, which Caetano is equally well known for.

I am your songbird
It doesn't matter where you go
I'll seek you out
I'll sing to you
I'll go, I'll give, I'll go and give to you.

What a pleasure it was to listen to this voice again. I thought
about the mornings at the Anglo-Americano many years before, when
I had dreamed of entering the lusophone world, of being visited by
tongues of flame. There's a sense in which the miracle of Pentecost
does indeed happen, though it does not come in tongues of flame. It
is a slow-burning thing, like a glowing coal, nurtured by breath, by
speech itself, little by little, until it gives you light enough to see your
way in a new language. Translating Caetano was an opportunity to
rekindle this light, to recover my memory of the city and the country
he personified, to experience again the swooning sensation of long
ago, in Salvador, when the sounds of the city were cries of love.

Caetano had been down that road, exploring the idea of
translation in a song called 'Trilhos Urbanos' (The Tracks of the City).
In it he sings of streets and tramlines and lines of verse that lead back
to old times, to the cityscape of childhood. The act of translation
becomes a metaphor for memory itself, for the redemption of the past.
Sitting at my desk, on those cold, dark mornings, with *Northern
Nights* on the sound system and the distant rumble of trains on the
Hammersmith and City line, the lyrics seemed apposite enough:

A streetcar runs on the tracks of the city
The years are passing by
Yet I've not lost you
My work is to translate you.   □

Now that everyone lives as if in a movie, we begin to forget that once it was only special people who did. In Glasgow such people were famous and they were called 'characters'; they seemed to absorb more light than other folk and their patter was original and they wanted for nothing. My mother's only sister was like that: when she walked into a room or a pub everybody smiled.

Famie might seem like a figment of the sentimental imagination. She wasn't: she lived at 50 Skerryvore Road, Cranhill, where the tenements had concrete verandas, and where Famie had a bar in the living room that Joe built one time they came back from Spain. Famie lived generously and open-heartedly; children followed her across the playing fields because they knew she would open her purse to anyone. She liked a drink, and, after her son Stephen died in a brawl in London, she drank too much. When she died at fifty-seven everyone who knew her felt darkened by it. I can still see her lying dead in a room at Glasgow Royal Infirmary. I just couldn't believe the silence coming from her.

The song she always sang was 'Does Your Mother Know You're Out, Cecilia'. Growing up I don't think I knew what the term 'bring the house down' really meant. I came to think it meant what happened when The Jesus and Mary Chain played at the Barrowland, but more perfectly it describes what happened when Famie sang that song. As a teenager I lived outside Glasgow, and I used to go there to see bands with names like Big Flame and Wire, but often enough I'd sneak out of those clubs, and walk eastward to find Famie. One time I went to the Shettleston Railway Club, on the off chance, and there she was in mid-flow, singing 'Cecilia' in that way of hers, the whole room up on its feet, ablaze with approval.

There isn't a recording in the world of anyone singing that song like she did. She didn't have a very good voice, she wasn't that steady on her feet, and I don't think she even knew all the words, but Famie invested feeling and character and place in that song like nobody else. The original song is whimsical and flapperish—a cheapskate product of Tin Pan Alley—but Famie had the gift to put manners on it. She put cadence into it. She slowed it down and made it a song about yearning.

Nobody knew who Cecilia was, but Famie seemed to know: it

was herself and it was everybody in the room, and it was everybody in the world outside the room, if such a thing existed.

'Cecilia' was written in 1925, the words by Herman Ruby and the tune by Dave Dreyer, a couple of vaudeville songsmiths who sometimes worked for Al Jolson and Fred Astaire. (Ruby later wrote the 'Charlie Kane' song in Citizen Kane.) The song was made famous by Whispering Jack Smith, the susurrating crooner of the jazz era, who got his vocal style from being gassed in the Great War. Whispering Jack's career, and the career of 'Cecilia', was tied to the growth in home phonographs, and those old discs marketed by Victor and Columbia, some of which made their way into the houses where Famie grew up. 'Cecilia' also survived by becoming a favourite on the old Wurlitzer Band Organs; the company's records show it was on Roll 20, one of the earliest, next to 'Beer Barrel Polka' and 'Alice Blue Gown', songs that have no doubt disappeared into the personal histories of God knows who. Nowadays you can download Whispering Jack Smith's rendition of 'Cecilia' from the internet, and you find all its dapper romanticism is there, with static as well, crackling down through cyberspace.

There are hundreds of places where Famie sang that song, few of them more than twenty-five miles from the house she was born in. She sang it at the Eastmuir Social Club and the Firemen's Club in London Road. She sang it on the beach at Seamill in 1975. She sang it on top of the counter of Mario's chip shop in Kilwinning two years later. She sang it walking down Sauchiehall Street one night after a wedding. And she sang it more times than you can count on the number 62 bus. She sang it to boys in football scarves, to the bus conductress, to avid readers of the *Evening Times*, to bar staff, to half-familiar men down on their luck and selling razor blades in Argyll Street, and she sang it most of all to her husband Joe, whose name comes up in one of the verses, and who always loved Famie singing and would just smile and look at his watch.

One Hogmanay we were traipsing through the snow in Carntyne looking for a party at the house of somebody called Cathy Bow. Famie had forgotten the address and she chapped on the door of a well-lighted house to use their telephone. After fifteen minutes hanging around outside we went into the house to find Famie sitting on the woman's sofa, holding her hand, with a tumbler of whisky in the other hand, halfway into 'Cecilia'.

Famie and Joe eventually dismantled the Spanish bar and moved to a high-rise flat east, in Sandyhills. Joe worked away a lot. I remember lugging a Nat King Cole box-set to her flat because I knew we could spend a night listening to them, drinking illicit lagers and telling stories. It wasn't long before she died, and I see Famie now, sitting in the corner surrounded by all her ceramic ornaments, singing her favourite song, eyes glistening in the dark. ☐

LA MER
Nicholson Baker

Nicholson Baker

One day after school, when I was thirteen, my bassoon teacher told me that the Rochester Philharmonic, where he played second bassoon, was rehearsing a piece of music called *La Mer*. *Mer* didn't mean 'mother', he said, it meant 'sea', and the remarkable thing about the piece, according to him, was that it really and truly did sound like the sea. He played me some bits from the score while I put together my instrument. What he played didn't sound like the sea to me, but that wasn't surprising, because nothing sounds like the sea on the bassoon. A few months later, I bought a record of Pierre Boulez performing *La Mer* with the New York Philharmonic. I put on the heavy, padded headphones, that were like inflatable life-rafts for each ear, and I heard Debussy's side-slipping water-slopes, with cold spray blown off their crests, and I saw the sudden immensity of the marine horizon that followed the storm, and I was amazed by how true to liquid life it all was. It was just as good as Joseph Conrad's 'Typhoon', then one of my favourite stories—maybe even better.

Later, after I'd applied to music school, I bought the pocket score of *La Mer* and tried to figure out how Debussy did it, but the score didn't help much. What gave Debussy the confidence to pick up half a melody and then flip it away, like a torn piece of seaweed, after a moment's study? How did he turn an orchestra, a prickly ball of horsehair and old machinery, into something that splashed and surged, lost its balance and regained it? There may be things about *La Mer* that are slightly dissatisfying—there may be too much of the whole-tone scale in a few places (a novelty then, worn out by cop-show soundtracks now), and Debussy made a mistake, I think, when he revised the brass fanfare out of the ending—but this piece has so many natural wonders that you drive past the drab moments as if they are convenience stores, without paying attention to them, looking out at the tidal prodigies.

Debussy finished *La Mer*—adjusting its orchestration and correcting proofs—during a month in England in the summer of 1905, in Eastbourne, a late-Victorian summer resort where he had gone with Emma Bardac. Emma was married to a well-to-do banker at the time, and was very pregnant with Debussy's only child. A few years ago, paging through one of the biographies, I stopped at a picture of Debussy frowning down into the viewfinder of a camera, on the stone-parapeted balcony of the Grand Hotel, Eastbourne. The camera was pointed out at the English Channel. I was living in Ely at the time, north of Cambridge, but it occurred to me, as I consulted a map and a schedule, that I could easily go to Eastbourne and return the same day.

I rode the screeching, battered local train out one March morning; I walked into town and stopped at a used book store, which had nothing about Debussy, and then at the tourist information centre, where a kind woman pulled out a red notebook entitled FAMOUS PEOPLE, with entries for Wordsworth, Tennyson, Swinburne (who wrote 'To a Sea Mew' nearby, at Beachy Head), King Arthur and Debussy. The woman pointed me in the direction of the Grand Hotel, and when I finally found it, after turning the wrong way on the shore road, I was told that room 277 was the Debussy Suite, but that they couldn't let me in to look out its windows because it was almost check-in time and that night's guests might arrive at any moment.

So I sat in the garden on a white bench, with my back to the sea, looking up at the balcony where Debussy and Emma had, not so many years ago, looked out over the channel toward an invisible France. The balcony was directly above the main entrance, under the letters that spelled GRAND HOTEL. In the pale sunlight, I sketched the facade of the hotel, with its eye-guiding beaux-arts urns and scrolls (designed by R. K. Blessley in 1876); it seemed to me that Debussy, often penniless and foolish about money, had felt industriously rich here, perhaps for the last time, as he put the final touches on his ebullient sea poem. A few months later, back in Paris, his wife, abandoned and heartbroken, shot herself near the heart, and though she recovered, everyone's life was different afterwards.

I went back inside the hotel and up the fire stairs to the second floor. (The stairs had nicely carved banister-knobs.) It was one of those buildings in which the flights of stairs and the placement of windows are out of synchrony: in the stairwell, the top of the window frame was low to the floor, so I had to bend way down, my head pounding, to get a proper view. I had only a minute or two before I needed to leave to catch the train back. There was dried rain-dust on the outside of the glass, but I looked out over the water and saw, near to shore, an unexpected play of green and gold and turquoise waves—not waves, really, because they were so small, but little manifestations of fluid under-energy. The clouds had the look that a glass of rinse water gets when you're doing a watercolour—slowly diluting black roilings, which move under the white water that you made earlier when you rinsed the white paint from the brush. But the sea didn't choose to reflect the clouds that day; it had its own private mallard-neck pallet, the fine gradations of which varied with the slopes of the wind-textured swells. Through the dirty window, I thought I saw, for a moment, what Debussy had seen. ☐

GRANTA

THE SEA
Michael Collins

TAKEN BETWEEN WEST BAY AND
EYPE, WEST DORSET, 2000-2001

STANLEY KAUFFMANN

REGARDING FILM

CRITICISM & COMMENT

FOREWORD BY MICHAEL WOOD

"Stanley Kauffmann cares, valiantly, ardently, about movies. He is—doesn't everyone know this?—one of our national treasures."
—SUSAN SONTAG

"I can't think of any other film critic in the world whose criticism I find more thrilling, provocative, and thought-provoking. I enthusiastically recommend this book to anyone who loves to go to the movies."
—ANDRÉ GREGORY

PAJ Books: Bonnie Marranca and Gautam Dasgupta, Series Editors

$21.95 paperback

The Johns Hopkins University Press • 1-800-537-5487 • www.jhupbooks.com

PLAYS BY MAC WELLMAN

cellophane

FOREWORD BY MARJORIE PERLOFF

Celebrated for his dizzying linguistic inventions, his experimental narratives, his biting social and political critiques, and his absurdist sense of humor, Mac Wellman has become one of America's leading avant-garde playwrights. In *Cellophane*, Wellman offers the eleven plays that he considers his most important.

$22.50 paperback

"**What Wellman does best [is] approach the mystery of things without succumbing to the mute darkness.**"
—Charles McNulty, *Village Voice*

"**Wellman is our latter-day Brecht, providing the *Verfremdung*, the 'making strange' that makes us see what has been before us all along.**"
—Marjorie Perloff

PAJ BOOKS • Bonnie Marranca and Gautam Dasgupta, Series Editors

THE JOHNS HOPKINS UNIVERSITY PRESS
1-800-537-5487 • www.jhupbooks.com

HIS VARIOUS
SELVES
Mark Holborn

Portraits by
Richard Avedon

132nd Street, New York, November 4, 1963

In this year of Bob Dylan's sixtieth birthday and forty-third album, *Love and Theft*, more biographies have been published, further domestic details have been revealed, yet little is known about the man beyond his presence on the stage and his voice. Despite the never-ending tour, his enigma grows, based on his art of self-invention and his fervent denial of whatever mantle is thrust upon him. At twenty he sounded like the greatest white blues singer ever recorded. His various voices were raw, tender and angry. He once snarled that he could sing like Caruso. His recent recordings include a duet with the bluegrass legend, Ralph Stanley, and a song, partly in Italian, for the soundtrack of *The Sopranos*. He has many disguises. Along the way his influences have been drawn from Nashville, Kentucky, Dublin and the Delta. He has been both Rock God and prophet in the wilderness. In this first age of the recorded voice, his has been one of the most prolific. He has changed vernacular language. His various selves constitute not just a portrait of an artist but of American popular music itself.

Photographs of the man are nearly always inadequate. He escapes the net. His early *Self-Portrait* album, containing few of his own songs, but covers of 'Blue Moon' and 'Copper Kettle', was adorned with a painted self-portrait. The album and its sleeve were no more than a mask. His portrait on his most harrowing album, *Blood on the Tracks*, camouflages his features in the grain of the image. Photographs appear to elevate him to icon or veil him. The exception are those by Richard Avedon, who has famously penetrated the masks of celebrity. He first engaged with Dylan in 1963 and returned to photograph him in Los Angeles in 1997 at the time of *Time out of Mind*. Avedon was familiar with the multiple selves of artists. In the course of his rise as a celebrated fashion photographer and portrait photographer, his own various selves were being released.

In an essay written in May 1970 to accompany an exhibition of his portraits in Minneapolis that summer, Avedon wrote, 'I work out of myselves.' He went on: 'All these photographs are linked through me and each is like a sentence in one long inner argument.' He confessed that after 1965 he could make no more portraits for four years. He had to start anew. He was experimenting with multiple portraits or an ongoing series recording the same face over the passage of time. The power of the method was movingly evident in his portraits of his father exhibited at the Museum of Modern Art in New York in 1974.

Avedon's first book, published in 1959, was titled *Observations*. In his 1970 essay he quoted Virginia Woolf in despair at her end, 'Observe the oncoming of age... Observe my own despondency. By that means it becomes serviceable.' But Avedon wanted more than observation. He described his photography as if it was alchemical, involving a transference of part of himself. He wanted confirmation. 'Because I don't feel I was really there,' he wrote, 'at least the part of me that was...is now in the photograph. And the photographs have a reality for me that the people don't. It's through the photographs that I know them.' So, too, it is through the photographs we might know Avedon. When in 1993 he published his epic *An Autobiography*, a self-portrait with the emphasis on the indefinite article, it was an assembly of nearly 300 portraits of others. It includes two significant pictures of Dylan.

On November 4, 1963 Avedon photographed Dylan on 132nd Street and the East River in New York. Dylan's face is very young, his head tilted and his eyes lined. The buckle of his belt round the faded Levi's forms a big D. A pen sticks out of the pocket of his shirt. His boots look worn beside a battered guitar case. This is Dylan in his first public incarnation, having come out of the mid-West and made it to New York. Dylan had invented a persona incorporating elements of an American myth—the road and a wandering tradition—followed by a quest to the hospital bedside of his idol, Woody Guthrie. Behind the invention lurked truth. Not only did he sing the Guthrie repertoire to the man himself, but at only twenty he was recorded on harmonica with Victoria Spivey and the great bluesmen, Big Joe Williams and Lonnie Johnson. He had shared gigs in Greenwich Village with John Lee Hooker. This was not just a white boy with an adopted drawl and a good twelve-bar pattern, he was playing the real thing and was recognized for it by those he emulated. An early account of his performances describes him as 'Chaplinesque', fidgeting through the ironies of his 'Talking Blues'. His first concert, upstairs in a side room at Carnegie Hall to an audience of fewer than a hundred, was taped. He was a nervous but mesmerizing performer, sounding like a stand-up comic who occasionally broke from a laugh to deliver an impassioned, driving blues. A few weeks before the Avedon photograph he had played to a sold-out Carnegie Hall. He had moved on from the Village. His repertoire had shifted. He had already written and recorded 'A Hard Rain's A-Gonna Fall', a prophecy layering Old Testament language with his apocalyptic visions. He had not only discovered the great lineage of American songs, he had found his own voice. He was twenty-two years old.

In the summer of 1963 Dylan travelled down to Greenwood, Mississippi and sang 'Only a Pawn in their Game', the ballad on the death of Medgar Evers, to the cotton workers in the fields. Civil rights were the greatest issue facing America. Dylan had performed beside Martin Luther King at the Lincoln Memorial. He understood the power of the broadside and was about to be transformed from balladeer to writer of anthems. He was unwittingly becoming a spokesman.

Early in 1963 Avedon went south to photograph the mental patients in East Louisiana State Hospital. In March he photographed Julian Bond and members of the Student Non-Violent Coordinating Committee in Atlanta. Three days after photographing a former slave in Algiers, across from New Orleans, he returned to New York to photograph Malcolm X. Two days after photographing Dylan in New York, he photographed Governor George Wallace. His photographs of racists and civil rights workers appeared the following year in *Nothing Personal*, accompanied by a text written by James Baldwin. In retrospect, the historical momentum of the year is daunting. Within three weeks of the Dylan portrait, John F. Kennedy had been assassinated. Any youthful innocence of the postwar years had vanished.

On February 10, 1965, beside Central Park, New York, Avedon made a second portrait of Dylan. In the interim, Dylan's trajectory had left a trail across American music and—according to the photograph—on the man himself. He had been lauded in Europe. His shirt and suede jacket look like he's been down Carnaby Street. His frame is gaunt, his boots big, his eyes deeply ringed, and his head slightly stooped under the wild mane. Avedon's portrait is a study in the price of fame or the sheer weight of accelerated creativity. Dylan is finding his stride in the middle of a tumultuous decade. He has left a lot behind. His 'wild, mercury sound' is yet to come. The previous month he had recorded *Bringing it All Back Home*. The great electric trilogy of albums, including *Highway 61 Revisited* and *Blonde on Blonde*, had begun. He was about to hear the booing. His output was furious. There is no trace of a smile. He is, of course, impossibly cool.

What seems like another lifetime lies between Dylan's creative climax of the Sixties and a further Avedon portrait—a passage from youth to middle age. Dylan crashed a motorcycle, withdrew, became the father of a large family, adopted biblical language and morality, recorded in Nashville, went down to Durango to work as an actor in Peckinpah's *Pat Garrett and Billy the Kid*, playing a character called Alias, made a film about Bob Dylan and called himself Renaldo, separated, divorced, hired Elvis's bass player, stood on the stage as if it was a pulpit, recorded a multitude of new songs and released albums of cover versions, both profound and banal. A vault of unreleased material is rumoured to exist—the secret Dylan. Now his solace appears to be to go out on stage. Although the huge repertoire is largely defined, he flourishes through rearranging his past songs. No two performances are alike. He can wear any of his various selves if there is sufficient adrenalin to carry him.

Avedon ended the Nineties in a retrospective mode. *The Sixties*, his collaboration with the writer Doon Arbus, a portrait of a decade conceived some thirty years before, was published in 1999. The two pictures of Dylan were essential to the project. Then in Los Angeles on September 11, 1997 he photographed Dylan again. The result, when placed with the previous pictures, forms a triptych. Maybe they fulfil what Avedon was looking for when he gave up portraiture in 1965— the subject through time, the observation of the oncoming of age. In the text accompanying the final portrait, Dylan, looking back, says:

I'm still the same. I'm still the same person. I still feel like the same person. The music I listen to, it's still the same music, a whole list of names of people who aren't around anymore, you know? Those people, they were the first. They were like the clue to it. That was the world I came East to find, which was like a long odyssey in

Central Park, New York, February 19, 1965

itself, just trying to get there. And these people I'm speaking of, they knew about the older people who'd been there in the Forties. And the Thirties. That stuff was real obscure, but they knew what it was and they had the stuff, they had it. I knew it rubbed off on me. In a big way.

Despite the trajectory and the legend surrounding it, Dylan confirms his constancy. His passion for his forebears has never been concealed. He openly declared it in his first song, 'Song to Woody'. Before the success of *Time out of Mind*, he had released two stunning solo records which included material ranging from versions of 'Delia', 'Sitting on Top of the World' and Blind Willie McTell's 'Broke Down Engine' to songs by the Mississippi Sheiks and Irish ballads. By *Time out of Mind* his sound, despite the virtuosity of the musicians and the production, was still that of one man and a guitar located somewhere well south of Memphis.

At the beginning he admitted he couldn't carry himself like the masters. When, as a twenty-year-old, he sang 'Fixin' to Die', how could he have known the loss that enabled Bukka White to write it? At the time of Avedon's third portrait he'd become what he'd set out to be. He could 'carry' it. The picture is reduced to his face against a white background. The loss and beauty that touched his predecessors have marked his face as surely as they marked his voice. The weary eyes stare back at Avedon and at us.

To make a portrait of a figure so enigmatic, a composite had to be constructed. Avedon's pursuit of the single face over time provides a revelation no others have achieved. Dylan's face became a sentence in Avedon's inner argument. He too has seen Dylan's world 'of paupers and peasants, and princes and kings'. The final portrait of Dylan has yet to be made. It will be prescribed by his voice not his face. It will stretch from the depths of the Delta, through the ballads of Kentucky and Virginia, along Highway 61 to Memphis, and all the way to Chicago and the north country. Such is the power of one man and a guitar. In Dylan's selves, of course, we see our own. His voice is played out against the shared background of tumultuous decades. Such is the power and the burden of an idol. □

Los Angeles, September 11, 1997

Medtner   Philip Pullman

Not long ago I tried to explain to a friend the effect that Nicolai Medtner's music has on me. I spoke with eloquence, passion and wit; analogies of the most ingenious kind sprang to my lips; I found myself stirred to a frenzy of admiration for the profundity of my insights.

'I don't know what you're talking about,' said my friend.

Discussing music when you have no technical knowledge of it is to be reduced to finding more or less fancy ways of saying, 'I like that bit when it goes da-da-da-DUM.' However, we have to try, or be silent; so I shall try to say why I love Nicolai Medtner, and why his piano music satisfies me so deeply.

He was born in 1880, and educated at the Moscow Conservatoire. He had some success as a concert pianist, but his calling was always towards composition. After the Revolution he left Russia, and for the rest of his life he lived in exile—for the last fifteen years of it in London—struggling against poverty and the indifference of the public and the critics. He wasn't without his champions ('Why nobody plays Medtner?' said Vladimir Horowitz. 'He is wonderful composer'), but he was never fashionable: he loathed the modernism of Schoenberg, Stravinsky and Prokofiev. The only contemporary he truly esteemed was Rachmaninov, who returned the compliment, and gave him generous and unstinting help throughout his life.

The first piece of his I heard was the Sonata 'Reminiscenza' in A minor, from the *Forgotten Melodies*, Op. 38. It was on a second-hand LP of a Carnegie Hall recital by Emil Gilels. The first notes held me quiet: a slow steady rocking melody that climbs and returns and climbs again and then just as steadily goes back to its beginning and falls still. Then after a moment's silence comes a different melody which flowers into a third, and...this is where description fails, of course, so I have to resort to assertion instead, and say that the melodies you can hear in the Sonata 'Reminiscenza' are some of the loveliest in any music. There's one that consists of a series of falling phrases of six notes with a little hesitation after the first note of each (a dotted note?), which has the sort of tentative quality of a blossom coming out just a little early, beautiful, unsure, not quite safe... The mood is tender and lyrical and suffused with a graceful melancholy, without the slightest bitterness.

Anyway, I fell in love with it. And I began to search out Medtner wherever I could: scouring the BBC Radio 3 listings was the best place to start, since there were hardly any records available at that time. Gradually I accumulated tapes of broadcast recitals, and became more and more absorbed in Medtner's world. I can't have been the only person this was happening to, because after a while it became easier to find him in the record shops: there are at least two very good boxed sets of the piano music available now, by Geoffrey Tozer (clear, unfussy, strong) and Marc-André Hamelin (pyrotechnic, delicate, brilliant). It's not hard these days to find out what he sounds like.

So here we are again: I shall have to try and describe the impression he makes on me. I think it boils down to three things.

Firstly, those melodies. Melody, of course, is the one thing even musical dimwits can come away humming. The sonatas are full of melody, brimming with it, and they're subtle, complex, unexpected melodies, each strongly characterized with a vivid emotional flavour. Furthermore, they're not like anyone else's, and I haven't the faintest idea why. Occasionally you'll hear a passage or two that might sound (from a distance) a bit Rachmaninovian, or perhaps Scriabinistic, and once or twice a sequence of harmonies that's faintly Chopinesque, or even Alkan-like; but his tunes are entirely his own, and unique. Listen to the broad, serious, passionate yearning of the tune in the third movement of the Sonata in F minor, Op. 5. Or the lovely fresh poised grace of the second movement of the Sonata 'Skazka', Op. 25, No. 1. Or the simple, lyrical, delicate first movement of his last piano sonata, the Sonata 'Idyll' in G, Op. 56. Wherever you listen, something entrancing is happening.

Secondly, the notes behind the melodies. These untutored ears couldn't distinguish a canon from a fugue in an identity parade, but they can hear that something polyphonic is taking place, and Medtner is rich with it. It's *interesting*. Phrases are passed from hand to hand; little pieces of tune break off to spin up the keyboard two, three octaves higher, and then return again; out of the thunder of a fast and complex passage in the left hand (for instance, in the 'Night Wind' Sonata in E minor, Op. 25 No. 2, over thirty minutes of stupendous surging energy) will emerge the tune you heard a minute ago higher up, but something's happened to it, it's transformed—and then it's gone again. It feels like being a child in a room where adults are having a deep and passionate conversation about important things: you have the impression of profound intellectual engagement without being able to follow it fully, but you trust the adults, and it's clear that they know what they're saying even if you don't. So somebody does, and that's important.

And finally, the stuff that isn't music at all. I love Medtner because of his photograph, because of his appearance in old age: almost invariably wearing an old-fashioned wing collar right up to his death in 1951, bald, craggy, noble, his expression serene and resolute. I love him because his friends loved him, as Rachmaninov did. I love him because of the fact that in a semi-detached house in Golders Green, troubled by financial problems, weakened by ill-health, this 'firm defender of the sacred laws of eternal art' (in the words of Glazunov) went on calmly writing music in an idiom as out-of-date as his clothes, completely untouched not just by fashion but by common sense as well, and listening only to his conscience and to the themes that came, as he believed, from God.

But does that non-musical, biographical stuff really make a difference? *Should* it, even? Yes, I think it should. We should respond to art as we should respond to life, with every particle of knowledge and feeling we have, leaving nothing out. When I listen to Medtner, I'm glad I have his photograph to look at; I'm glad I know what I do about his life; and over and over again, I marvel at the chance that led me to this lovely, passionate, endlessly refreshing music. □

FREE ISSUE OFFER

Special deal on orders for two or more subscriptions: The first 1-year subscription (your own or a gift) is $37. Each additional 1-year subscription is just $29 (a $22 saving).

Please enter my:

○ Own new subscription, ○ Renewal order, or ○ First gift, for:

- ○ 1 year (4 issues) $37   Save $14
- ○ 2 years (8 issues) $65   Save $38
- ○ 3 years (12 issues) $95   Save $60 (39%)

○ Additional 1-year gift(s) for $29 each (save$22)

Payment information:

○ Check (US Dollars drawn on US banks)

○ MasterCard   ○ Visa   ○ AmEx   ○ Bill me

Credit Card Number

Expiration Date/Signature

$_____ total for _____ subscriptions/gifts
(add additional foreign postage if necessary).

For faster service, fax credit card orders to (601) 353-0176.

Additional postage outside the US: Canada (includes GST): $11 surface, $19 airmail; South America and Mexico: $8 surface, $19 airmail; Rest of World: $19 airspeeded.

My Name: _____
(If renewing, please attach issue label.)

Address _____

City/State/Zip _____ N601004NC

○ Send gift(s) to:

Gift 1: _____

Address _____

City/State/Zip _____ N701004NC

Gift 2: _____

Address _____

City/State/Zip _____ N701004NC

www.granta.com

FREE ISSUE OFFER

Every issue of Granta features outstanding new fiction, memoir, reportage, and photography. Every issue is a handsome, illustrated paperback—because the writing itself endures. Every issue is special. That's why Granta is published only four times a year: to keep it that way. Subscribe and you'll get Granta at a big discount, delivered to your home. (Granta makes a great gift, too: thoughtful, personal, and lasting.)

- A one year (four-issue) subscription is $37. You save $14. That's better than getting a whole Granta, FREE.

- A two year (eight-issue) subscription is $65. You save $38.

- A three year (twelve-issue) subscription is $95. You save $60.

"Essential reading." —The Observer

NO POSTAGE
NECESSARY
IF MAILED
IN THE
UNITED STATES

BUSINESS REPLY MAIL
FIRST-CLASS MAIL   PERMIT NO. 115   JACKSON, MS

POSTAGE WILL BE PAID BY ADDRESSEE

GRANTA
P O BOX 23152
JACKSON MS 39225-9814

CLARA
Janice Galloway

An engraving by an unknown artist of Clara Schumann nee Wieck (1819–1896)

MARY EVANS

Halflight and rain. The path of the street shines along the rim of guttering. Look up.

Behind the glass, a girl, a little girl, a young woman, maybe, is looking back. She can't see you, she won't object. You can look as long as you like. The light is bad and she's distinct enough, hair pulled back and her eyes full almond shapes, the size of bay leaves. Wide. She has a generous lower lip, a gypsy mouth; skin pale as cheese. You see braids and ribbon, the sheen of dark hair slatted with something that might be pearls, can almost smell the lavender, pomade. Nine, perhaps? This dark, at this distance, it's impossible to be sure. She shifts, half in shadow. Whatever else, she's certainly a child. No one is with her. Nothing moves and rain glints on the paving. Once in a while, she presses a hand against the glass, blurring an outline on the pane. Her mouth opens a little as though she might speak. But nothing comes. There is only stillness, the silent house. This curiously undiverting, undiverted child, watching. Waiting.

Listen! You can hear it plain.

Someone is playing exercises.

His hand, the solid pressure he exerts upon the keys. Not Czerny, not Hummel—he plays his own. Simple but effective, the same half-melodies over and over, designed for discipline, the honing of muscle. Aesthetics be damned: training is what comes first. His fourth finger sticks and it starts again, staccato next time, contrary motion, evanescing between major and minor, just to keep his fingers on their toes. No pauses: no sooner does one finish, than it turns on its heel and starts again. The little G minor triplets passage runs into the distance, vanishes like a mouse. He catches it by the tail and drags it back, backwards. Clever, a mental arithmetic that falls into place quite naturally after a while, happens almost without thought. And while it's happening, something else is too. Listen again and you hear it too, something married to, but not one with, the keys. Something human for a start. Take a moment, allow yourself. All it takes is listening and it's there, quite clear. A woman, singing. Her voice is high, expressionless, saving itself for more. A voice that puts itself through its paces: a ladder of five ascending notes, tonic to dominant, back again. That done, it cranks up a semitone, does it all over again: a five-note bloom and fade again, another semitone, again. Soon it's as high as you think it can go and—it does it one more time. Whose voice? Mother. Her mother's voice. There's no one else's it could have been. Does knowing make the voice more beautiful, more keenly felt? Perhaps. Another, surely there will be one last flourish, and the woman will appear entire around it, if only in your imagination: the voice will come into itself. So you wait. Your ears strain, waiting. Only the piano keeps going, churning the same cycles, oblivious. For whatever reason, the voice has gone. You can't even remember it. The texture of the sounds, the edge of it against the ear. Gone.

Sound. That memory is made of sound before it's made of anything else, she has no doubt. That it is not as ephemeral as it appears she has no doubt either. After the kiss, the glass of lemon water, the scent of orchids is gone, it's gone. But a fragment of music, somehow remains. And she knows that when she is alone in bed, in the early hours before dawn, music comes whether she likes it or not: a sliver of Chopin, one stubborn phrase of Beethoven, the edges and elbows of countless songs. Numberless songs. And these. Her earliest memories, maybe, but something etched inside the skull, heard again and again till they stuck forever and one in the same. Father raising his inventions to the sky. Mother, in another place entirely, singing.

Sing. One word. *Sing!*

She doesn't speak, has never spoken. Four years old and not a word.

Some people say she's deaf or simple; others that she's both. *Poor Herr Wieck!* She hears them herself. Leering down with faces like owls, mouths open wide so the rotted places in their teeth show. *Hello!* they roar. *Hello little lady!* in warm clouds, heavy with pig fat, garlic, tobacco. She peers out at them, protecting her nose behind the grey mask of someone's skirts, unblinking. Unfocused. After that, they give up. They turn to Father, the baby with a face like a bloater, knock horseshit from their shoes—anything but persist with this awkward child. Never speaks. Never smiles. Thin as a stick with monstrous eyes; they can't even say she's pretty. Never mind. They give her sweets anyway, let her father take them away, wag his finger in mock-warning, let the talk turn to Other Things. Weather, they say. Who's married, who's sick, who's died. Business, ah! Business. The fascinating Subject of Business and How it Thrives. And even at four, she knows what Business means. Business means pianos. It also means Mother and all those notes, tickets, money and students but mostly pianos. This talking, mouths chewing verbal cud, always runs for some time. After that, there is remarking about the weather, who has dropped in or out of the subscription series, concerts and optional cooing at Gustav—this last always brief. Gustav is only a baby and by definition, not interesting. Then what? They scan with their eyes, working out the farewell strategy and she's still there, oblivious to the blatancy of it, staring. Every time they turn around, eyes. The child's entire repertoire. She watches them put their hats on and knows it's nearly over. When Papa puts his on too, it's sure: the talking is done. That's what Hats-On means. *Done.* To prove it there are farewells, the looking-over of shoulders, waves. Then there is walking. The sound of walking is footfalls to the Eilenburg Road, brass keys clanking in Father's pocket. Nothing but footfalls for miles.

Herr Wieck's is a plain house, neither elegant nor grand. Sufficient is the word that springs to mind: this house is pleasingly adequate. There is a door and matching shutters in dutiful loden; ten solid apartments and loft-space, all necessary. There are music rooms, workshops, the warehouse; a spread of bedrooms, a sitting room, parlour, kitchen. One servant's room, one servant, three big windows, eleven pianos. That's what bulks up the space. Pianos. They're not slight beasts, not dainty. Varnished edges sharp enough to cut, snap-shut lids, shin-battering pedals, stops, stands. Watch boys lifting them for transport and you'd see—pianos, even small ones with painted lids and silver candle sconces, all nymphs and weeping trees, are brutes. Unwieldy lumps. Stand between them and they crack, moan, breathe out wood: a little girl could get lost among their brown bull legs. That she never does is just as well, for the pianos keep coming. He trades one, puts one out for hire, two more appear. Teaching, trade, sale and barter; livelihood, aspiration: this house is made of pianos. That's what people come here for. They knock and

Janice Galloway

Johanna opens the door, green door, Johanna has a weather-brown face. Inside, she takes your coat and you wait in the hallway to see *the professor*, perusing the frames. Silhouettes; cheaper than miniatures. Representations of people. One bears a passing resemblance to Schubert, another Beethoven. Everyone has these. As for the rest, Lordknows who. But trying to concentrate, to *think* in this place is impossible. This house has no peace. It rings and resonates, echoes from all its corners. Pianos. Voices. *Sound.*

Sing!
Someone does. She has never heard anyone refuse. The very idea.
Sing!
Girls come with their hair curled tight, sheet copy under their arms; young men with more hope than talent, and what they come for is Him. For Father to tell them what to do and he does, he certainly does. *Sing!* It's the same for everyone, even the pianists, especially the pianists. *Sing!* They make scales and arpeggios, domino shapes of sound to make their throats and fingers supple, their pitch true. *The voice is your beginning!* he shouts: it's how every lesson starts. They sing till the whole street can hear them, it carries through walls. Later there are only pianos: the same pieces faltering, recurring, snipped into bits. Bad days, there are crashes and howls, even curses. Father is a passionate man. He kicks things, usually instruments. The old ones. Better that than Other Things, he says and you know he is offering a joke. It's also not a joke because he's right. Father is always right. This is how it is: a reliable constant. He takes full responsibility, he says, for being in the right. If he is not, they may apply for refund of fee and no one ever does. Proof. During the day, all day, the music rises. Standing over the practice room ceiling, upon the floorboards of elsewhere, she can feel it buzz beneath the soles of her canvas shoes. Music makes sensation, it vibrates along the bones.

Clara.
It means limpid. Light.
Her father chose it.

Clara. Say it. Clara. He holds a watch in front of her face. It swings to and fro on a chain. Gold or brass, perhaps, beautifully polished. The child's eyes make half her face dark. They tilt at the corners like a Slav's.

Clara. You may hold Papa's watch if you say it.

The reflection in her pupils shows the face of a man, doubled; twin timepieces, swinging.

No one at home thinks she's deaf. Not in their heart of hearts. The child takes instructions, clears her plate, comes when she is called. Eventually. She doesn't laugh much, and thank God seldom runs. She is not as clumsy as most her age, can walk good distances unassisted, and has no perceptible need of toys. As for her silence, (here the man of the house raises himself to his full height) some would say that an admirable trait in a woman. Then he looks at his wife. He looks hard. Family, he says, that's what matters: people in town may say what they like. People are always saying something. It's beneath his dignity to say anything back. Time will tell, he says. *We'll see.*

What he sees before long are the lines between her brows. He notices them more than once, little furrows. It seems they only appear when he does. He tries experiments, watches her with Johanna, Alwin and it's true. With them, there's nothing. Her forehead's flat as a field. When he comes back—so do the lines. He does it several times for sheer curiosity, to see this semblance of adult concern on a little girl and it makes him smile. They make her look like a spaniel, he says, a pup. The lines are consistent, however: as though she is trying to make sense of the unfathomable. She knows I take her intelligence for granted, he says, not like some. Here, he says, gives her a penny. The frown stays put. It has to be admitted: something about the observation is infinitely pleasing.

Not long after this, he decides to act. This plan has been waiting its moment and the frown-lines are it. He will use the concentration he inspires and to begin that use, he reaches for the dead centre of the keyboard. One note, clear and resonant. C. He looks her in the eye. He plays it again, sings it.

He plays it again, waits. Waits. Then her face lights like sun from behind a cloud and her mouth opens. She sings. C, she sings. C for Clara! Again. Again. He does this for three minutes, choosing five different notes. He times it, never strays more than a sixth, returns to where he began. Then he smiles. What's more, she smiles back. A very small smile, true, but discernible. Her brow, he notices without even trying, is completely smooth. *We'll see*, he says. *We'll see*.

There is no mistaking her paternity: she has her mother's nose, which forever means her mother's profile, but the rest of her face is all Friedrich God help her. That apart, she doesn't give much away, which is, after all, as it should be: he would give nothing away if he could help it either. Diligence, Patience and Craft, he says, these are what matter; not what idle people say. They have a counted stitch motto of these very words beside the mantel, low on the wall so the child can see. A pattern of browns and blues, nothing she can read. But the words are shapes she knows already. She can touch the threads with her fingertip. Meanwhile, her father says—he looks at his watch—work on the concerto, the second movement in particular. Attend to your poor arpeggios. Sewing can wait. Directives before he leaves. It's a habit. Frau Wieck has a concert in two weeks, then she always has a concert in two weeks and the rest of the time there is plenty else to do. She puts the dress down, the panel she is stitching unfinished. Her needle glints in its dark blue folds. Herr Wieck looks at his daughter, addresses her alone.

Apply the highest principles and expect favours from no one, child. No one.

No-one. A vast word for a small head.

He looks at her watching him, her hair parted like a split damson. Whether she hears him or not, she understands. He is sure she understands.

No one save Papa, he says. He smiles, broad, wide. His eyes glitter. Save me.

When he calls her he calls her by name.

Clärchen, Little Clara. My Clara.

Friedrich lusted for Clara irrespective of her sex. Before he knew what she was, who she was, he knew what she would be: the greatest pianist he could fashion, his brightness, a star. He never allowed himself to think she would not survive. He had worried for Adelheid and what had it meant? The crunch of his tiny fists, the blue cast of his lips. Adelheid had died before there was much to see, but what there was, Friedrich remembered. He remembered very clearly. White-blond, unlike either parent. Some children are like that; they lack a stamp of physical belonging. As though they were built in error. His firstborn, then, was a failure. Clara arrived on the first day of the working week, full head of dark hair first, eyes open if the midwife was to be believed. The weight of her in his arm, when he held her, was solid. His true firstborn, he thought. He felt her struggle against the shawl. And there and then a tightness in his chest welled up so sudden, so powerful, he was forced to sit lest he fall. It was a sensation he had never experienced before and it frightened him more than a little. He sat with his eyes closed, listening to his own breathing as it shuddered under control, steadied itself. The smell of her, like warm fruit, soothed him. But soothing was softness, and softness counted for nothing in this life. His eyes still closed, the moment suggesting itself, Friedrich prayed. He absorbed the supple scent of her, and prayed for iron. She would see strength, this child. She would acquire it, too. This time, it would be different. Done, he looked down at her wide-open eyes, her jet-black head, saw her looking back. It was not foolish to think so. This child was here for the duration.

After three months of screaming colics and night-feeds, Marianne bound her breasts and handed the child over. Johanna it was, then, who saw to feeds and chewing rusks, the awkwardnesses of mittens, bibs and bonnets. She boiled wetting-cloths and nightdresses, tiny pinafores and gruel. She worked the baby's legs and arms, kept an eye on the stair-edge, placed ornaments on higher shelves, cleared up vomit, spills, shit and fingerprints; saw off wind and night-terrors with equal capacity if she heard them. By the time of Alwin's arrival, she was practised, by the time of Gustav's, mechanical. When Marianne took to sleeping in the afternoons, Friedrich found the little girl trailing him. Stopping when he stopped, waiting. What's more, he let her. He had plans for the child and they could begin now, more unconventionally than he had imagined, but

certainly now. He showed her the workrooms, let her sit in on
lessons, encouraged her to listen if she could not articulate. He swung
his watch like Mesmer, repeated her name.

Father. Father taught. Father talked a lot in a noticeable voice. He
instructed. He had a straight back, a scratchy face. His boots were
shinier than any other boots she had ever seen or could imagine; they
made music on the cobbles from their leather soles. Father walked.
He walked off tempers and to increase his joy of living. He walked
to cafes and meeting houses, to avoid excessive coach fares and to
enjoy the Rosenthal. Walks were lessons and discipline, sound
preparation for a sound and godly life. And walks were silent.

The memory is clear to the end of her life and why is no mystery.
They did this every day. Father and daughter, she from the age of
four with her white baby bonnet and loosened strings. When it
rained, his coat (mud green, the colour of a river in spate) smelled
like wet chickens. His skin stunk of leather and the stick he carried
in his hands. Her memories carry blisters, the sensation of skin
loosening, tearing away from the tissue beneath at every step, the tang
of wet woodland filling her nose. Her feet were damp: the price of
owning only one pair of stout boots, of not drying them as fully as
she might. But she would not complain. She bit her lip as she saw
her mother often do, did it without thinking, and kept going, the hem
of her pinafore turning darker every step, the trackless mud paths
splashing. Up and overhead, however, was a lattice of leaves with
light razing between, a watery sun promising more. Up, there was
the whole sky, and Father himself, lofty as a monument, his hat brim
an eclipse. Grey hair flared at his temples, the studs on his heels
clapped like hoofs and he was handsome, she thought; a man not to
be trifled with.

Once he caught her looking at him, not watching her feet at all
but him and whether he was pleased or not was hard to say. His face
changed not at all, but he stared down the length of his considerable
nose and spoke. The sky is growling, listen! *The sky is growling.*
These words, their strangeness. That the sky might *growl*, might be
a threatening thing despite the fact that God lived there was
impossible to believe. For a moment, and only a moment, doubt

made a trap-door in her stomach. What, she wondered, split-second dazzled and terrified, what if God did not help them when the growling came? And then, as she thought it, it did. Thunder. The sky rolled darker, and the low rolling noise of a coming storm made her turn her head and single spits of rain smacked close to her eyes. Seconds later, the sky opened like a tear in a shop awning and she heard his footfalls behind her, picking up speed as he moved away. Afraid of being left here, she turned on her heel, saw him ahead of her, and started running. Perhaps her foot caught on her skirt hem, perhaps she slipped on rotted leaves; perhaps she had no excuse at all. But she remembers falling, tumbling headlong, the trees flipping over her head and a cracking of twigs loud in her ears. There was pain, but nothing pressing; a peppering of dirt on her hands. And when she raised her eyes, sure that now he had marched away without her, there he was, raised to his full height, looking back. He glanced at her hands and eased back his shoulders. *Up*, he said. *Up*. And Clara stood. She refused to cry out despite the stinging, refused to allow any halt in her stride. She hitched her dress to her ankles and merely walked. In the time it took to reach him, something was decided. *You'll do*, he said gently as she reached his side. *You'll do*. Whatever it meant, it pleased him. Only then did he reach out to her. He dusted her hands, smoothed her coat over her flat child-hips. When they set off once more, he walked closer to shield her from the rain. She was quite sure now. Father was not afraid of anything. Everything came right. Lest he feel forced to slow down, be disappointed that he had misjudged her, she widened her step. He looked down then, watched her doing it. She was quite sure he was smiling.

And Mother? Ah. Mother.

Mother sang. Mother rocked her sometimes, rocked without her sometimes. Mother stayed at home with Mozart, swollen as a sow. Mother played. Mother played.

There was a journey to see Grandma in Plauen, her mother all in grey. She recalls the colour, the scrub of the cloth against her face, the cold crush of its linen folds. It must have been summer because of the flowers, something fresh and yellow in a vase, Easter long gone. That something serious had happened, something to split a life in two, did not show. Plauen was only Plauen, they had been to see Grandma before. Viktor, in the crook of Mother's arm, still feeding from her body when he got the chance, Grandmother throwing a ball. Alwin and Gustav had not come, but this was nothing new. The baby was new, he required to be shown: his brothers were not an issue. Mother smelled of blood and the dog followed her. The dog would not sit still if she came near. People visited as ever but their talk was lower, more hushed and someone, someone unplaceable, took her on their knee and rocked her. It made her uncomfortable, a stranger swaying her back and forth. Over days, the whole visit became uncomfortable with it. It was too long, too purposeless. Too clearly Not Home. The birdsong was too loud and the air was always sticky, pending thunder. After a while it dawned. There was no music. Home was stuffed with it: the same phrases of the same concerto for days on end, ringing on in echoes in spaces in your own head. Here in Plauen, the piano lid stayed shut. Mother didn't touch the keys at all. A book appeared in Clara's mind, red morocco covers with embossed lettering, W-E-B-E-R, each figure raised and dusted with gold. The pages inside were thick, their edges curled and dark with use. Perhaps she missed the book, the music it held inside. Sometimes she was almost moved to speak, but didn't. Not more than a baby herself, but she knew already. This terrible hiatus. There was only so much longer it could go on.

Saxon Law, Napoleonic Law. It's all the same.
Children are property: men are property-owners.
It was certainly the Law.

Soon Clara, newly five, sits next to strangers at the open window-spaces of a post-chaise. She wears the new boots that were the present from her grandfather, her best pinafore, the apron Grandmother stitched with her own hands. A gift, brand new. It's not cold but Mother's face looks bitten and her hands shiver. All Grandmother does is sniff. Someone opposite wears a coat like a ploughed field, doesn't speak for the whole journey. He spits on the floor and Mother moves her feet. Blots of phlegm shine like eggs, sliding as the chaise rocks. He says nothing, this man, only coughs and spits and does not admit anyone else is there. Mother, however, talks a lot. Look, Clara, the trees! The rabbits! Soon you'll see Alwin again, won't it be good to see Alwin? talking far too much, truth be told, wrapping Viktor tighter in his cowl. How Gustav will have missed you! For a moment when she says this Grandmother seems to laugh but it isn't that. Nothing feels like a joke. The man with the coat has a yellow face, and when his eyes meet hers, an accident, she looks away. When the man coughs again, she fetches a scarf up to Clara's nose, holds it there, tight. Grandmother takes the baby and Mother fusses in the bag beneath her feet. The bag has stockings and dresses, pattens, a winter cape. She saw them packed. Why, she has no idea. The winter cape stays in Plauen, too awkward to ferry back and forth, but not this time. This time, everything, everything of Clara's at least, is coming too. Where Mother's bags might be never occurs. They will be somewhere. They're not a child's concern. Through the open window-space, a distant steeple hoves into view, back out again. The trees turn russet, horses run in the fields. The coat-man coughs. His whole body rattles. There is nothing to play with, nothing to see.

Then comes Altenberg. Altenberg with fresh horses and pie-sellers, pumps for water, an inn. This time, there is also Hanna, Hanna in her old cap and dun skirts with a bag on her arm, her knitting and the sight is so pleasing the child breaks rules and runs. Johanna stands there, laughing to see her do it—as if she would forget her Johanna even after these months! As if! And Johanna strokes her cheek as though they had arranged to meet here, as though nothing was unusual in this place, this happenstance, at all. She has bread and apples in her bag, a pastry twist. Clara may choose. Since no-one says they are not, she assumes them birthday presents, maybe from Papa too, and thinking it fills her up so she wishes only to own them, not eat. In any case, there's the rest of the journey to go and the carriage rattles. It would not do to be sick, the same length of journey to go. For that's what's coming. It's clear now. What else can they be doing in this place? Altenberg, a crossroads, the way to somewhere else. All five together; they are met up as they should be and they're going home. No-one else seems to know, however.

Janice Galloway

Mother and Johanna stand apart: don't greet each other. Even
when Clara holds up the pastry to Viktor's lips, knowing he is asleep
and can't eat pastry in any case, no-one smiles. When the porter shouts
for passengers and it's time, Clara turns to wait for their first move.
She watches their faces. The horse brasses clank. Mother and
grandmother do not move. Something calls in the wood, one bird to
another, and everyone stands as still as a picture. The driver tests his
whip. Just as Clara is begins to be uncertain they are leaving at all,
begins wondering why no-one speaks, Johanna's hand slips into her
own, tugging. Tugging the wrong way. Clara watches her mother and
grandmother stay put, feels herself inched forward, away from them
without her cooperation. Johanna keeps pulling, more definitely now,
and Grandmother, still within touching distance, calls as if from far
away. *You'll see Mama soon*, she says; *very, very soon*. Viktor is held
out, a package being shown off, and Clara can't understand. Why
should she look at Viktor now? And despite her rheumatism, her
weakness in the joints, grandmother kneels. Clara has never seen her
Grandmother kneel and is faintly appalled. What is she doing? *Viktor
is staying with Mama*, Mother says. *Goodbye, Clara*. Johanna's hands
are clinging like mud, sucking her away. *We will see you soon. Very
soon*. Without being able to account for the footsteps that take her
there, Clara's boots find the first of the coach-steps and begin to
stumble upward out if habit. Grandmother is struggling to her feet
again, and Viktor is waking up. Clara can see a hand emerge from the
layers, its scorched redness against the white. He cries and no-one
comforts him, no-one says anything at all. The horses move from hoof
to hoof and from inside the carriage, someone's hands are reaching
down. They bracelet her arms and Clara pushes up on her toes to help.
It is what a good girl does. She helps. As she rises, lifting out of sight,
the child checks over her shoulder one last time. There is a glimpse of
Grandma folding like paper, hands lifting to cover her mouth, Mother's
face the colour of milk then nothing but arms, black woollen sleeves
against, the scent of leather. Something is wrong. Johanna pushes,
someone in the carriage hauls. Something is terribly wrong.
   After that? The sound of rain.
   The cold seeping through the woollen blanket over her knees.
   Johanna, silent as stone. That's all.

Presumably he collected her. Presumably someone held her, even if in passing, as they helped her down. If only for that short period of time, it's something. If she had not been so sure on her feet they might have carried her, which affords embrace by default but she seems to have had no aptitude for that kind of artifice, no way to ask. Her father's daughter, she returned to the house at Leipzig on her own two feet, blisters starting on her heels. A new house. Papa was up and waiting, of course. He did not ask where her mother was. Maybe he knew. Maybe everyone knew but her. Her brothers were already asleep, he said, leading her up stairs she only half-remembered. He would take her to her room. *Brother. Her room.* She had been in Plauen too long, could picture only Viktor, her grandmother's bed, yet that was not his meaning. For here she was, going up different stairs entirely, to a room that smelled like staleness and crumbs, not babies; a room that was nonetheless hers. *Hers.* You are home now, he said. With Papa. Home with Papa where you have always been. And he drew the shutters. And always will be. She heard them thud shut. A jug of cold water sat near the bed, a blue flannel. One candle. Johanna prised what was left of the pastry from Clara's hand, pushed gently till the rim of the mattress was near enough to lift her towards in one swoop. Her feet did not reach the floor. Slowly, one eyelet at a time, Hanna worked on the laces of her boots.

Next day, she ate no breakfast. Her father noticed but did not force. A man who was once a domestic tutor, who understood children, he knew best when to leave alone. The violent shaking of the coach, airless interiors and poor roads—the after-effects of travel on a child's system were only to be expected. Besides, fasting had its limitations: he saw no need to insist when Nature would do it without his intrusion. In time, he told Johanna, in time. She'll eat when she's hungry. Soon after, he found her standing at the window, her chin barely reaching over the inside sill. What held her attention? Outside, he saw only a man grooming a dray, carters unloading wood. No carriages. No-one coming. She kept looking out nonetheless. He fetched his hat then issued Johanna with the day's directions. The housekeeper now, the only woman of the house, she needed little telling, but checking was never wasted, in his opinion. The sky was clear, cloudless. Herr Wieck would not show it was anything else. He walked to the CoffeBaum, ticking lists in his head, making plans, many plans. First, Exercise: the best medicine for a troubled digestion. It was clear the child's digestion was at fault. After lunch, whether she had eaten or not, he would take her out. He would take her out for four miles. After that, sleep. After that? He made many plans.

Six days after her fifth birthday, then, near four o'clock in the evening, her father led Clara to the piano. He pulled his daughter, his brightness, next to him, tilted her chin, raised her right hand close to her face and looked at her. Hard.

Five, he said. Five. Look.

He raised his hand to her window that she might see the spread of his fingers, the bright translucent blood-colour in the spaces between.

The thumb is ONE. This here is TWO. This, THREE. He counted out loud till each was called something. FIVE, he said. ONE. TWO. THREE. FOUR. FIVE. Then he raised her left hand and did the same again. Clara, *Clärchen*, this child chosen for greatness, waited till he was done, then she looked at him, her face steady, her mouth a tight line.

I know this, her eyes said. *I know this already.*

To his credit, Friedrich laughed.

Except for Sunday which is the Lord's day, mornings are lessons. Every day, the same. Lessons are in the room downstairs, where other girls take theirs. The other girls, that is, the ones that pay. She waits for him like anyone else in the corner of the stair-head room, a pupil waiting for her teacher. Which she is. He is. Now. There must have been a time when music, staved and stuck to the page, was something unfamiliar. It stands to reason. no-one begins with the page. Yet these seed-pod heads, their sticks and legs, attenuated hairpins and crack-backed rests have always been there: strewn on tables and piled in corners, scattered on the music-stand. Falling ringlets of stave-brackets, the arcs and bows of phrasings, time-signatures, random confettis of sharps, flats and naturals seemed always to have been comprehensible; stair-runs of semiquavers, more loaded with meaning than any alphabet. It's how things are, have always been. So is the room in which one waits: familiar, unchanging, known down to the chips in the painted window ledge. An empty vase, two candlesticks, a wooden box stuck over with shells, an ornamental porcelain in the shape of a dancing shoe: the same five things on the mantel shelf. And just as she reflects, as she reflects every week, that there is nothing interesting whatsoever about candlesticks, there he is. Punctual. Watching his watch to prove it. *The Mind and the Tree, Clara*, he says, opening the door for her to come in. *What do they have in common?* She doesn't know. *They bend*, he whispers. *They bend.* She looks intently when he tells her here is a new language to learn. French as well as mother tongue, Italian too—she will not believe how much Italian. And, of course, singing. Clara, the child who almost never speaks, tries to think about language, singing. Mother. Tongue. The two words come easily together for her. She sees how they fit. Her eyes meet his and lock there, saying it. She understands.

So. Lessons. Practice. Handwriting and study of theory.

Sometimes in the evenings there are house-concerts.

She may listen, she may watch, she may sit. Sometimes she may just sit, restraining her extremities as a matter of course. A musician must learn to sit still and expressionless, waiting their turn. Grimaces are the province of hopeless amateurs. This is a Lesson too. Everything, it seems, is lessons. Aphorisms. Notes. Sit still and watch. These are the materials of all learning.

DUTY IS THE HIGHEST HAPPINESS.

LITTLE AND OFTEN IS THE SUREST WAY.

PLAY ALWAYS AS IF YOU PLAYED FOR A MASTER.

TRUST GOD AND YOUR TEACHER.

THE MIND AND THE TREES ETC.

The street is two floors down, only a sliver of it visible. The glass creaks in its frame when pressed, a rusty sound like ice, not enough to pull away. Up, the sky is bright blue, buzzing. It's full of beasts; hairy black blots that rise on warm currents from the nostrils of coach-horses, flies the size of thumbs. They zoom into your mouth if you hold it open, Papa told her, but they can't come through brick, through glass, so in here is safe. Two floors up, a vantage point on the whole world. Down there on the paving, someone invisible is whistling. Behind her, without turning, she can hear Johanna wheezing, Gustav baby-snoring, Alwin scraping on a slate. Audible warmth. Thick, slow, torpid, a heat-dazed fly hovers just outside, eye to eyes with her on the other side of the glass. Then the door opens. And everything, everything changed.

Papa was filling the room, enormous somehow, waving his arms and mouthing and for a moment, one horrible, stomach-clamping, moment, she thought he was weeping. Then she realized he was laughing and felt so blessed with relief that she laughed too. But there was something not right hanging in the air, a disturbance the laughter didn't shift. Despite the laughing, maybe because of it, Father didn't look like himself. His cheeks were too red, everything about him was too loud. Then she heard the words. Your mother, boys! he shouted. The pianist, Fräulein Tromlitz of Plauen!

Alwin's eyes were round as plums.

We shall have to become accustomed to her new name! He arched an eyebrow, catching his breath and in the moment's silence, Clara felt her smile having nothing to do with her, unfixing from her face.

Madame Bargeil! He roared, his face like an actor in a play. Madame Bargeil!

Startled by the noise, the suddenness, Gustav woke. He started crying.

Your mother, Clärchen! he shouted, not even looking like her father any more, laughing all over again, *Madame Bargeil!* This time so loud that Alwin joined in, squealing like a piglet, almost dancing with delight while Clara struggled to understand exactly what it was she had been told. For one inspired moment, she looked down at her dress, hoping the answer was there, but there was nothing but blue cotton. Then Gustav started wailing, the same terrified monotone he made in the middle of the night and Johanna lifted him up one-handed. Though Alwin was in no distress, her free hand seized him too, and before either of them had any idea they were going, she careened both children out of the room. Clara glimpsed the tail-ends of Johanna's skirts, Gustav's legs dangling, before the door closed and there was only her and Papa. The laughter, inside and out, stopped dead. Clara heard Johanna's heavy footfalls fading on the stairs, Alwin beginning to scream. She did not look up. When the screams faded too, the only sound was her father's breathing, so close she felt it gusting on her arm. After a while, it levelled out. When he no longer sounded like a horse, he walked to the window, stood as though looking into the distance. Perhaps, the child thought, looking at her father's back, perhaps Johanna would come back to fetch her. She kept her breathing shallow, noiseless, and waited. From outside, beyond glass, came the thrumming of monstrous flies. Soon, she thought, if she kept very still indeed, someone would fetch her. If she waited like a good girl, someone would come, very, very soon.

Pot-bellied Herr Bargeil.
Mother and Herr Bargeil. *Frau Bargeil.*

Wieck is working late. Students staggering home see his gangly shadow through the ground-floor window, pacing, not at peace. They point it out to each other, snort like pigs with cider-apples. Wieck is burning candles! Whatever's on his mind, it's serious—he's spending money to see it by. Inside, the teacher hears every word. Law students, he mutters. He says it under his breath like it's a nasty disease. Tonight, though, he doesn't really care. He has more to think about. He has Logier: *His Method.* Friedrich likes this word, *Method.* He likes *System* too, but *Method* is better. And who these days thinks of Logier without thinking of his Chiroplast? The whiff of science in the very name excites. A length of wood with little straps of canvas and leather; buckles, tiers and hollows: it's simple enough. From what he has read, he has grasped the idea very well. The board attaches to the piano and the child attaches to the board, each finger caught like a ferret in a trap, then the restraining band is clamped in place over the knuckles. Result? The hand held *just* so every time—without the pupil being able to disrupt the fact. Now! If the importance of hand position cannot be overestimated— and it can't—this peculiar little pillory has its attractions. To hell with finger-stretchers, thumb-belts and lordknew what else—this, they say, is the Coming Thing. In Vienna, people were queuing to have their children strapped to it, paying excellent money. If he introduced it here, persuaded Logier himself to give a lecture or two, it might work untold good for the hands of the town, especially for little hands, little, malleable hands. He thinks of Clara's fingers, her wrists that need all the help they can get. Then his eyes water. The candles are sending out distress signals, smoking their last. Rather than light more, he should make up his mind and get to bed, just choose. Kalkbrenner had already endorsed the thing. The French liked it, the Italians; even the Austrians, who preferred dancing to hard work, who abhorred anything remotely new-fangled unless it was a recipe, had taken the Chiroplast to their hearts. Only the English had reservations and what did they know about music? Besides, applied properly and with the right addition to fees, the thing would pay for itself in a matter of months. Enough thinking. He snuffs the last limp wick, sniffs with satisfaction. Law students! Ha! He wouldn't light a fire with a law student. Let none say Herr Wieck is not a man of action, a man to be reckoned with! Herr Wieck, the innovator, is buying.

Clara has a class. Not just lessons any more, a class. Three together, they will learn from each other and reduce Wieck's new pupils list. These days, everything is advantage. The other girls have beautiful hair. It's pleated and coiled like ear-muffs. They have pale skin the colour of ham rinds and their eyes are pink as potatoes. Side by side with Clara, they play scales in triplicate, petticoats rustling as they stretch for the pedals, miss. Girls in lace-for-lessons frocks, smelling of outside and hairdressing. Rich girls. They speak even when they are told not to, and on occasion, rare occasion, when Papa is out of the room, Clara speaks back. Mostly, however, they play, which is to say they work, and straight ahead of them sits the same book. LOGIER it says, white on black cover: THE METHOD. It sits on the stand, so much a part of the hours at the keys they can see its chapter-headings, its smooth list of contents, even when they close their eyes.

Her first book. All her life, Clara will be able to conjure the frontispiece with its attendant angels; the warm and gingery smell of its paper pages. The words would rise before her eyes when she could not sleep, recall the feel of the leather straps against her knuckles, reining her in. She would run them in her head till her eyes grew heavy again, fade away with her father's voice repeating them in her ears.

RECKONING A CROTCHET REST.
THE PAUSE.
DURATION OF SILENCE.
SILENCE.

An envelope arrives from Plauen. Inside, white ribbons. He tears the letter up, instructs Johanna to add the ribbons to the child's stock of clothing, not to mention the sender. He can think of no immediate reason why the child may not have ribbons. Later, he returns with a sack. Kittens. Little boys, he says; they'll need smacking. He sets them down and they huddle, shivering. She must flick their noses when they are naughty, he says. Feeding will be her responsibility: Johanna and Lise have enough to do. He lifts them by the scruff to show how it's done. Handfuls. She is astonished by the blue of their eyes, the slightness of their bones, like twigs inside a fur purse. They squeal. Of course, he says. He's surprised by the question. Of course they are hers. No-one else wants them. Their legs flail in mid-air, trying to reach solid ground.

He takes her to the opera and the theatre is vast. It has stars on the ceiling. When she was small, she might have thought it was the sky itself, but now she knows that's not true. Now she's rising seven and she knows many things. She knows Czerny's Toccata and she knows the sky is very big indeed. People can disappear into it. Men come and shake her father's hand, hold it tight, and even with no-one's skirts to hide behind, she is not afraid. She can stand her ground. The opera is full of people hiding, being lost and frightened. There's a Bad Queen who sings high enough to shatter plate china. Her Husband hates her because he hates all wickedness. The Daughter gets lost but is found again, this time—hurrah!—by the Father who will surely teach her to be Good. She likes this opera but is afraid of the Queen, of what might have happened to make her

so terribly wicked, and is really quite pleased when it's over. They
go home in silence, just the two of them, as they always do after an
evening out. After music, her father says, is no time to talk. Next
day she plays the Toccata and he says nothing, but he smiles. He calls
her *Clärchen* for the rest of the day. *My Clara.*

Duet	Schubert	Friedrich and Clara Wieck
Songs	Schubert	Francilla Pixis and Clara Wieck
Duet	Clementi	Emilie Reichold and Clara
Trio	Hummel	Rapscallions (not Herr Matthäi)
Solo	**Of Unknown Origin** (i.e. by C. W.)	

Pause for supper, rapturous applause and congratulation before
realization the second half is to come wherein will play yr Host Fr. W.

Fans and summer evenings. The men lit cigars and the music
and flies escaped together through the windows into the street. In
winter, the windows steamed, music stiffened on the stands. If
happiness matters, these were significant days. She knew at the time.
They were hers for the taking and she took. Already the boys
mattered little. She certainly took.

The night of her first concert in Leipzig, she waited alone at home,
watching her own hand melt a pattern of mist on the cold
window. The sheen on the guttering, his words in her ears: *Glass
Coach, it will be a glass coach.* And already late. He had gone ahead
to prepare, trusted her to be there, and all she could do was wait. It
will come, she promised herself. What else could she do? He had said
so: it would come. She imagined a carved gemstone drawn by white
horses, its insides exposed through the transparent sides like a lidless
watch, only velvet and herself inside. Snug. By the time something
arrives she didn't question: anything would do. A plain brown affair
with a dray and a loud man roaring her name barely waited for her
to get inside. There was no glass, only other girls in cheap dresses,
but they had been waiting for her. They said so. Before long, the
houses outside looked not only unfamiliar but alien. She tried to
memorize the slant of these roofs, wondering if it was some kind of
test. *I am Clara Wieck and I have a concert at the Gewandhaus.* She

couldn't even say her name. *I am to play the piano with Demoiselle Reichold. People are coming.* Not a word. She imagined her father at the hall, staring at his two watchfaces, screwing his eyes up to see the nothing that was arriving on the Gewandhaus road, and that finished her. She had no choice. *I am an artist.* Six faces turned to look at her. *And I have a concert at the Gewandhaus.* And the frowning child with the awful eyes burst into shivering, face-drenching, silent tears. It was simply enough resolved. The wrong coach had the wrong Clara—mistaken identities, that was all. The Gewandhaus coach handed over a footman's daughter when pursued, laughing at the luck of it, carried the grey-faced little piano-player to her concert only sixteen minutes late. She was here, at least, the coachman said, she was here. She had to be lifted down, not able to take her hands away from her face, her new fan dangling from her wrist by a cord. *Clara. Clara.* The voice he used in public, winkling her out like a whelk. *Clärchen.* Softer still. *People are always taken to the wrong house the first time they play in public.* She looked through the lattice of her fingers to see if anyone was looking at the baby who needed to be humoured in this way. *It's the law!* he whispered. His smile in the dark made his teeth long and yellow, and he held out a sugar-plum. Too sticky, even with gloves; she knew the rules. So she opened her mouth like a bird, let him feed her instead. Chewing, she let her hands fall, smoothed them on her new white dress. He dusted sugar from her lips, straightened, lifted his head up, up and she did the same. She recalls clearly his blue velvet collar back, his profile as he turned, waited in the wings, the drop in his smile as he glanced beyond. Mlle Perthaler was finishing her third solo. *Mlle Perthaler plays like a child*, he said, easing her gloves off, dusting chalk on her palms. *Like a monkey in a dress.* He moved aside and there was the stage. The piano. Mlle Perthaler leaving as the clapping rose, huge in the room like random gunfire. He took her by the elbow. They walked together towards the light.

Students come and go. They come thicker, faster, some of them grown men. She hears their lessons from other rooms and knows something. She plays better. Father spends time with some of them, though; goes out to student lodgings to hear their music, music they write themselves. They all compose, some better than others, and she must too. It's expected these days: it's part of the training. *New work,* he says. *Lifeblood.* In the coldest part of the year, she learns there will be no more lifeblood from Schubert, not this season, not any season. Some of papa's students turn up weeping on the doorstep; another doesn't come for lessons at all, just stays in his room, howling like a dog. If genius were proof against dying it would not have happened, he says, but it's not. Demonstrably, it's not. Schubert is as suddenly dead and buried and that's an end of it. When Alwin plays badly, Wieck cuts his lesson time and gives the extra to her. All Schubert. Work is the cure for grief, he says. Most of these young pups wouldn't know grief if it hit them in the eye: they use death as an excuse for laziness. Most of them don't know they're born. Alwin, nursing a bruise, his mouth tight shut.

The night he took her to see Paganini, she wore blue. He remarked on it, dropping the second watch in his waistcoat. *You will remind him of Italian skies.* He strode up and down the same bit of rug, ranted about the Miracle of the Age, the privilege of being alive In This Hour. *Some people,* he said straightening his waistcoat front, dusting off invisible crumbs, *some people said he hadn't many concerts left in him. He was sick, they said, dying! Ha!* The boys' eyes grew round as eggs, watching him. He sawed with two knitting needles, pretending a bow and a fiddle. His hair stood on end. They had never seen him so jovial. *The devil! Lightening!* he said. *People say anything—most of it stupid.* Then he demanded the boys get ready for bed. If they weren't so stupid themselves, they might be coming too. Paganini was a virtuoso to redefine virtuosity, he said, adjusting his best cravat, yet even Paganini began with scales. He grabbed his hat, fought his gloves, took Clara by the arm so suddenly it hurt. *Your sister will hear something tonight, not because she is lucky, but because she is industrious!* he roared, then rushed them both downstairs. Halfway down the street, he stopped, spoke back for his sons, for Clementine, the cats—whatever was sure to be hanging on his every word, to hear. *And another thing— prayers. Ask God for an end to idleness. Make them long prayers.* Tripping over her own feet, blue suiting her better than it ever had before, Clara followed him. *Eh, Clara?* he wheezed, somewhere between a laugh and a cough. *Long prayers!*

Of the concert, however, all she recollects is enormity, astonishment, an overpowering welter of sound: nothing that broke into distinct elements to tick off on a list. How did he look? A chalky face and black eyes. A spider. How did he play? Like three men at once. What did he play? Things she had never heard the like of before, impossible to describe. And his nose! The most Jewish-looking man you will ever see, they said, and she supposed they were right. Jewish or not, the applause was endless. Outside in the low fog of late hours, her hands still burned. They went backstage and a skinny four-year-old with his father's pallor though not his nasal dimensions, welcomed them in. She gave him two bunches of grapes, one white, one black, and the Great Man squeezed her hand, his tendons tight as punches, his skin damp as dough. His face was hollowed with missing teeth, his hair lank, his shirt soaked through. The child held on to his leg and Paganini kissed him, exhibiting his foreignness for all to see. Nonetheless, her father was happy; he was demented with happiness. Invitations to the rest of the concerts, invitations to sit on stage, invitations to play, invitations to receive letters of introduction through which would come more invitations— he and Paganini might be lost brothers. From nothing, he said, from *less than nothing*, M. Paganini has made himself a life. He has *earned for himself*, Clara. Only those of us not born into money know what that means. He has a talent and by God he *earns* with it, he makes an independence and forces their respect! Remember, Clara, what you earn by yourself is yours. You need depend on nothing, no-one else. You have a *means to prosper* and, he sniffed, to save your family should the need arise. This is what Great Men teach us. Spite them! Prosper! And look what you may become!

Clara listened and said nothing which was what she was meant to do. He was not talking to her now, in any case, but to himself. Or a Clara some years later, someone who would know what he meant one day. Clara thought about the Great Man's terrible thinness, the smelling-salts and brown lotions in his dressing-rooms, the bandages and sleeping masks. His kind looked sick. She thought of those cold hands touching hers, the kisses of a skull-face. *Dying?*

father said, swinging his cane as he walked. *People will say anything!*
As they did. They do.
Before long, they say them about Clara too.

Next time in Dresden, their letters open doors. If the girl played
for Paganini, she could play for Dresdeners too. Dresdeners, like
everyone else in this respect at least, are not averse to Paganini. And
when she plays, she does it so well they are suspicious. They say
things the like of which she has never heard before. She's really a
dwarf in her mid-twenties; a midget in a childish dress, a shooting
star that will fade. They say she is forced to practise till she drops,
can't read, can't write; is the tool of a tyrant out to make his own
name and a fortune. Even if she's none of these, the sophisticates
observe, she's not very pretty and will probably (here they snap their
fans) *never marry.* Wieck hears the stories; he saves them up. What
a joke! He'll dine out on these. She chases butterflies in the park, his
little girl, and no-one notices her; sit her at the ivories and they notice
so hard it hurts. The difference makes him laugh till he cries. *He tells
lies about her age, you know*, someone whispers in a salon bulging
with stuffed beasts, glass-eyed birds; *that's him over there. Really?*
says Friedrich, screwing an eyeglass in place to look at a man he's
never seen before, that no-one's seen before. *Ugly fellow!* Lisped at
by aristocrats, Friedrich roughens his speech on purpose, rubs his
hands in sheer delight. It's a game and he's winning: they can say
what they like. He's confounded the lot of them. Counts tell stories
about her, titled women and their daughters give her earrings, stroke
her hair. She's invited to the palace by Princess Louise. Twice.
Princess Louise looks like a frog, Friedrich thinks: who is she to wear
a coronet? What talent do these people possess? There is no stopping
his revolutionary zeal, his desire to show them their heredity is
nothing at all next to ability. This is the coming world! he says, he
writes it home. But he wears the proscribed clothing when he takes
her through the palace gates, bows when he must. It pleases him to
toss his hat at flunkeys who may not complain, who must call him
sir. What do they look like in their ill-cut livery, their awful wigs?
Ha! Not like him, that's for sure. Next time, while he looks on
dressed to the nines, the sensation proceeds entirely to his liking.

During her improvisation—the *Wundermädchen* also improvises! she composes!—someone swoons. It could be the unusually warm spring weather, the claustrophobia of the small room, it could be the new vogue for tighter stays, but Friedrich doesn't think so. He knows what he thinks. If they're reeling now, what will they make of her next time? The time after that? *The teacher must be a lion, a genius!* they say, and he is forced to agree, but he's in no hurry. Only fools rush and Wieck is no fool. Not yet. To date this is his finest hour and the best thing about it is his certitude. He knows without doubt. He's just begun.

D resden, theory and distant guns fill the summer. There's fighting in Warsaw, Alwin says: a post-boy told him. He has no idea where or what Warsaw is, but ignorance in these matters is no drawback. Fighting, he says, and his whole face shines. Before he's tired of soldiers, there's news from Paris too. Revolutions. The French are making the very word their own. *Gun manufacturers and undertakers,* her father says, *they're making a killing.*

Clara's heard stories, too. Father tells her not to listen. Artists are above such things. War, he says, is not our concern. Meanwhile, people close their shutters, build stronger doors. Some leave altogether and the question of who will play at the next subscription concert at the Gewandhaus—*her first paying concert and all her own*—occupies no-one. no-one but Friedrich. Art stops for nothing, he growls: it never concedes. When the music press closes down, all advertisement with it, his rage is thick. It fills up rooms like porridge and every one gets a taste. One morning, when Clara stumbles on a simple triplet passage, he snatches the sheets from the stand and tears them to snowflakes before her eyes. The rest of the day she must spend writing a list of adjectives that best describe Bad Girls which, by coincidence, describe Bad Mothers too. All night, and for several nights after, the sound of ripping sheets makes her thrash in her sleep. Alwin has no trouble sleeping: his playing, however, is helpless. One day, it's bad; even for Alwin, it's bad and he confesses he didn't practise. When the swelling won't go down, the doctor comes to look at Alwin's eye. It will get better, he says; no more stumbling on the stairs, eh? He chucks Alwin's chin, gives him an apple. And no peering at notes till it passes!

Everyone smiles till the doctor is out of sight. Doctors know nothing about music, says Friedrich, and anyhow, there's nothing wrong with the boy's fingers. Alwin keeps the apple and plays with his eyes bound, resting. His scales, however, get no better. Alwin is as musical as a pig, father says and Gustav laughs. Briefly. Sit up! he roars out of the blue at Clara one afternoon, Straighten your face! And Clara sits. She straightens perfectly.

One week later, after a week of solid fighting that can be heard as near as the outskirts of town, the Gewandhaus closes until further notice. Friedrich understands—a concert hall can't live without an audience, when tickets won't sell; all the same his face is set like a bear's and his knuckles are white. Alwin's next mistake is pure folly. The same phrase fails him but he keeps restarting, tucking the violin back under his chin. He hasn't the sense to stop, so his father does it for him. He reaches, takes the violin, turns his son slowly. He looks directly into the boy's eyes. And Alwin, stupidly, asks to try again. Everyone in the room knows before it happens that something will. Even then, when Alwin's head tilts suddenly to one side and his legs crumple beneath him, it takes her by surprise. He looks like a calf in an abattoir, she thinks, something taken by a vast, unpleasant surprise. She almost laughs, then wonders if he's fainting, but that's not it. It's his hair. Staring makes it no different, simply more the case. Her father is pulling her brother's hair. The nine-year-old is almost kneeling now, tangled round the man's fingers as he's pulled lower still. With his remaining free hand, Wieck removes the violin to keep it safe, and hands it to Gustav, who simply take it. When Alwin yells, stumbling lower, his father tugs harder, and the boy begins sliding on the loose rugs, his feet churning in little circles. Even when he's prone, it doesn't stop. It changes. Hauled by the hair, like a dog on a lead, the boy begins sliding across the polished floor. Clara can see the skin of his neck stretching as the hair begins to snap, her father's hand clutching tighter as he drags. *I want to play*, the child shouts, his voice splitting; *I want to try!* and they all know it won't work. Even Alwin knows it won't work, but he begs despite himself. Well-trained, Clara and Gustav do not look at each other, do not react at all. Anything at all might make it worse. There is nothing to do now but wait. While her father begins in earnest, pacing the room with his burden whimpering behind him, Clara picks up the music on the stand. WEBER, it says. Sonata. She reads the words over and over, rocking slightly on the stool, trying to keep her face expressionless. WEBER. Other people, she thinks, ignoring the thuds behind her, the whimpers and shouting; other people are coming tonight. There will be fairy-tales and laughing, food and wine. Tonight, she thinks, she'll play. Close to, something crashes. Even when the piano-lid rocks and threatens to fall on her still fingers, she doesn't flinch. *Is this the way you repay a father?* he roars. *This ingratitude? You children will be the death of me!* and Gustav bites his lip. Tonight, she thinks. She keeps her eyes on the pages, the word *Sonata*, the serried ranks of notes. She'll play flawlessly, with all the meaning in the world. She concentrates, fighting her own eyes. She waits.

The concert comes, eventually. They remember her. The little girl with the *doppelgänger*—even the driver jokes. This time, there's no mistake, no other little girl with the same name. All the way without mishap, without diversion: the night is all her own. The pianos are tuned, the programmes in plentiful supply, the orchestra sitting silent for a nod from her head. She concentrates, certainly. Clara Wieck does not play, has never played, without focus. All the same, she is aware of the black suits that surround her, the kindnesses of so many men. The only dress during the four-piano finale is hers. The Herz is faultless, they tell her; her Variations clever, for a girl. Did she write them all by herself? they ask, look at her father in a knowing way. Nonetheless, Dorn calls her a *true servant of music* and kisses her hand. When they take their bow together at the close, she is aware hers is awkward, not assured but they don't mind. Her father remarks on it of course, but he's pleased. He even says so. *Work on your composition, Clärchen, the public want more!* She doesn't mind if they do. Her own concert in front of so many is a different affair, more different than she had expected. That it would give her this feeling of alertness, this fizz in the head, was something she could not have anticipated. It's a difference she likes and it keeps her awake. She waits up, making conscious acts of memory: that her sash was grey, that the satin of her dress glowed almost yellow under the stage-lamps, that she felt no tiredness at all. Tomorrow it will turn to dictation. *Tickets at sixty groschen*, he'll say, *outlay and return* and she'll write it down. Outside, the bells of the Nicholas Church chime midnight. It's moonless, the sky too cloudy for stars, but the lodger's lights are still on. Herr Schumann staying up late again. She sits at the window in her nightdress, hanging on to what she can. Already, it's tomorrow. Applause ebbs in her ears. His window flickers.

G one six months, what did she do?

Weimar	Erfurt	Gotha
Eisenach	Arnstadt	Cassel
Frankfurt	Darmstadt	Maintz
Paris	Metz	Saarbruck
Frankfurt	Hanau	Fulda

She learned faces, times of day, the different smell of another country's streets, the mean disposition of foreign hotels. She travelled with her father. She played the piano.

Let Clara tell the story exactly as she recalls.

Cold, unsprung coaches and no sleep, the acrid stink of piss-hardened whips and ancient horses, dragging another mile, another mile. Arriving late in the evenings with the towns shut and nothing to see, nothing to eat, almost never a welcome or a porter to carry bags; new rooms with old sheets and the noise of Papa snoring in the bed beside hers till morning filled up the window, if there was a window, to see what lay ahead: breakfasts of bread and afternoons of hiring and haggling, demanding and blustering, of contracts, bookings, accounts. She had studied, sung, composed. She had stood by while Papa made himself known to music-society presidents, administrators, critics, tuners, dealers, bodice-fitters, clerks, censors, town-officials who took three days to process a request then asked for another signature, another fee. And every day, after her three-mile exercise, she had made trips to hotel ante-rooms, the backrooms of dealers' warehouses, schoolrooms, parlours in rich people's houses, to beg an instrument to play till the time came to view the brute they'd provided for the concert. Sometimes she wished she played the violin, the flute, something portable, most times she didn't. Pianists played pianos: this was how it was with her kind. From out-of-tune dustboxes to shipped-in Pleyels, they took what was afforded, they played. Pianists gave concerts, that was the correct word, they *gave*, and she had given a great many; in halls little more than barns with not enough light to see by, others in palaces, with Royal Families in matching sets waiting round a piano so patterned with inlays and painted landscapes it seemed an affront to touch it at all. She had played for Goethe with all his hair after eighty-one years, who fetched her cushions and sweets; for Spohr who held her hands and told her they were *treasures from God*; for Mendelssohn and Chopin who looked like princes till she saw them bear-fighting, giggling like boys in a salon ante-room. Yet how beautiful—she could think of no other word for it—Herr Chopin was when he listened! How fragile yet determined his face! And she had played for Kalkbrenner and for Herr Hiller and for Paganini, who remembered her and showed her his three more missing teeth; for officials and generals and countless teacup-rattling Philistines, supporters and sniffers, for boors, bores and the merely curious. She had seldom been asked for an opinion. She had been given jewellery, medals, accolades, keepsakes, locks of hair from lovesick girls; gold clasps, emerald combs and money. Most of the jewellery was money now too. But this was nothing to say. It wasn't a *story*. She had travelled with her father, she had played the piano—that was the long and short of it. She said so—and they laughed. Father too. Relief lightened the air in the room like orange zest.

The things you say, her father smiled. He shook his head in a manner indicative of incredulity. *Ce n'est pas dire!*

And he told it himself, as he knew he would all along.

Weimar was full of snobs. Gotha housed only ignoramuses and farmers. Eisenach and Frankfurt were miserable. They could tear down Frankfurt and he'd not weep. There of all places she played like an angel till Darmstadt, where perfectly tolerable people were served cold playing, this time *not the piano's fault*. Never mind! Performances aren't rewards. Not for anyone. And Paris? Where to begin? Paris stank. One tiny jug of water for washing in the morning and no more all day! Clementine's brother, however, couldn't be faulted, had even drawn an official portrait—Clara with no waist at all and her neck bare—that earned a few thaler *thank the Lord*. A new dress for *each appearance* and everything white, flat-soled shoes, only fresh flowers or seed-pearls for her hair which should *always* be up. For himself, three pairs of yellow kid gloves, as many white stocks and half a dozen shirts *in one week alone!* Add laundry bills, hairdressing, wraps, and shawls and one wondered why people put their daughters to touring at all. Salons reeked of smoke, stale cologne, and Frenchmen. Programmes didn't start till after ten at night then everything was lumped together like stew—Spaniards lying full-length on the table with flowers between their teeth, chicken-faced sopranos with their dresses cut so low their nipples showed, divorcees reeking of cigars—he'd seen it all. And the crush! Four hundred in Kalkbrenner's tiny front rooms to hear Chopin play for fifteen minutes! And that hellish piano! What was it like, *Clärchen?* Eh? Kalkbrenner's instrument? A bag of bones, that's what, a disgrace. Yet Chopin thinks Kalkbrenner a magnificent fellow, so what is to be made of that? Now, listen to what an honest German had to say, and in his own home, not to impress multitudes. In Weimar, Goethe himself said our Clara had the strength of six boys. *Six boys.* And she needed it in Paris! You don't play these French uprights, you fight them! You fight to win! And the true connoisseurs, of course, knew it. They knew the difficulties. Spohr, Pixis and Mendelssohn, Paganini—all Great Men, Good Men. Heine, however, was an arrogant pig and Kalkbrenner was worse. Kalkbrenner was a precious, self-adoring sort, a prig like Heine but without the talent to back it up. *In Paris we love Beethoven*, he said. *Programme her without Beethoven and with only the claptrap you push upon her presently and you will reap little here.* Ha! Do you know what I said? He looked around the room fiercely. I said this! She plays Beethoven as she plays Schubert—at home and not for the mass until I say so, sir. He sighed. Until I say so.

For the first time since he'd begun, he leaned back in his chair.

Of course it was a regret not to have spoken to Chopin. You should see him—the way he looks them in the eye. As though he has never asked for their money and never will. They say he does not care if he only ever plays for a handful of people in his life, he will not be *liveried entertainment*. Ha! He repeated it, savouring the idea or ridiculing it, it was hard to know which. *He will not be entertainment*. Well then. He slackened his collar. Well. A pity. People of spirit should stick together. Then the young man is naturally reticent.

Clara watched him sink back further, drop the tension in his shoulders. He is reticent. That's all.

Ferocity seemed to have been all that was holding him together. Now he had allowed himself to spit it all out, he looked smaller. He looked thin and old and tired. The way, in fact, he had looked for weeks. She had recognized his story as she always recognized his stories. He had told what he saw. But she had seen other things, things around the edges of his vision; mere detail of course, nothing so important as what his own eye had lit upon. But certainly Other Things. Many of them about Father himself. She had noticed his incredulity at the Paris protocols, his spluttering humiliation at being unable to afford the rate for the hotel found by Fechner, his face reddening in the accumulated heat as the evenings went on and on; the hateful French salons full of stuffed leopards and embroideries and paintings and peacock feathers and whispers that he never seemed to notice. She heard the content of the whispers, too, sometimes wondered if she was meant to. But that wasn't it. That would have been to give her too much credence. They talked out loud like that because they thought her more or less insensible, because they assumed she had not a word of French to her name. And what they said! The father's infelicitous turns of speech, the passé colour of his coat, the not-quite fit of his yellow kid gloves. Lord, my dears, do you not pity her! Chopin thought him stupid, they said; Kalkbrenner thought him a buffoon, and everyone in the world, it seemed, made fun. Oblivious, his French not up to French as spoken by French persons, he led her to pianos, his velvet-covered arm under hers solid as truth. And inside the cocoon of whispering snobbery, his voice had sounded good, like the Voice of God. *Artists are your own; be in awe of none. As for the rest? Remember that none of these sorts, no matter much they think of themselves, not one of them can do what we can do.* Then he left her to what she had come for, left her alone at one keyboard after another. And she had played.

She had played very well.

For all that, they seemed to see her as an amusement, someone so young playing so maturely, a girl playing with such *masculine strength*. That they thought her *pretty* seemed to matter more than any of it. She met the poet Heine, who, for his politics and other things besides, had packed himself out of Saxony before Metternich had done it for him. But he and his companion, knowing nothing of the applause she had received in Weimar and Cassel, thinking nothing but the applause of the city in which they stood counted, appraised her like a vase while she stood there in front of them: *Poor child! It seems as though she could tell us all a long story woven out of joy and pain, yet what does she know? Music.* Her face burned recalling it even now. And this was not the worst, not by any means. Audiences of aristocrats—well. It seemed they couldn't help themselves. Anyone who was paid for a living they assumed no more than a servant. They talked through the music, petted dogs, ordered tea and yawned. If French, they smirked at her speaking in her own language because it was not theirs and asked how on earth she had learned so much *so far away*. How Chopin endured it, she had no idea. She certainly understood why he hated to play. But Clara and Father endured it all for just four concerts in small rooms, the sense of being a tolerably amusing entertainment. This, then, was the Capital of the Musical World.

When word of cholera made him pack their bags, she was almost glad. Through Metz and Saarbruck, swathed in flannel, a heaviness grew in her stomach, her head. In Frankfurt, another name for hell, she woke with night-sweats and her bones ached: no more than a passing chill but her father prayed and his face was grey. Shortly after, she bled. There was no hiding it. Her father said nothing but he ordered her bed stripped and demanded fresh sheets, let her patch herself with rags as best she could. This was something that happened, she knew, it was not cholera. Not, despite its awfulness, an illness at all. Sharing the room together, however, was becoming unbearable. As soon as she could dress herself, a cheap overnight coach and four had rattled them home.

None of this had much to do with what people wanted to hear either, but it was what made the deepest ridges in her memory.

Applause and performance she took for granted, yet they were triumph, success, the Real Story. She must learn to refocus her priorities, *then* she'd have something to say. Thinking it through made her feel restless. She made her excuses, left the company in the sitting room, put on her oldest pinafore and headed for the kitchen. Lise gave her salts and vinegars, soda and lemon juice, a recipe for metal paste. That made, she worked. Hair scraped back, a necklace worth two years of Lise's wages round her neck, she set herself to polishing knives. Next time, she thought, scouring, when Papa said, *Tell Dr Carus how Paganini played, Clärchen; what Goethe said; what that rather stuck-up fellow Heine looks like; what refinement Mendelssohn, the son of a Jewish banker, can display*: she would say something dazzling. The reflection of her face appeared in the blades as she worked, her lips parted as though ready to speak. She was Clara Wieck. These hands had been kissed by adult men. *Parisians.* The great, the good, and the very rich indeed had looked her in the eye and she had looked straight back knowing she had something to give. More to the point, that she worked and she *earned* and that mattered, dear goodness, that mattered. One day, she thought, buffing till she broke sweat, she'd say something dazzling. *Ce n'est pas dire.* One day, she'd say something to surprise them all. □

LOVING MONSTERS

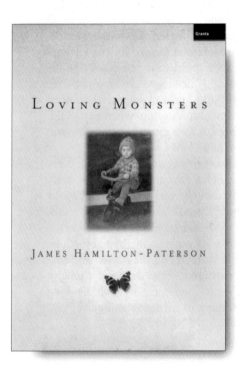

"The book is fresh with the imaginative vigour and moral urgency that make him an important writer . . . It is a tribute to the power of *Loving Monsters* that, on finishing it, I ignored the plaintive pile of unread books on the bedside table and instead hunted down and read some of the author's earlier work."

—*Spectator*

"A LITERATE, NABOKOVIAN LARK. BRILLIANT."
—Time Out

JAMES HAMILTON-PATERSON

HARDCOVER • 308 PAGES • 1-86207-425-9 • $24.95
www.granta.com/monsters

Granta Books

I'm Like a Bird   Nick Hornby

Of course I can understand people dismissing pop music. I know that a lot of it, nearly all of it, is trashy, unimaginative, poorly written, slickly produced, inane, repetitive and juvenile (although at least four of these adjectives could be used to describe the incessant attacks on pop that you can still find in posh magazines and newspapers); I know too, believe me, that Cole Porter was 'better' than Madonna or Travis, that most pop songs are aimed cynically at a target audience three decades younger than I am, that in any case the golden age was thirty-five years ago and there has been very little of value since. It's just that there's this song I heard on the radio, and I bought the CD, and now I have to hear it ten or fifteen times a day...

That's the thing that puzzles me about those of you who feel that contemporary pop (and I use the word to encompass soul, reggae, country, rock—anything and everything that you might regard as trashy) is beneath you, or behind you, or beyond you—some preposition denoting distance, anyway: does this mean that you never hear, or at least never enjoy, new songs, that everything you sing in the shower was written years, decades, centuries ago? Do you really deny yourselves the pleasure of mastering a new tune (a pleasure, incidentally, that your kind is perhaps the first in the history to forego) because you are afraid it might make you look as if you don't know who Foucault is? I'll bet you're fun at parties.

See, the song that has been driving me potty with pleasure recently is 'I'm Like a Bird', by Nelly Furtado. Only history will judge whether Ms Furtado turns out to be any kind of artist, and though I have my suspicions that she will not change the way we look at the world, I can't say that I'm very bothered: I will always be grateful to her for creating in me the narcotic need to hear her song again and again. It is, after all, a harmless need, easily satisfied, and there are few enough of those in the world. I don't even want to make a case for this song, as opposed to any other—although I happen to think that it's a very good pop song, with a dreamy languor and a bruised optimism that immediately distinguishes it from its anaemic and stunted peers. The point is that a few months ago it didn't exist, at least as far as we are concerned, and now here it is, and that, in itself, is a small miracle.

Dave Eggers has a theory that we play songs over and over, those of us who do, because we have to 'solve' them, and it's true that in our early relationship with, and courtship of, a new song, there is a stage which is akin to a sort of emotional puzzlement. There's a little bit in 'I'm Like a Bird', for example, about halfway through, where the voice is double-tracked on a phrase, and the effect—especially on someone who is not a musician, someone who loves and appreciates music but is baffled and seduced by even the simplest musical tricks—is rich and fresh and addictive.

Sure, it will seem thin and stale soon enough. Before very long I will have 'solved' 'I'm Like a Bird', and I won't want to hear it very much any more—a three-minute pop song can only withhold its mysteries for so long, after all. So, yes, it's disposable, as if that makes any difference to anyone's perceptions of the value of pop music. But then, shouldn't we be sick of the 'Moonlight' Sonata by now? Or the Mona Lisa? Or *The Importance of Being Earnest*? They're empty! Nothing left! We sucked 'em dry! That's what gets me: the very people who are snotty about the disposability of pop will go over and over again to see Lady Bracknell say 'A *handbag*?' in a funny voice. You don't think that joke's exhausted itself? Maybe disposability is a sign of pop music's maturity, a recognition of its own limitations, rather than the converse.

A couple of times a year I make myself a tape to play in the car, a tape full of all the new songs I've loved over the previous few months, and every time I finish one I can't believe that there'll be another. Yet there always is, and I can't wait for the next one; you only need a few hundred more things like that, and you've got a life worth living. □

THE FIRST SENSE
Robyn Davidson

Robyn Davidson

Hearing, they say, is the first of the senses we develop in the womb. For a certain time, inside our mothers' bodies, the entire universe is a soundscape, nothing else exists.

As soon as we are born, our mothers speak to us in a special lilting way, and we respond to those sounds—to their rhythm, pitch, intensity and timbre—the musical or prosodic features of speech. Our brains are already organized to decipher them. They convey emotional rather than grammatical meaning. Perhaps, back in the shadows of geological time, such exchanges between mother and infant arose in order to bond them still closer, and, from this, evolved into a form of communication between adults. Perhaps this is the ancient root of music and of speech, the first, musical language lying coiled beneath the later, gatekeeper to more primal realms.

My career as a concert pianist ended with the two final chords of Brahms's Rhapsody in G minor. The chords, delivered fortissimo, sound something like 'Take that!' I was nineteen.

Three years previously I had won a scholarship to the Queensland Conservatorium of Music, but it was not quite enough to live on, even with part-time work. My father, suddenly aware that he was the sole parent of, and therefore somehow responsible for the future of, a girl, declined to contribute financially, suggesting that I get a job as a secretary, or something, anyway, respectable, until marriage. Instead I hitched a ride on a truck going to Sydney and lived, initially, on the streets and in the parks of that sparkling city. Eventually I found work as an artist's model, then as a croupier and poker player, then as the de facto manageress of an illegal gambling club. This gave me enough money to enrol at the Sydney Conservatorium of Music, in order to rejoin the path my mother had set me upon long ago, in an infancy beyond conscious recall.

I trudged along it for about a year. I was obliged to transform my technique, by carrying out single-finger exercises requiring transcendent patience and concentration. The playing of actual music was forbidden. Surreptitiously, I had learned the Brahms Rhapsody—a troubled, passionate piece that suited my temperament and style. Buñuel's heroine plays it stark naked in *That Obscure Object of Desire*. Fortunately I had not seen the film at the time of my own performance.

I am sitting at a concert grand halfway through the Rhapsody. There is an audience of sorts, I don't remember who, or where. The epiphany arrives during a difficult passage which I am not confident I have fully mastered—'You do not have the makings of a great pianist, and you are revealing that fact in front of a lot of strangers.'

My body carries through to the end, but my head has completely vanished. Take that! I bow, walk away from the piano and do not touch another for over two decades.

In all that time I did not experience one moment of regret. I was not, in any case, given to dwelling in the past. I seemed always to be in a present that sheered off from the past like an iceberg, and floated into the future carrying a new version of myself.

But one evening, I was listening to Glenn Gould playing Bach. I closed my eyes and gave myself over to music I had heard before, but this time it was almost unbearably moving.

I suppose I was already primed. My mother died when she was forty-six. As I approached that age, an indeterminate sadness began to settle over my life. I began to wish that she, a stranger to whose scanty memory I had previously felt indifferent, could be retraced, reconstituted, as the person I must once have loved.

I was sitting in my father's old chair which had travelled in his family's wake all the way from Scotland to Australia, accompanied him through all our various Queensland houses, and had now ended up with me, a dreg of the Davidson line, back in Britain. Through large industrial windows, the view was of an east London skyline. There was a familiar bittersweet sensation in my body, characteristic of musical attention—states of anticipation, deferral and reward which seem to occur all at the same time.

As I penetrated deeper into the sound, or it into me, I began to 'see' the music—a 'hearing' of architecture or landscape, as if sensory channels had misfired and were hitting each other's targets. I had always experienced mild forms of this phenomenon—assumed that everyone did—but nothing as intense, or as unnerving, as this. Then, the main event—a bolt of awareness which tore open memory all the way to the root.

It is shimmering over the downs country. A white sand river bed ascends from the house towards the brigalow ridge. The banks are lined with eucalyptus trees, their grey leaves hanging vertical to the sun. A man on a horse moves along the river bed towards the brigalow forest. Every day he sets out early from the house, with his axe and saddlebags. A cattle dog follows behind. Every evening they return, along the same track, always stopping at the same bores, the same gates, trailing the same spume of dust, and again, the next morning, as before.

Brigalow wood is springy and hard. The percussion of iron on brigalow produces a unique timbre. You can hear the wood's elasticity and resistance, blunting the axe with each strike.

The man whistles without awareness, always the same tune, ground into his memory when he was a boy, and unleashed into immediacy by certain kinds of concentration. His attention is cut by a bird's call. He looks up to follow the sound which breaks into smaller and smaller fragments until it disappears into the midday silence of insects and a friction of leaves.

On his way back from ringbarking the brigalow, he catches sight of a building undulating on the horizon, but this is an illusion created by heat pouring into the sky. When the real house comes into view, it is no more than a rent in a curtain of eucalyptus trees on the far side of the river of sand.

A woman is singing, accompanying herself on a piano. She sings beautifully and without inhibition—an 'aria'. As he approaches the lonely house, other sounds stir in the air—the luffing of sheets on a line, a windmill creaking. The sounds of her world have their silences too, just as, at midday in the forest, there is a silence of the axe, of insects and leaves.

I sit beside her on the piano stool, in front of the German upright. I press the keys with her hand over mine. Now she is at the window staring out at the drought which penetrates the house as a fine powder, as if the house itself were a wreck beached far from shore, into which sand seeps threatening to bury the survivors...

No, these are not the memories that erupted out of me that night in London. I don't recall now what, specifically, I remembered then, if indeed it was as straightforward as that. Certainly the sites of my childhood and the people who lived there returned to me, and the sensation was something akin to a mental avalanche. But a lot of time has passed since that night, and much work has been done breaking the crust of the past and fathoming its depths, the consequence of which is that I now have a facility for calling up its contents. I could have gone on and on with the 'ringbarking' sequence, pulling scenes from my mind with the ease of a magician pulling scarves from a pocket. It is perhaps the same mechanism by which dreams become easier to recall if you make a habit of noting them down.

The scenes seem to exist as if a flash of light had fallen on the original episode, illuminating and congealing it. Each scene sprouts, as it were, tendrils of story which link it to the next, giving the illusion of a seamlessly flowing sequence. Sound pervades the memories like a mirage.

That child who, glimpsing her father setting out on his horse, or who, hearing her mother's voice, was perhaps already transforming 'father' and 'mother' into actors, on some imagined stage adrift in time, was perhaps already making stories to contain the emotions stirred by certain sounds—an axe's thud, a piano, sheets on a line; was perhaps already creating images out of such fertile new words as 'ringbarking', 'brigalow', 'aria'.

Inside the pocket of bone, beneath blonde curls caught up in a bow, an electrochemical gale was sweeping signals along loops and switchbacks of unfathomable complexity, embedding mind and world together in a configuration that, in spite of ceaseless changes wrought by new information, by experience, nevertheless would maintain a continuity that felt like me-ness, and in some way that seems even more uncanny, was laying down the basis for a past which could later be exhumed by music, and remodelled as a synthesis of fact and fantasy.

It is not important to me any more that my 'scenes' aren't true, though it was at first, when I thought the past could be reconstructed. Paradoxically, it was when I gave in to the inevitability of fiction that I gained insights which had a deeper and more subtle authenticity, were more valuable to me, than facts.

For example, if I look again at the sequence of story that emerged from the seed image of the man on the horse, sure enough, I notice something to which I had not previously given sufficient attention—the extent to which my parents' spheres were discreet, the rigidity and formality of the separation. The either/or-ness of it.

My father lived in the paddocks; my mother lived in the house. I see now that this segregation of the manly (free, outdoors, undomesticated) from the feminine (restricted, interior, tamed) has influenced me deeply, prefiguring the opposing inclinations in my own nature.

My father was born in 1900. The moral structures underpinning his personality and beliefs were formed before the First World War, that is to say, by the nineteenth century. The whole of his life's journey was an extension, a playing out of that epoch. One of his convictions was that certain beliefs amount to natural laws because they are upheld by science, notably Darwinism. Men are superordinate to women because natural selection made it thus, and whites are superordinate to blacks for the same biologically determined reason. These laws have predictable, though often regrettable, even tragic, consequences. For example, Aborigines were destined to die out in the face of invasion by a fitter race. My father was neither aggressive nor cruel—he admired and respected Aboriginal culture and knew as much about it as most anthropologists of the time. But admiration and respect, even friendship and love, were no match for Natural Law. Similarly, the self-evident truths of Darwinism informed his relations with women. Ambition and aspiration in females, beyond their biologically determined roles as homemakers, was folly and bound to lead to unhappiness and disorder.

His family were squattocrats who had opened up grazing land in Queensland during the previous century. The women tended to be eccentric, imperious and jealous. The men, evasive and good-natured. They were all tall and strong and led marvellously free lives. Indoors was where you resentfully went when you couldn't be outdoors, galloping bareback down a beach, going for picnics in the first Model T Ford in Australia, mustering cattle on some vast holding. They looked down comfortably from an elevation that was moral and social as well as physical. They despised weakness of any kind, hoarded and squabbled over money, and were constitutionally incapable of humility, introspection or self-pity.

My father's choices, however, made him something of a misfit in this milieu. He inherited the amiable indifference of the male line, but cleansed of snobbery. Just after the First World War, he slipped out from under female dominance and went jackarooing and dead-wool picking in the outback. Then, abandoning all responsibilities and betraying his family's expectations, he set sail for East Africa with his savings. There he lived a youth of high romance—prospecting for gold and diamonds, going on safari with his 'boys', harpooning crocodiles, wrestling with death in the form of blackwater fever and charging elephants, and looking breathtakingly handsome in pith helmet and khakis. He sailed a ketch home for the next war, met and, contrary to the wishes of both families, married a woman seventeen years his junior—and I was born in his fiftieth year, on a droughty cattle station called Stanley Park, in western Queensland. Being conventionally Victorian in his views he left all things domestic, including the raising of children, to my mother, without, however, allowing her ready access to his purse. In short he was an inadequate husband and father in many ways, but an adorable hero.

On those rare occasions when I was allowed to accompany him through the paddocks, reaching up to hold on to his thumb (half of it was missing), I would pester him to tell me, yet again, about igneous and sedimentary rocks, about stars and planets and Magellanic patches, about the conceptual difficulties of space and time, about the formation of crystals, about the Cretaceous period and malachite and radiolaria and basalt...and I would strive to impress him with my latest dilemma about my choice of futures— should I be a zoologist, astronomer, geologist, astrophysicist, botanist? He chuckled and seemed to approve though his attention, as always, was partially elsewhere. If we passed a snake, poisonous or not, he would quietly pick it up behind its head, so that it wrapped around his arm, and invite me to stroke it. 'No need to kill the poor old Joe Blakes,' he would say, and throw it far away from us. Thus by example rather than instruction, he taught me to be unafraid: of snakes, spiders, cyclones, ocean waves, solitude and the dark. He taught me how to listen to the silence of nature so that its silences opened all the way out to the rim of our exploding universe.

Of course I do remember him being in my mother's territory. But he had the status of a special visitor. He might sometimes, of an evening, allow me on to his lap as he sat in his armchair, or come to read to me at night—Edward Lear verses, most of which we knew off by heart, or essays from *Marvels of the Universe*, popular science volumes published in the Twenties. Yet there was always the sense that he was doing what was expected of him. She sat him at the head of our table (serviette rings, table manners), and tried to establish him as the disciplinarian. But he was hopeless. His authority inhered in him more subtly—by having the right to disappear to some inner place unavailable to us. That is what set him above us, like air above land.

Only once did I witness his anger. He was in the house paddock. He thought he was alone. I peeked at him from around the corner of the sheep shed. He had the reins of the horse in one hand, and with the other he was laying his stock whip, again and again, across the terrified creature's back as if he would flay it alive.

The atmosphere inside my mother's time is modern; her journey begins just after the First World War and her gaze is fixed firmly towards the fresh new century. I have a photograph of her when she was a girl, dancing in the style of Isadora Duncan. The possessions which defined my father—prehistoric stone axes, fossils, rare geological specimens, African spears and an elephant gun—were perfectly antithetical to hers—a silver fox fur, a crystal bottle of eau de cologne, a trunk full of sensational ball gowns that her children would use for dressing up, a piano. She was exquisite, comic and full of nervy vitality.

She was raised as a Protestant though her father, at least, was a Jew. Whether anyone thought this important I shall never know as it was never mentioned. But I sometimes wonder if it contributed to the disdain with which she was treated by my father's family, or whether they simply believed her the wrong class and temperament. It was not, after all, the 'barbarism' of Aborigines of which they were scornful. They related to their black stockmen as to aristocrats of a separate and doomed order. No, it was the 'civilizing' values of the middle class they disliked. My mother's aspirations—her concern with clothes and accomplishments, her care to define herself against all things 'common'—would only have compounded their disdain.

I know that by the time I came along she was ground down by country life and yearned to return to the city and all that it represented—lively conversation, light opera and friends; doctors who weren't a couple of days' journey away; opportunities for her daughters. I suffered croup as an infant and I know that she spent countless nights walking me up and down the corridor, willing me to breathe. Snakes terrified her and they were everywhere—on the path to our outdoor dunny, in the rafters of our bedrooms, coiled in the corners of her kitchen, basking on the verandas. Loneliness engulfed her and there was no relief from it. Except music and I suppose, to some extent, me.

Whenever she wasn't working—and both my parents were industrious to the point of illness—my mother was making music. She played the violin and the piano, and had a lovely soprano voice. The German upright that had followed her from her previous life was the hearth of all our houses.

For something that played such an important role in the family, music received very little of my curiosity. It was just there. A background accompaniment weaving in and out of our lives, as unremarkable as breathing. Yet one of my first uncontestable memories is being on the swing in the backyard of Stanley Park composing a 'symphony'. I must have been younger than four. The event exists as a series of seed memories—the swing, a hot sunny day, eucalyptus trees, the awe and exhilaration of creation, the enormous scale of the back veranda steps as I struggle up them to inform my mother. I hear her words, 'Hum it for me.' But when I listened for the melody again in my mind, it had vanished. She laughed and hugged me to her legs, but some losses are inconsolable.

I think as a child I provided some solace for my mother. I remember, quite vividly now that I attend to it, an afternoon that I presented her with a routine I had been working on. We had moved to the coast by then, so I was probably six or seven. I dressed myself up in her old ball gowns, led her in from the kitchen and made her sit in my father's armchair. I put Gracie Fields on the wind-up

Robyn Davidson

gramophone, and mimed... 'I'm a char and I'm proud of it too and that's that, though charin's a thing that I 'ate'... There she is, a little, elegant, worn-out woman collapsed backwards in an armchair, a tea towel across her knees, laughing, as she would have said, 'to beat the band'. And I can feel the echo of what I felt then—the open, willing sympathy that is a child's love. I notice too, with a little shock, that she is much younger than I am now.

It was some time after this that I began to be consciously aware of the rift between the two worlds, and of its implications. In my mother's world my vocation was obvious—I was a musician, singer, dancer, actress. In my father's world it was equally obvious that I would solve the riddles of nature through scientific enquiry. By then I was beginning to show real musical aptitude, but I was also finding my mother's realm stuffy and restrictive, and longing for the freedom of the paddocks.

And there was something more ominous in the air. A pressure, as if the two continents were grating against each other, and something was going to crack. There were little releases from time to time. As when my parents flicked each other with wet tea towels in the kitchen, and my sister and I joined in until we were all chasing each other around the house laughing so deliriously we ended up gasping for breath on chairs and floor.

Or when neighbours visited and we gathered around the German upright for a 'sing-song'. Then it was as if we all breathed an eternal air of friendship and goodwill. When we sang together, each of us, immersed in inner worlds as real to us as the objective world we shared, felt the boundaries of our individual solipsisms dissolve and we were one with each other and all things.

I watch us gathered there, through the transfiguring light of years. It is the late Fifties. The colours are a little muddy. There is a new twenty-two-inch-screen television in the corner which will gradually parasitize our sing-songs. But for now, it's 'Roll Out the Barrel' and 'How Much Is that Doggie' and 'Bimbo Bimbo Where You Going to Go-e-o', and everyone has forgotten their wounds and worries and is warmed through. Music is a kind of compassion, I think. It lives in the depths of us as a subtle solidarity, consolation for our separation from each other and from the Supreme.

In the afterglow we offer our solos. My sister is doing her 'Vilia, Oh Vilia', and then my red-letter moment arrives with 'I Heard a Robin Singing'. It is touch and go whether I will hit that top A or land a good half-tone below it.

And then it is my father's turn. He is self-conscious standing there beside his wife, with his pipe clutched in his right hand, singing 'Sarie Marais' in what is probably bad Afrikaans. Surely anyone can see what we in the family already know, have always known. That our beloved hero is ashamed of his own gentleness, which he thinks of as effeminate, a weakness. The man's man, unwilling to burden you with his emotions, is an idealized version of himself; and his need to prove (to himself) that he is not afraid is what makes him obdurate. The general remoteness of his bearing is in fact the expression of an impregnable obstinacy, and it is wearing her spirit out.

By the time we moved to the suburbs of Brisbane, she was very ill. Her eyes held a perpetually bewildered and haunted look and she did not make music any more. We lived in a new sound collage— the silence of ticking clocks, of stifled weeping, of a car passing slowly down a tarmac road, of things going wrong quietly, and very fast.

I remember one day she came home from an appointment with a psychiatrist. She said, 'He told me I should be happy. I have everything a woman needs—a husband, two lovely children…' She trailed off as if I would not bother to listen. I was ten years old, and even if I had not been distancing myself from my drowning mother, trying to save myself, I was still too young to have been able to find the words to comfort her, to assure her that I perfectly understood the sadism of the doctor's words. A sadism induced by anxiety—a woman who was not satisfied with a husband and two children was, by definition, unnatural, diseased. And coded into his words was the message that she could never be happy unless she agreed to be docile, to be asleep to her own predicament. I don't imagine my mother was much of a thinker, her rebellion was instinctive and therefore profoundly honest. I wish to hell she had chosen to live, yet if, for her, it was a choice between the death of her body, or the death of her meaning, then I admire her for choosing the former. It is not necessarily true that where there is life there is hope.

I have never assumed that my mother's suicide made my

existence worse than it might otherwise have been, only different. In fact it would be just as legitimate to describe the act as her last gift to me—the gift of becoming a puzzle to myself.

I was sent to live with my father's twin sister—my mother's bitter enemy. I barely saw my father again until I was in my twenties.

Under those circumstances it was inevitable that I would lose trust in the world of appearances—the so-called 'real' world—and withdraw further into my private world, the key to which was the secret of how things really are. Early on I understood that most people are happy because they do not know how things really are. They are happy in the way that dogs are happy. By the time I got to boarding school I was in the grip of a paralysing inertia and I don't think anyone had an inkling of the magnitude of my retreat from life.

Those years are obscured by a kind of mental fog. Through the fog the only glimpses I catch are of a faintly autistic girl hiding out in the music rooms, missing classes and playing Chopin badly but with feeling. I did not shed a tear for my mother, I don't recall ever thinking of her. Yet somehow the music mothered me, by playing an essential part in my emotional development. It was like a hand to hold until I had passed safely through a perilous place, and reached the shore of adulthood.

There are assets to every liability, and one of the assets of my fractured childhood was that I had no regard either for the securities of the status quo, or for conventional ambitions. And such things as identities which people with normal histories took for granted as a natural unfolding of first causes, as something contiguous with the past, I could invent from scratch. It took time to grasp that I could make myself over, but when, at the age of seventeen, I hitched a ride on a truck that would take me away from my past, I was laying the first stone in the creation of an individual.

In his final years, my father's emotional life rose closer to the surface. He strove to conceal it, yet it was that never fully disguised vulnerability that had always made him so lovable to me. We had grown very intimate by then, yet he never referred to my mother except in the most oblique terms. Once, on a trip back from London, I gave him a tape of Willie Nelson songs—*Stardust Memories*. We sat together in the lounge, he in his old chair, me at his feet. The music, sentimental and nostalgic, which I had hoped would give him pleasure, instead opened a vent. He began to weep, that old man's weeping that comes from some unreachable cavern deep within. The music had brought her back to life in him, and at the same moment, made him aware, again, of her loss.

I suppose you could say that something similar happened to me. Music gave a mother back to me but also made me aware of an irreparable loneliness, the asset of which was a greater range of thought and feeling. What Bach's music made possible that evening in London was an imaginative or literary engagement with a past that had been so undisturbed by contemplation that it was stagnant.

For a long time afterwards, that engagement took up most of my mental life. I had been exiled too early from childhood and, like all exiles, found myself obsessed with a place that could never be reached. It was as if those who could not be reconstituted as they truly were, were now represented by actors whom I brought on stage to help investigate the meaning of a text—a scrappy, incomplete document of traces and clues. How many combinations and variations we experimented with in that theatre, how many arguments and contradictions, tantrums and reconciliations we endured. Any final understanding was an illusion of course. One has simply to live with the fundamental ambiguity that is the nature of all things.

I have less and less to do with my actors these days, but I came to like them very much. □

PATRICK MCGRATH

In *The Designated Mourner,* there is a sense that the liberal intelligentsia may be impotent, irresponsible, hypothetical, but at the same time, when they go, everything of value goes with them.

TWENTIETH ANNIVERSARY

BOMB

WALLACE SHAWN

My dear fellow, you've summarized my work so beautifully that I don't need to say any more or write any more.

TO SUBSCRIBE CALL: **1-888-475-5987** OR VISIT WWW.BOMBSITE.COM

MOZART, NOT
Alan Rusbridger

Alan Rusbridger's Fazioli piano

Sometimes when I sit down to my morning piano practice I wonder what my neighbour makes of it. Or rather, I try not to think what my neighbour is making of it. Gillian's kitchen is just through the wall from my piano and I know that she knows something—possibly a lot more than something—about music.

'Not that Beethoven again? Why doesn't he just admit he can't play it?' Is that what she's thinking? Or is she thinking: 'Bach again. I expect we'll have the same old shambles around bar 23?'

Does she groan when I fumble my way up and down scales? Is she sick to death of a particular piece of Mozart that I keep coming back to? Is she astonished at my effrontery at tackling that Shostakovich? Or possibly she doesn't listen at all? Sometimes I see her going to the gym in the morning. Have I driven her out of her house?

When I tell people I've taken up the piano again they always ask, 'Are you any good?' And I never know quite what to say. Some days when my spirit and fingers are in sympathy with each other I think I make a reasonable sound. On other days spirit and fingers aren't on speaking terms and the result is fumbling, dismal, depressing. I recently made the mistake of tape-recording myself the way middle-aged amateur golfers video their swing. They hope to see Tiger Woods and see instead a portly form waving a stick in an uneven arc. I hoped to hear Mitsuko Uchida or Angela Hewitt—I didn't. It was an effective exercise in delusion-stripping.

I can play some passages from some of the greatest works by Beethoven, Mozart, Schumann and Brahms. But there are not many pieces by those composers that I can play in their entirety. I can please myself in the morning by playing a piece that I've been working on for some time. And then I can go for a lesson in the evening and within minutes it's apparent that I was fooling myself. Passages that flowed perfectly in the morning dissolve into fudge under the scrutiny of my teacher. I've misread chords, failed to work out reliable fingerings and I play everything too fast.

So I never know what to answer. Am I any good? The honest answer is no, I'm not very good. But if the questioner is not especially musical a plausible answer might be—not bad. I recently played a Bach Prelude and Fugue to a friend who knew little about music and the friend didn't run from the room. The notes were the right notes. There might even have been flashes of phrasing and touch. But I know that anyone even moderately knowledgeable about music would have tiptoed off to make the tea.

It shouldn't matter, I suppose. I'm just playing for my private enjoyment. But somehow it does. Most days when I practise I end up in some degree of despair at my inability to progress. Most days I ask myself what's the point? What is the point of hacking through a piece of Schubert so badly that nobody with even a minimum of musical sense would want to listen to it? It's not like playing tennis badly. At least with tennis you can play with a friend who's equally bad and have some enjoyment together. You don't have to serve like Sampras to have fun. At least with tennis you're not murdering a creative masterpiece. Music is different: there is an achievable ideal. You've heard it in recordings—and how to do it is there, in precise detail, on the page in front of you.

Other days I astonish myself. A piece that seemed impossible the previous day suddenly comes together. The fingers move gracefully and fluidly. Most of the notes are in the right order. I won't sell the piano after all. It is a moment of quiet, utterly private satisfaction.

Or it would be utterly private if I could be confident that Gillian couldn't hear it through the wall. But of course I could never ask her. What if she said 'yes'? Then my little act of morning indulgence would no longer be private. I would be conscious of another ear hearing what I am hearing. My fantasy life would be destroyed. It is better not to know.

I first started playing the piano when I was about six. My mother played, though not, I think, particularly well. When she was feeling sad she used to sit down and pick at the opening bars of Debussy's 'Clair de Lune'. It reminded her of her mother, who used to play it to comfort herself after her husband had left them. The story of my deserted grandmother—and my mother's tears—became the programme for the music. I, too, wanted to learn how to play the piano.

We lived in a leafy road in leafy Surrey. And soon I was making my way up a leafy drive to piano lessons with a Miss Dunn Davies, who lived with a companion in a large Edwardian house. I went every week and my mother made me practise every morning for twenty minutes. I now can't remember a single piece I learned with Miss Dunn Davies. She liked to teach short pieces ('Fireside Tales' or 'Sunlight over Haystacks') by English composers of the Twenties. But I suppose I must have picked up some technique. I took Grade One (the lowest grade of the Associated Board of the Royal Schools of Music exam) in 1966, when I was twelve, and passed with distinction. The yellowing certificate shows that this was in spite of the examiner coming close to failing me for my aural tests—singing tunes, clapping rhythms and so on. But he scrawled at the end 'very musical'.

Musical or not, I soon added singing to piano, and followed my brother into Guildford Cathedral Choir, which involved about two hours of music a day, six or seven days a week. I also took up the clarinet. At my secondary school I had a teacher who was very glamorous and about a hundred years younger than Miss Dunn Davies. She didn't think much of the English inter-war composers. She did think a lot of Beethoven and started me on his simple sonata Op. 49 number 2. From that we moved on to Schumann's *Kinderscenen* and the 'Pathétique' Sonata. In time I switched to a new teacher, who made me play Mozart's C minor Fantasia. I was now playing great music, albeit indifferently, and I became obsessed with trying to master it. But two things did for me in the end: one was the fact that piano-playing was a solitary occupation and the other was that I was allergic to scales.

The first mattered because, like most fourteen- or fifteen-year-olds, I longed to be part of some crowd—even if the crowd was the uncool classical music crowd. By now I was quite good at the clarinet and I had begun to play in chamber groups and orchestras. I was not sporty. Music was simultaneously my escape and my belonging.

The second defect was more troublesome in the long term. I discovered I could sight-read well and play the piano plausibly, if not accurately. But I was not building the infrastructure of a technique. Anything involving fast finger work I either slowed down for, or

Alan Rusbridger

simply jammed down the sustaining pedal and hoped that the litter of wrong notes would be absorbed in a blancmange of dissonance. (The sustaining pedal lifts the dampers off the strings, thereby allowing them to go on sounding, even if you've moved on to another note. Fine in Chopin, frowned on in Scarlatti.)

I sort of gave up. Sort of: I still played the same old pieces time and time again at home when no one was listening. I went through university playing piano duets with my friend Philip: he was much better than me and my technical incoherence mattered less. Later still I would play songs for my children—nursery rhymes, Pooh songs, Broadway numbers. But any ambitions I ever had to play the piano even slightly seriously had long since been extinguished.

And then, two or three years ago, they came back.

First I started playing the old pieces which I knew so well, if so inadequately. I was no better, but, it seemed to me, no worse. In the intervening twenty years of listening to music my tastes had moved on. I began toying with some truly great music and with the idea of getting a teacher.

One day I found myself at the home of Michael Shak in north London. Shak is an intense, clever and instantly likeable American whose concert nerves had brought a career as a soloist to an early end.

I played him some Bach. He listened politely and agreed to teach me. He asked me to begin again. After about four notes he stopped me. 'Alan,' he interrupted in his New York–London drawl, 'if you're going to play seriously you're going to have to think about fingerings—work them out and stick to them.'

Ah yes, fingerings. Useful, of course, but somehow not for me. I should explain: fingering is the way composers, or subsequent editors, make piano music playable. Only by writing the number of the digit above the note can you guarantee to make your eight fingers and two thumbs arrive on the right note at the right time. My big red Beethoven books at school announced that they had been 'fingered by Donald Tovey', which—unhappily for the late Reid Professor of Music at Edinburgh University—had always caused a teenage smirk.

It was plain that if I was to get anywhere with Michael I was going to have to approach the whole business of fingerings with a new

250

seriousness. Of course, it should have been obvious even to a teenage know-all that there was something in it. Try this—a basic scale (eight notes) in the simplest key, C major. Your thumb is 1, your little finger is 5. Play a scale on the table or your knee that goes 1,2,3,4,5—a straight run up. You've got as far as G. To finish the scale you have two options. One is for your hand to do a little hop to the right after 5 and begin again on 1,2,3. But you will find it almost impossible to do that leap from 5 to 1 seamlessly. The smoother option (though not one universally used) is to tuck in the thumb after 3, so that it plays the fourth note in the scale. 1,2,3–1,2,3,4,5. The act of moving the thumb automatically pivots the hand to the right, where it covers the rest of the scale.

After a while fingering scales becomes fairly automatic. Actually, that statement needs qualification. Scales involving black keys—sharps or flats—require different fingerings. And, of course, left hand and right hand are not at all the same. And minor keys are, again, different. And melodic minor scales are different from harmonic minor keys. So it would be truer to say that fingering scales in some of the simpler keys becomes fairly automatic to a moderate pianist.

Before I started with Michael I had never given much thought to fingering a piece in advance—that is, sitting at the piano writing in pencil above many, if not most, notes, which finger to use. Michael convinced me that to play a smooth line it was necessary to work out in advance which finger was going to play which note—and to stick to it. The faster you played, the less time there was to make snap decisions and the more important it was that you sorted it out at the beginning. And he quickly spotted, and banned, my own technique for playing slow movements fluidly, which was to slam on the sustaining pedal and hope for the best.

Michael approached fingering with the seriousness a mathematician might approach higher calculus. One lesson on a Beethoven sonata might cover only twenty bars. Thirty seconds in he'd quibble over a particular sequence of fingers suggested by Sir Donald and try different variants himself. If not satisfied he'd reach for his own editions—one of them fingered by Schnabel—and try another sequence. Tovey would be crossed out and replaced by Shak. Schnabel might then be pencilled in brackets above Shak and Tovey, and I would be instructed to go home and work out which suited me and to make my own definitive mark on the score. Fingered by Rusbridger.

To begin with, this obsession with details irritated me—I just wanted to get on and play the music, and it was taking weeks to get through half a movement of one sonata. But after a while I did begin to hear a difference in my playing. Michael was right: using the same fingering every time greatly simplified the business of getting the fast notes evenly in the right order. And I was beginning to be able to play a legato—i.e. smooth—melodic line without the safety net of the loud pedal.

Things which had seemed impossibly unnatural began to seem natural. Try this: play a note on the table in front of you with the little finger—number 5, the fifth finger—of your right hand. Now, keeping that finger down, play a note to the right of it with your fourth finger without unduly tilting the hand itself. Feels weird? It is weird, but it is a surprisingly useful little piece of digital yoga to practise during dull meetings. Or try this: play a note with the third finger of your left hand. Now, with imaginary key still depressed, move your second finger on to the same imagined key—i.e., tucked just in front of, and slightly under, it. You have switched fingers on the note, without sounding it twice. This frees your third finger to play the next note down without the slightest gap. Watch a pianist's hands closely the next time you—or a television camera—are close enough and you'll see this all the time. But you'll have to watch closely. The best pianists have magicians' hands.

A few months into my lessons with Michael I had an expensive midlife crisis: I bought a new piano. It really was the classic midlife crisis—it came from nowhere, I couldn't explain the grip it had on me, and afterwards I felt a little foolish.

I had been playing on a baby grand Challen that my mother had bought for me and my brother nearly forty years ago for £350. It was immeasurably better than the old German upright we'd had previously, and I'd always imagined that it was a rather fine instrument. But Michael had a six-foot Steinway and there was no getting round the fact that—though I was always slightly nervous when I played in front of him—the noise that I made at his house was incomparably rounder, richer and deeper than anything the poor little Challen produced.

One day Michael was in a state of rare excitement. Another pupil of his in Kentish Town had just bought a new piano by a modern Italian maker he'd never heard of. It was, without doubt, the finest piano he'd ever tried. It was something called a Fazioli. I could see he was in love.

That night I sat down at my computer and typed Fazioli into a search engine. There was the maker's website, which told of the extraordinary ambition of a mechanical engineer from Sacile, a town north of Venice. This Fazioli had not quite made it as a musician and had decided instead to build the best piano in the world. I searched further. A pianist in north London was selling a second-hand nine-foot long Fazioli. I emailed him. He emailed back. He'd just sold it that morning to Christ Church Cathedral, Oxford, but I was welcome to try it before it went.

The next day I went to the modest terraced house of Mark Swartzentruber, an American pianist settled in Finsbury Park. In the front room—where normally you'd expect the standard sofa, armchair and telly—there were not one, but two nine-foot grands, a Steinway and the Fazioli. Mark discreetly left me alone with these intimidating black hulks. Eventually I summoned up the courage to touch the Fazioli. From the first chord I played I, too, was in love.

The usual metaphors do not help in trying to describe such moments. It has been said that playing a Fazioli is like driving a Ferrari after driving an Austin Maestro. This may very well be true. But, although I did once own an Austin Maestro, I have never been behind the wheel of a Ferrari so this does not help me much. There is certainly a feeling of power such as I imagine you experience when you first depress the accelerator on a Ferrari. The lightest touch on a Fazioli produces a sound of effortless clarity and depth. The further down the scale you go the notes begin to blossom, then growl. On cheap pianos the note begins to die the moment you touch it. On these pianos the note seems to swell, like an organ.

I imagine there is that same sense of only just being in control of a sports car if you step into a souped-up Porsche after a lifetime driving Volvos. Gone is that reassuring sluggishness: now you're on your own, the wind in your hair, the lightest touch producing the most dramatic results—and no seat belts! Hit a street light on the other hand and you're a goner.

A panic crept up on me in that Finsbury Park sitting room because I knew I could not resist this thing of beauty beneath my fingers. It was not the sort of thing I could keep secret. Of course, I would have to confess all to my wife. But even the children—who do not, as a rule, see much of the house during the hours of daylight—would eventually notice that the piano had acquired an extra two yards and would begin to ask questions. Like, how much did it cost, Dad? (roughly one and a half Volvo estates, since you ask).

My Fazioli arrived about a month later. When I came home one night it was there—draped in a maroon cover with FAZIOLI embroidered in distinctive gold letters on the side. The cover came off and the lid went up, exposing a burst of colour—the deep red spruce soundboard from the Val di Fiemme and the golden walnut inlay around the inside of the case. That night I played the piano for four hours.

The Challen went to a good home in Battersea and I set about rebuilding such technique as I had. On this piano the good sounded wonderful, the bad sounded appalling and there was no forgiving middle ground in between. It was impossible any longer to conceal the slightest unevenness of touch or rhythm. Hold the pedal down for a fraction of a second too long and the bell-like clarity turned to mush. It was time to get serious: but getting serious takes time.

I have a day job, editing a daily newspaper in London. The day job requires me to listen to the radio and read the papers early in the morning, and keeps me away from all but a computer keyboard for, on average, twelve hours a day. The paper arrives at home shortly before midnight. And then there is the odd glass of wine in the evening. Alcohol does not generally coax one's fingers into acts of flawless coordination and subtlety, so that rules out most evenings. The only option was to set the alarm clock to buy another twenty minutes in the morning.

Twenty minutes a day is, of course, pitiful, but it is just enough to get perceptibly—if very slowly—better over time. But only just enough. My bedtime reading has recently been a 1924 book on the basics of piano playing by Josef Lhévinne which tells me that a 'smattering' of technique in playing scales simply won't do. 'Don't pay a teacher a high fee later in your musical life to have him point out something that you should have learned in the musical primary class.' A good point, Josef, well made. If only you had been my bedtime reading when I was seven.

Just as I have never driven a Ferrari I never go to the gym, so this may be another unreliable metaphor. But I imagine that what I am now doing to my fingers in my twenty minutes a day is roughly what other people do to their quadriceps or deltoids down at the LA Fitness Centre. All amateur pianists despair of their fourth finger, which—because it shares a tendon with the fifth—is the weakling. While other people are working on their abs or triceps I'm doing a spot of pump-'n'-burn on my flexor digitorum superficialis. But, obviously, not as much as Schumann, who famously invented a special piece of gym equipment to work out his fourth fingers, and ended up paralysing them.

Of course, scales and exercises are as boring in a man's late forties as they were when he was in short trousers. Besides, by the time his midlife crisis arrives his musical tastes are rather more sophisticated than they were, and the time he has ahead of him is rather shorter—too short, in fact, to be practising any music that is less than great.

So the next challenge is finding music that is emotionally and intellectually absorbing without being frustratingly unplayable. This is, needless to say, harder than it sounds. Music that—to the casual ear—feels as though it should be approachable is almost inevitably trickier than it seems when put to the fingers.

Try, for example, the fugue at the end of Beethoven's extraordinary, mystical Op. 110 Sonata. Part of the paradox of most late Beethoven is that—while the ideas and technical realization are so complex—the music itself is often spare. The fugue at the end of this, his penultimate sonata certainly sounds as if it should be playable: though it is marked *Allegro ma non troppo* a great many pianists take it at a stately walk. The fugal theme is simple enough— you play it evenly, quietly and smoothly with your left hand.

It is really only when the third entry comes in that the fingerings require a bit of Sir Donald's assistance.

By bar 32 life starts getting tricky. Look at bars 31 to 33.

You'll see that—at the same time as keeping two other lines going—Beethoven wants the melody to sing out at the top. That means weighting the outside of the right hand (fingers 3,4,5), so that those fingers play louder than the thumb and the lower fingers. But if you are to make the fugal line smooth you must play each note in the upper line with a different finger. This is going to make for some awkward stretches. And at the second beat of bar 33 you're going to have silently to switch fingers—4 to 5—while quietly playing 1,2 underneath. That leaves the fourth finger free to play the next note with the fourth without breaking the legato line. It is the pianistic equivalent of scratching your head and making circular motions on your stomach while simultaneously raising only your left eyebrow. But it has to be done.

You've managed that? Well, in truth, it wasn't that hard. Now try bar 39, where Beethoven requires you to:

a) manage an even trill with the (weedy) fourth and (much stronger) fifth fingers of the right hand (or, alternatively, use 3 and 5) at the same time as

b) playing two other quavers with the third and second fingers (or 2 and thumb) and

c) readying the left hand to play the organ-like fourth entry of the fugue in the bass, while

d) catching the last quaver beforehand with your left hand, even though it looks as though it should be really played by the right hand.

The point is that this music is not even especially difficult. It doesn't present any of the technical Everests of a Chopin étude, a Rachmaninov prelude or a Lizst sonata. All it asks of you is to play four individually simple lines reasonably evenly, with the ability to weight both inner and outer sides of each hand, depending on which line needs the most emphasis. It shouldn't be impossible. Indeed, it's not impossible, even for an amateur pianist. The technical challenges above are all individually surmountable with a bit of quiet thought and by endless repetition. But it probably is impossible on twenty minutes a day.

B uy a really good piano and you enter a new and bewildering world of piano aesthetics. Much better pianists than you call round to give it a run round the block. They ripple their fingers up and down it, peer inside the case, waggle the pedals and suck air through their teeth.

'It's beautiful,' they say, shaking their heads sadly, 'but the hammers are too soft/too hard/too bright/too dull.' They may love the tone in the middle octaves, but not the upper octaves. They think the lower register needs 'revoicing' to match the middle register. They're not sure the dampers are quite meeting the strings as fully as they should.

Alfred Brendel has written an entire essay on the voicing of pianos, in which he remarks that the problem stems from the 'ignorance of pianists, who are unable to perceive clearly and put into words what worries them about an instrument'. He means proper pianists: we amateurs are even more inarticulate about the little niggles that enter our minds about the instruments we love. And any shadows of doubt we do have we tend to suppress on the grounds of impertinence: who are we to cast judgement on such astonishing feats of mechanical engineering?

And yet, after a few months of swooning at the sound of the Fazioli, a little worm did creep into my mind. Some parts of the overall sound were undoubtedly brighter than others. The odd note did stand out from the crowd. I had become used to expecting perfection of output, if not input.

A proper pianist who has studied these things came and tried. He shook his head. It was indeed a beautiful piano, but it was not quite perfect. He would, he said, send round the technician who worked on his own pianos. The technician arrived soon afterwards on a large BMW motorbike. He made me play to him while he watched my fingers intently. He asked me how I liked to play—lid up or down? He then sat down to work without even taking off his leathers. I came back ten hours later and he was still at work, and still in his leathers. My stomach lurched when I saw the floor: it was ankle deep in hammer felt.

When you press the keys of a piano, it is the hammers that make contact with the strings. Scores of books have been written on that moment of impact. On the whole, pianists tend to concentrate on how they touch the keys—the position of the fingers, the height of the hand, the weight of the forearm, the push from the shoulders. But some pianists—and many tuners and technicians—have spent years of their lives working out how to compress, decompress, shape, iron, tease, prick or flatten the felt covering the wooden hammer so that, once you have got finger, hand and shoulder precisely where you want them, the note emerges precisely as you imagine it. Doctors use the word 'auscultation' to describe the act of listening to the minute internal sounds of the body with a stethoscope. Pianists use the same word.

The man on the BMW auscultated away and then packed up and

went. I hoovered up the discarded hammer felt and tried the piano. Another stomach lurch: it sounded quite different. The tone was softer, rounder, more 'boomy'. It was more even. But it was...different. Just as I was getting used to every little auscultatory idiosyncrasy of my beloved piano, I would have to start all over again.

A week later I was reading Svyatoslav Richter's diaries: 'Nothing is worse for a pianist than to choose the instrument on which he's going to have to perform. You should play on whichever piano happens to be in the hall, as though fate intended it so. Everything then becomes much easier from a psychological point of view.'

I remembered a story BMW Man told me about two internationally famous pianists playing together at a piano festival in London. The technician prepared three pianos. Pianist A rejected the first two as unplayable and went for the third. Ten minutes later Pianist B rejected the second two as beneath his dignity and went for the first.

BMW Man's moral: 'You can't leave pianos in the hands of pianists.'

There are many reasons why I will never be more than an averagely competent pianist, but among them is my memory. Pianists tend to divide into two categories—the sight-readers and the memorizers. Or maybe this is just a classification system I have invented for my own comfort.

I am not even talking here about the ability professional pianists have to memorize entire pieces. My problem is much more basic. Put a completely unknown piece of music in front of me and the chances are I will not make a complete hash of it—I will read it more accurately and/or impressionistically than many pianists who are much better than I am. It is a useful attribute on the rare occasion when, late at night after a few bottles of wine, someone suggests belting out some Jerome Kern. On the other hand, take away the sheet music for a piece on which I have been working for months on end and I'll be helpless. I will not be able to play three bars together.

I have no idea what is going on here. I also play golf to a mediocre standard and know that the game is almost entirely about muscle memory. Success depends on being able endlessly to repeat the same arc, so that the club head never departs from the perfect parabola.

The same—squared or trebled—is true of music. Some combination of psychology, neurology and physiology is, or should be, at work to coax your fingers to 'remember' combinations of notes, phrases, fingerings, dynamics, chords, touch etc. And clearly—with sheet music in front of me—my fingers are not completely amnesiac. They broadly know what to do next, where the next bar but three requires them to be and which upcoming chords have which flats and which naturals in which places. But with me this memory is either rooted very shallowly, or it is rooted in the wrong hemisphere, or nourished by insufficient RNA protein structures or suffering a sluggish interaction of synapses. Take the sheet music away and the neuronal connections fuse.

I have realized for some time that this is a problem not confined to music. I have an appalling memory for films or books, which tend to go in one frontal lobe and out the other. I cannot recite poetry nor remember plots, characters or endings in dramas. It is not, I think, age-related: I had the same problem while trying—not very successfully—to study English literature at university. And in other areas of my life I have a quite good memory for names, events, newspaper cuttings, faces, details.

I also have no problem remembering the pure, unapplied sound and shape of music, in the sense that I must have thousands of pieces I've heard over the years stored in my memory, more or less recallable in full and hummable at will. But I can't translate that kind of memory to the sort that makes the fingers do the right stuff.

I used to wonder why this mattered. I could see that having an entire piece in the mind would certainly help a pianist—if only so that he/she could concentrate on the fingers without constantly shifting the eye from music to keyboard. On the other hand plenty of pianists—Richter amongst them—have managed to play with the sheet music in front of them. In his diaries he writes: 'What's the point of cluttering up your brain when there are far better things to do? It's bad for your health, and it also smacks of vanity…it's easy enough to memorize a Haydn sonata, but I prefer to play twenty while reading the music rather than limiting myself to two performed from memory.'

But then Richter had perfect pitch 'and [he says] could reproduce everything by ear'. I realized I was up against something like musical apraxia when trying to learn a Schumann piano quintet to play with a bunch of out-of-practice friends who meet as much for the chat and the wine as for the music. I began studying this with Michael and continued it with Margie Scott, a pianist friend of the viola player, and—such was my love of the piece—really worked on the first movement. Twenty minutes a day was never going to do it, so I set aside hours at weekends to get to grips with it.

Most of it is medium to difficult—with the exception of the development section which is (for those of us with the wrong kind of brains) difficult to impossible. Schumann takes the same shaped phrase of quavers and for eighty bars or so repeats them time and time again in every imaginable key. No two bars have the same combination of flats, double flats, naturals or sharps. The suggested metronome speed is minim = 108, which means each minim is nearly half a second. There are four quavers to a minim, so if played at the 'proper' speed, you should be rattling through this passage at a speed of, say, seven notes a second. Try it on the table top in front of you. Tap a rough second beat with your foot and—using seven fingers of two hands—try fitting in seven 'notes'. Then imagine the impossibility of reading those—real, constantly changing—notes as you play them. The only possible chance is to have them—all 600-odd quavers—burned into your memory and for your memory to be hot-wired to your fingers.

At the end of about two months of practice I managed to play the passage, more or less note-perfect, at about half the marked speed. Margie had given me Czerny's Velocity Exercises to get more flexibility into my wrists, rightly spotting that my fingers on their own would never be up to the task. But, on the night, the quartet wanted—especially after a bottle or two of Rioja—to play it faster, so I ended up fudging my way through. It was not a disaster, but it was not what Schumann wrote. I put the piece on one side. Two months later, when we met to play again, the development section had gone from the fingers—almost complete amnesia. I'd have to start all over again.

Why bother? Why labour against these insuperable odds to do something that thousands upon thousands of people can do so much better and which I'll never master? Most art involves a process of communication. But, while I enjoy playing the piano *with* other people, I have no great desire to perform *to* anyone else. Even in my most satisfying moments I don't flatter myself that I have any profound insight into the music I'm playing. And yet playing the piano—or trying to play the piano—is now such a part of my life that a day now feels incomplete without my having sat at the keyboard for even two minutes.

The same 'why botherness?' obviously troubled the British psychoanalyst Marion Milner, who in 1957 wrote a famous book, *On Not Being Able to Paint*:

> For years I had had to decide each weekend, should I shut myself away and paint or should I just live? It was perhaps less of a problem for the professional painter who could live in his spare time. For the Sunday-painter it brought the need to balance up the various renunciations and gains. I had so often come away from a morning spent painting with a sense of futility, a sense of how much better it would have been to get on with something practical that really needed doing. And I had often felt, when out painting, both exalted and yet guilty, as if I were evading something that the people round me, all busy with their daily lives, were facing, that their material was real life and mine was dreams.

Her attempt to find an answer led her to a psychoanalytical exploration of her attempts to free herself from the conventional 'rules' of drawing in order to express the bubbling-under unconscious. Had she tried the piano rather than painting she would, I think, rather early on have stubbed her toe on Sir Donald Tovey.

There may well be a psychoanalytical explanation for this wanting to lose oneself in a private realm of musical expression. Neurologists may one day find the answer in combinations of peptides and amino acids; in the metabolic affinities between specific neurons. They may eventually be able to explain why it was that Casals could not begin a day until he had played one of Bach's forty-eight preludes or fugues on the piano. They may also be able to explain to me why my musical memory is so dysfunctional and why my brain is so inadequately wired to my fingers. All this may one day become clear. Until then I shall stumble on, feeling that the act of playing the piano each day does in some way settle the mind and the spirit. Even five minutes in the morning feels as though it has altered the chemistry of the brain in some indefinable way. Something has been nourished. I feel ready—or readier—for the day.

The other day I heard Alfred Brendel play two Mozart concertos in one evening at the age of seventy. I could never hope for a thousandth of his talent, but if I could be confident of having some of his physical and mental agility and energy at the same age then I would have twenty years ahead of me, sitting at my Fazioli. And, surely, in twenty years I could at least master just a few pieces—truly master them—fingerings, pedallings, phrases, tone, touch, the lot? That, at any rate, is the idea that sustains me. And if those pieces included Beethoven Op. 110—from its quiet opening chords to the final notes where (Brendel again) 'the "chains of music itself" are thrown off'—then it would not all have been wasted. □

"A strange and graceful work, of rare imaginative drive and richness of intellectual reference."

—Gopul Balakrishnan, NEW LEFT REVIEW

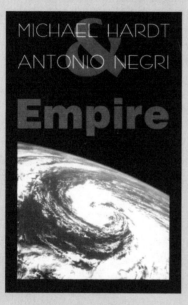

"So what does a disquisition on globalization have to offer scholars in crisis? First, there is *Empire's* broad sweep and range of learning. Spanning nearly 500 pages of densely argued history, philosophy and political theory, it features sections on Imperial Rome, Haitian slave revolts, the American Constitution and the Persian Gulf War, and references to dozens of thinkers like Machiavelli, Spinoza, Hegel, Hobbes, Kant, Marx and Foucault. In short, the book has the formal trappings of a master theory in the old European tradition... [It] brims with confidence in its ideas."

—Emily Eakin, NEW YORK TIMES

"*Empire* is a sweeping history of humanist philosophy, Marxism, and modernism that propels itself to a grand political conclusion."

—Ed Vulliamy, THE OBSERVER

NEW IN PAPERBACK

MICHAEL HARDT
is Associate Professor in the
Literature Program at Duke University.

ANTONIO NEGRI
is an independent researcher and writer and
an inmate at Rebibbia Prison, Rome. He has
been Lecturer in Political Science at the
University of Paris and Professor of Political
Science at the Univerity of Padua.

HARVARD UNIVERSITY PRESS
US: 800 448 2242 • UK: 020 7306 0603 • www.hup.harvard.edu

SONGLINES
David Oates

A challenge: overleaf are extracts from four famous songs by four famous singer-songwriters, each transposed into pictographs by the artist David Oates. The lyricist's name is the last picture in each. What are the lyrics? (Some help towards the solutions is on page 320.)

© DAVID OATES 2001

"What makes such
a book so attractive?

Carson's carefree and marvelously
chaotic tone, his exquisite use of language,
and his delight in reminding jaded readers
of the rich and various ways in which
our world can be imagined."
—Alberto Manguel

SHAMROCK TEA
CIARAN CARSON

Hardback • 308 pages • 1–86207–398–8 • $19.95
www.granta.com/tea

WHITE LIES
Amit Chaudhuri

JOHN VINK/MAGNUM

He rang the doorbell once, and waited for the door to open. It was an ornate door, with a rather heavy, ornamental padlock. When the old, smiling maidservant opened it, there was a narrow corridor behind her which revealed a large hall and further rooms inside, like shadows contained in a prism.

It was a particularly beautiful flat. He sat on the sofa, as the maidservant went inside and said, 'Memsaab, guruji aaye hai.' He glanced at the Arabian Sea and the Marine Drive outside; and then looked at the brass figure of Saraswati, from whose veena all music is said to emanate, on one end of a shelf. When ten minutes had passed, he briefly consulted his watch, its hands stuck stubbornly to their places, and then desultorily opened a copy of *Stardust*. Now and again, he hummed the tune of a devotional.

After another five minutes, a lady emerged, her hair not yet quite dry. 'Sorry, masterji,' she said, but, glancing quickly over her shoulder, was clearly more concerned about the 'fall' of her sari.

The 'guruji' shifted uncomfortably. Although he was, indeed, her guru (and without the guru, as the saying goes, there is no knowledge), he had also the mildly discomfited air of a schoolboy in her presence and in this flat: this had to do not only with the fact that she was older, but with the power people like her exercised over people like him.

'That's all right, behanji,' he said; from the first day, she had been his 'respected sister'. 'We'll have less time for the lesson today, that's all,' he said, chuckling, but also asserting himself subtly. Then, to placate her, he said quickly, 'Maybe I arrived a little early.'

This morning was quiet, except for the activity in the kitchen that indicated that the essentials were being attended to. In the bedroom, next to the huge double bed, the harmonium had already been placed on the carpet by the bearer, John. The air inside had that early morning coolness where an air conditioner has not long ago been switched off.

'A glass of thhanda paani,' he said after sitting down.

This request materialized a couple of minutes later, the glass of cold water held aloft on a plate by John, while Mrs Chatterjee turned the pages of her songbook unhurriedly, glancing at bhajan after bhajan written in her own handwriting. They were too high up—on the fourteenth floor—to hear the car horns or any of the other sounds below clearly; the sea was visible from the windows, but too distant to be audible. Sometimes her husband, Mr Chatterjee, would be present—and he'd shake his head from time to time, while sitting on the bed, listening to the guru and his wife going over a particular phrase, or a line. Sometimes he was content doing this even while taking off his tie and waiting for tea, his office-creased jacket recently discarded on the bed, beside him.

Indeed, he had married her twenty-two years ago for this very reason; that he might hear her sing continually. Not everyone might agree about the enormity of her talent; but something had touched him that day when he'd met her in the afternoon in his still-to-be in-laws' place in one of the more distant reaches of a small town, and heard her sing, not the usual Tagore song, but a Hindi devotional by Meerabai. He was the 'catch', then—a medium-sized fish that had the potential to be a big one.

Fifteen years they'd lived together in Bombay now, and for ten years in this flat that gave the illusion from certain angles that sea approached very near it. And for fifteen years, almost, he had wanted his wife's voice to be heard more widely than it was—what he thought of as 'widely' was a hazy audience comprising mainly colleagues from his company, and from the many other companies he had to infrequently, but repeatedly, come into contact with—though it wasn't as if he'd mind terribly if the audience extended beyond this group of semi-familiar faces into the unclear territory of human beings outside.

She had a weak voice, admittedly. It managed one and a half octaves with some difficulty; it was more at ease in the lower register, but quavered when it reached the upper sa and re, something the guru had grown used to. When she sang 'Meera ke prabhu' now, towards the end of the song, there was, again, that quaver. It was something she met reasonably bravely, head on, or ignored altogether, as did the guru. Neither could continue their respective pursuits, she, of being a singer, he, of being her teacher, if they took the quaver and its signal too seriously; they knew that one or two of these limitations were irremediable, but without much significance in relation to the other dimensions of their partnership.

'How was that?' she asked after she'd finished. She needed to know, in a perfunctory but genuine way, his opinion.

'It was all right today,' he said. He was never quite ingratiating in his response, but never harshly critical either. They had reached a silent mandate that this was how it should be. He went over a phrase as the servant brought in a tray with teacups, and a small plate of biscuits.

It was always a pleasure to hear him, even when he was humming, as he was now. And he was always humming. There was no denying his gift; but he probably still didn't quite know what to do with it. He was almost careless with it. He sipped the tea slowly, and carefully selected a biscuit. Sometimes they might give him a gulab jamun, towards which he'd show no lack of intent and no hesitation, or a jalebi.

He was certainly not the first teacher she'd had. He was the latest in a line that went back these fifteen years; he'd arrived to take his place at the head of the line, and to succeed his predecessors, roughly sixteen or seventeen months ago. She had interviewed him, of course, or conducted a little audition in the sitting room, during which she'd asked him, respectfully, to 'sing something'. He had descended on the carpet self-consciously, between the glass table and the sofas, and enchanted her, humbly but melodiously, with a bhajan she couldn't remember having heard before. She shook her head slowly from side to side to denote her acknowledgement of his prowess, and his ability to touch her, and because she hadn't heard anyone sing quite so well in a long time; and yet it *was* an interview, at the end of which there was a silence; and then she said: 'Wah! Very good!'

At first, she'd called him 'Masterji' (which she still did at times), as she had all her former teachers. There was no formal, ceremonial seal on the relationship, as there is between guru and shishya; he was there to do his job, to be a teacher, and she to learn. Nevertheless, the relationship had its own definition. They'd grown dependant on each other; he, for the modicum of respect he received here (fit enough for a guru, even though he might be a mere purveyor of knowledge rather than a repository of it), and the by-no-means negligible amount he got paid; there were also the little ways in which Mr Chatterjee helped him out, with his official contacts. As for Mrs Chatterjee, she liked the tunes he set the bhajans to, and could also recognize the presence of accomplishment; and she was too tired to look for another teacher. She used to change teachers every three or four years, when they began to dominate her too much; or when they became irregular. But he was much younger than her, and she'd grown fond of him— he was very mild and had none of the offensive manners that gurus sometimes have; she'd come to call him 'Masterji' less and less, and addressed him, increasingly, as 'Mohanji' or 'Mohan bhai'.

Mr Chatterjee came home at a quarter to seven, and called out to his wife, 'Ruma!'

Later, they had tea together in the balcony, facing Marine Drive, and watching the sun set at seven-thirty, because it was late summer. Everywhere, the glow of electricity became more apparent as the swathe of pink light permeating the clouds above the sea slowly disappeared; now darkness, and with it a different, artificial, nocturnal light, was coming to this part of Bombay.

'Sometimes I feel we have so much, Ruma,' Mr Chatterjee sighed.

She didn't know what he meant; she didn't even know if it was a complaint or an uncharacteristic confession of gratitude. Of course it wasn't true; that was obvious—they didn't have children. Towards the beginning, they'd tried out various kinds of treatment; and then they'd given up trying without entirely giving up hope. Now, as you slowly cease to miss a person who's no longer present, they no longer missed the child they didn't have. They gave themselves to their lives together.

'We should go to the party by nine at least,' he said. In spite of the tone of alacrity he used with his wife, the idea of having to go to a party exhausted him tonight. To change the subject, and also to allow the communion they'd had with the evening to survive a little, he asked: 'What did he teach you today? A new bhajan?'

Today was Thursday, the day the 'he' in the enquiry came to the house. She thought briefly, half her mind already busying itself with the social activity ahead, with the new sari to be worn, and said:

'No, the one he gave me last week. It still needs polishing. The one about the Rana—"My Ranaji, I will sing the praises of Govind." It's a beautiful tune.'

'Well, you must sing it for me,' he said, sighing as he got up from the sofa, resigned to the evening ahead. She looked at his back with a sort of indulgence.

The song, which she'd once sung to a different tune, and which she'd been practising assiduously for the last ten days or so, was about how Meera had given herself from childhood to her one lord, the Lord Krishna, and couldn't bring herself to live with her husband, the Rana, the king. The Rana, said the song, sent her a cup of poison, which became nectar when she touched it to her lips; if the Rana was angry, she sang, she could flee his province, but where would she go if her lord turned against her? Mrs Chatterjee rather liked the song; in her mind, of course, there was no confusion about who her Rana and who her lord was. Krishna's flute was second fiddle for her, although it, too, had its allure. But its place in her life was secondary, if constant.

In another age, Mr Chatterjee, with his professional abilities and head for figures and statutes, his commitment to see a project through, might have been a munshi in a court, or an adviser to a small feudal aristocracy. Now, it was he who, in a sense, ruled; he ran a company; he was the patron as far as people like Mohanji were concerned. It didn't matter that, when he sang before him, Mr Chatterjee didn't understand the talas, that he simply smiled quizzically and shook his head from side to side in hesitant appreciation. That hesitant appreciation, to Mohanji, meant much.

Coming back home from a party, Mrs Chatterjee would be so tired that sometimes she fell asleep with make-up still on her face. At such times, she almost felt glad she didn't have children, because she'd have lacked the energy to look in on them. All the same, she couldn't sleep for very long, and was awake, although she looked as if she needed more rest, when the cleaner came in for the keys to wash their two cars. She stood near the balcony with a teacup in her hand, as the day began, not really seeing the sea, its water resplendent with sunlight. Then, she might remember the guru was to come that day, and begin to think of the last song she'd learned from him.

On these days, she'd sometimes be a bit listless during the lesson, and the guru would say, 'Behanji, you seem a bit tired today.'

'It's this life, Mohanji,' she'd say, preoccupied, but not entirely truthful in the impression she sought to give of being someone who was passively borne by it. 'Sometimes it moves too quickly.' And she'd recall the exchanges of the previous night, now gradually growing indistinguishable from each other. Mohanji would regard her with incomprehension and indulgence; he was used to these bursts of anxiety and lassitude; the way an evening of lights, drinks, and strangers, when she was transformed into something more than herself, should change back into this sluggish morning, when she was unreceptive to the lesson and to him.

In this building itself, there were other amateur singers. On the seventh floor, Mrs Prem Raheja sang devotionals. Her husband was a dealer in diamonds, and occasionally flew to Brussels. For her, singing was less an aesthetic pastime (as it was for Mrs Chatterjee) than a religious one; she was devoutly religious. Then there was Neha Kapur on the eleventh floor, who liked to sing ghazals. No one really knew what her husband did; some said he was in 'import–export'. These people were really traders made good, many times richer, in reality, than Mr Chatterjee, though they lacked his power and influence, and inhabited a somewhat different world from his.

The guru had increased his clientele, if his students could be described by that word, in visiting this building and this area. Mrs Raheja was now one among his students, as was Mrs Kapur; and there were others in the neighbouring buildings. When he came to this area, he usually visited two or three flats in a day. The 'students' were mainly well-to-do or even rich housewives, with varying degrees of talent and needs for assurance, their lives made up of various kinds of spiritual and material requirements. What spiritual want he met was not clear, though it was certain he met some need; and his own life had become more and more dependent, materially, on fulfilling it.

Mohanji's life was a round of middle-aged women, mainly in Colaba and Cuffe Parade, and a few in Malabar Hill; in his way, he was proud of them, and thought of them as Mr So-and-So's wife, or, where the surname denoted a business family, Mrs So-and-So. He moved about between Cuffe Parade and Malabar Hill and the areas in between using buses and taxis, glimpsing, from outside and within, the tall buildings, in which he ascended in lifts to arrive at his appointed tuition. This was a daily itinerary, before this part of the city disappeared, too temporarily for it to be disturbing to him, when he took the fast train to Dadar at night.

Mr Chatterjee's company (although he didn't own the company, it was known among his friends as 'Amiya's company' and among others as 'Mr Chatterjee's company') manufactured, besides other things, detergent, which was its most successful product; and, since the company had substantial foreign shareholdings—the word 'multinational', like a term describing some odd but coveted hybrid, was being heard more and more these days—he, with his wife, made occasional trips to Europe (he to study the way detergent was marketed there), every one and a half to two years.

Returning, the vistas and weather of London and Zurich would stay with them for about a week as they resumed their life in Bombay. They'd distribute the gifts they'd brought between friends and business associates; deodorants, eau de toilette, ties; for Mohanji, a cake of perfumed soap, polished like an egg, serrated like a shell. He, in his gentle, qualified way, would pretend to be more grateful than he was, but nevertheless wonder at this object that had travelled such a huge distance.

There were so many projects inside Mr Chatterjee's head; he had only a year to bring them to fruition. Yet, though he was to retire, he was inwardly confident he'd get an extension.

In other ways, he felt that he was entering the twilight of his life in the company; though there was nothing more substantial than an intuition to suggest this. He suppressed this feeling before it could become a concrete thought. Among the more minor and personal, but persistent and cherished, projects he had in mind was to present his wife, Ruma, before an audience of friends and peers, with the repertoire of new songs she'd learned from the guru. With this in mind, he'd ask her sometimes, with a degree of impatience: 'Isn't he teaching you anything new? I've been hearing the same two songs for the last three weeks!' This might be said in the midst of talking about three or four other things, after he'd returned, yet again, late from the office.

He asked the teacher the same question in the course of the week, when he happened to come back earlier than usual, and find the lesson midway, in progress. He'd had a distracting day at the office; and he was about to go out again. He said, looming in his navy-blue suit over the teacher sitting on the carpet with the harmonium before him:

'Do give her another one, guruji! I've been hearing the same one—the one about "Giridhar Gopal"—for about two weeks now.' He called him 'guruji' at times, not as a student or acolyte might, but to indicate a qualified respect for a walk of life he didn't quite understand. He used the term as one might use a foreign word that one was slightly uncomfortable with, but which one took recourse to increasingly and inadvertently.

The guru looked a little bemused, and embarrassed on Mr Chatterjee's behalf. He picked up a printed songbook.

'I did give behanji a new bhajan, Chatterjee saab,' he said, weakly, but not without some humour and his characteristic courtesy. 'Maybe you haven't heard it. It's a lovely tune,' he said, with a kind of innocent and immodest delight in his own composing abilities.

'Really?' said Mr Chatterjee, lowering himself upon the edge of the bed and apparently forgetting the appointment he had to keep. 'Do sing it for me, guruji.' He could spare five minutes. 'Your behanji doesn't tell me anything!'

The guru began to sing almost immediately, first clearing his throat with excessive violence; then an unexpectedly melodious voice issued from him; he looked up, smiling, twice at Mr Chatterjee while singing.

'Wah!' said Mr Chatterjee with unusual candour after the guru finished, the song fading in less than three minutes. He turned to his wife and asked, 'Have you picked it up?' She waved him away with an admonitory gesture of the hand. 'See? She doesn't listen to anything I say.' The guru was greatly amused at this untruth. On his way out, he looked into the room and said, 'It's a particularly lovely bhajan.'

The guru smiled, almost as if he were a child who'd entered forbidden territory; as if, through the bhajan, he'd entered a space, and a mind, generally reserved for official appointments and more weighty transactions than these; how else could he obtrude upon such a space?

Two months later, they had a party in the flat; it came in the wake, ostensibly, of a new diversification for the company, but it had, actually, little to do with that. There were parties every two weeks, sometimes for no good reason, except to satisfy the addiction to the same set of faces; though these events were justified as being necessary for off-duty chatter among colleagues and associates, and, more importantly, because there was a persuasive myth that it was an extension of business activity. Usually, however, the party turned out to be none of these, but an occasion for bad jokes, bickering, and mild drunkenness and indigestion.

This party was a little different, though; Mrs Chatterjee was to sing tonight. Of course, she could be found standing by the door, a small smile on her face, responding to the exclamations of 'Ruma!' and 'Mrs Chatterjee!' and 'Where's Amiya?' as guests walked in with little nods and smiles, half her mind on the kitchen. They didn't know yet that she was to be a prima donna that evening; going in, however, they noticed a harmonium and tables kept on one of the carpets, and continued to circulate loudly among themselves, exploding noisily at moments of hilarity.

No one was surprised, or took more than a cursory note of the instruments; 'musical evenings' were less and less uncommon these days, and were seen to be a pleasant diversion or a necessary hazard in polite society. Meanwhile, people cupped potato wafers and peanuts like small change in their hands; and a platter of shami kababs passed from person to person. The guru had come earlier, and was sitting with members of his family—his wife, his mother, his cousin, a shy and thin man who'd play the tabla today, and his son—cloistered in the air-conditioned guest room, semi-oblivious of the noise outside; they were having their own party, chattering in their own language, holding glasses of Limca or Fanta in their hands, unmindful of the party outside.

Mrs Chatterjee had hardly time to think now of the songs she'd rehearsed; she went frequently to the kitchen, her face pale, to see how the pulao was coming along, and to leave a regulatory word or two with the servants, whom she could never trust entirely. As she checked to see if the right cutlery was out, and the correct arrangement of crockery, a ghost of a tune hovered in the back of her head. She wasn't really missed; one was missed at other people's parties, but not at one's own; one was not so much the centre of attention at one's own as a behind-the-scenes worker. Other people became centres of attention, like the advertising man, Baig, who was holding forth now about the travails of advertising in a 'third world country'. Yet, forty-five minutes later, leaving the kitchen on autopilot, she had to suffer herself to be, briefly, the cynosure of all eyes.

The cook measured out the koftas, while, in the hall, Mrs Chatterjee lowered herself awkwardly on the carpet, the guru sitting down not far away from her, unobtrusively, before the harmonium. He looked small and intent next to her, in his white kurta and pyjamas, part accompanist and part—what? At first, it wasn't the guests who listened to them, but they who listened, almost attentively, to the sound the guests made, until whispers travelled from one part of the room to another, the hubbub subsided, and the notes of the harmonium became, for the first time, audible. Mohanji could hear the murmurs, in English, of senior executives who worked in twenty-storey buildings nearby, and knew more about takeovers than music; it must be a puzzling, but oddly thrilling, experience to sing for them. It was odd, too, to sit next to Mrs Chatterjee, not as if he were her guru (which he wasn't, not even in name), waiting for her to begin, indispensable but unnoticed. The guests were looking at her.

She began tentatively; she couldn't quite get hold of the first song, but no one noticed. Certainly, Mr Chatterjee looked relaxed and contented. The only doubt was on Mrs Chatterjee's own face; the second one, however, went off better than the first. 'You're a lucky guy,' said Motwane, a director in a pharmaceuticals company, prodding Mr Chatterjee in the shoulder from behind. 'I didn't know she had so many talents.' Mr Chatterjee smiled, and waved at another friend across the room. Now, in the third song, her voice faltered in the upper register, but no one seemed to hear it, or, if they did, to be disturbed. Once her performance was over, the shami kababs were circulated again; a faint taste of 'culture' in their mouths, people went to the bar to replenish their glasses.

That night, as they were getting into bed, Mr Chatterjee said, 'That went quite well.' It wasn't clear to what he was referring at first, but it was likely he meant the party itself. Mrs Chatterjee was removing her earrings. 'And the songs?' she asked pointedly, making it sound like a challenge, but only half serious.

'Those were nice,' he said. To her surprise, he began to hum a tune himself, not very melodiously—she couldn't tell if it was one of the songs she'd sung earlier—something he did rarely before others, although she'd heard him singing in the bathroom, his voice coming from behind the shower. He seemed unaware that anyone else was listening. Seeing him happy in this way—it couldn't be anything else— she felt sorry for him, and smiled inwardly, because no one, as he was so successful, ever felt sorry for him, or thought of his happiness.

'We must have one of these "musical evenings" again,' he said simply, following an unfinished train of thought, as if he were a child who spoke impulsively, trusting to intuition. Yet, if he were a child, he was one that had the power to move destinies. Not in a godlike way perhaps, but in the short term, materially. But she loved his childlike side, its wild plans, although it tired her at times. She said nothing.

In his childlike way, he could be quite hard. Not with her; but no investment justified itself to him except through its returns. That was because he couldn't run a company on charity or emotions; or his own head would roll. Nor did he believe that the country could be run on charity or emotion.

She, in the long hours that he was away, leaned more and more on the guru. It wasn't that she felt lonely; but no one leading her kind of life in that flat, her husband in the office, could help but feel, from time to time, alone. The best she could think of someone like the guru, given his background, was as a kind of younger brother, 'kind of' being the operative words—not as a friend; certainly not as the guru he was supposed to be. There was one guru in her life, and that was her husband. But she needed Mohanji. She might spend a morning shopping at Sahakari Bhandar, but needed also to learn new songs. And yet her mind was focused on a hundred other things as well. When her focus returned to her singing, it was sometimes calming, and sometimes not.

One day she said to him, mournfully: 'I wish I could sing like you, Mohanji. There are too many parties these days. I can't practise properly.'

Mohanji was always surprised by the desires that the rich had, a desire for what couldn't be theirs. It also amused him, partly, that it wasn't enough for Mrs Chatterjee that she, in one sense, possessed him; she must possess his gift as well. Perhaps in another life, he thought, not in this one. The guru was a believer in karma phal, that what you did in one life determined who and where you were in the next; he was convinced, for instance, that his gift, whatever he might have done to perfect it in this life, had been given to him because of some sadhana, some process of faith and perseverance, he had performed in an earlier one. Of course, there were advantages to the position he was in now; in another time, he'd have had to submit to the whims of a raja, with the not inconsiderable compensation that the raja loved music. That empathy for music was still not good enough, though, to make you forget the frustrations of living under a tyrant. Now, in this age, all he had to do was attend to the humours of executives and businessmen and their wives who thought they had a taste, a passing curiosity, for music; it was relatively painless.

'Why do you say such things, behanji,' he said, unruffled. He scratched the back of his hand moodily. 'There's been a lot of improvement.' His eyes lit up slightly. 'All those bada sahibs and their wives came up and congratulated you the other day after you sang, didn't they, behanji,' he said, recalling the scene, 'saying, "Bahut acche, Rumaji," and "Very nice".' He shook his head. 'If you'd come to me ten years ago, I could have...' He sometimes said this with a genuine inkling of accomplishment at what he might have achieved.

'They may be bada sahibs,' said Mrs Chatterjee, vaguely dissatisfied that this appellation should be given to someone else's

husband. 'But Mr Chatterjee is a bigger bada sahib than all of them.'
The guru did not dispute this.

'Bilkul!' he said. 'Even to look at he is so different.' He said this
because he meant it; Mr Chatterjee, for him, had some of the
dimensions of greatness, without necessarily possessing any of its
qualities. There were so many facets to his existence; so little,
relatively, one could know about him.

But the guru wasn't always well. A mysterious stomach ulcer—it
was an undiagnosed ailment, but he preferred to call it an
'ulcer'—troubled him. It could remain inactive for days, and then
come back in a sharp spasm that would leave him listless for two
days. To this end, he'd gone with his mother and wife to a famous
religious guru, called, simply, Baba, and sat among a crowd of people
to receive his benediction. When his turn came, he was only asked
to touch the Baba's feet, and, as he did so, the Baba whispered a few
words into his ear, words that he didn't understand. But, after this,
Mohanji felt better, and the pain, though he hadn't expected it would,
seemed to go away.

When his 'behanji' heard about this one day, she was properly
contemptuous. 'I don't believe in baba-vaaba,' she said. The guru
smiled, and looked uncomfortable and guilty; not because he'd been
caught doing something silly, but because Mrs Chatterjee could be
so naively sacrilegious. It was as if she didn't feel the need to believe
in anything, and affluent though she might be, the guru was not
certain of the wisdom of this. 'If you have a problem, it should be
looked at by a real doctor,' she went on. The guru nodded
mournfully, seeing no reason to argue.

Of course, the problem was partly Mohanji's own fault. As he
went from flat to flat, he was frequently served 'snacks' during the
lesson, the junk food that people stored in their homes and dispensed
with on such occasions. Sometimes the food could be quite heavy.
Mohanji could never resist these, eating them while thinking,
abstractedly, of some worry that beset him at home. This irregular
consumption would leave him occasionally dyspeptic.

He suffered from tension as well, a tension from constantly
having to lie to the ladies he taught—white lies, flattery—and from

his not having a choice in the matter. He had raised his fee recently, of course; he now charged a hundred rupees for lessons all around, pleading that a lot of the money went towards the taxi fare. In this matter, his 'students' found him quietly inflexible. 'I can't teach for less,' he said simply. And because he was such an expert singer, his 'students' couldn't refuse him, although a hundred rupees a 'sitting' was a lot for a guru; making him one of the highest-paid teachers doing the rounds. But they'd begun to wonder, now and again, what they were getting out of it themselves, and why their singing hadn't improved noticeably, or why they—housewives—couldn't also become singers with something of a reputation: it would be a bonus in the variegated mosaic of their lives.

'But you must practise,' he'd say; and when a particular murki or embellishment wouldn't come to them, he'd perform a palta or a vocal exercise, saying, 'Practise this: it's for that particular murki,' as if he were a mountebank distributing charms or amulets for certain ailments.

M r Chatterjee's office had a huge rosewood table; now, on the third anniversary of his being made Chief Executive of this company, a basket of roses arrived; after a couple of files were cleared away, it was placed on a table before him, and a photograph taken by a professional photographer arranged by Patwardhan, the Personnel Manager. 'OK, that's enough; back to work,' he said brusquely, after the camera's shutter had clicked a few times. Once the photograph was developed and laminated, its black and white colours emphasized, rather than diminished, the roses.

The guru loved this photograph. 'Chatterjee saheb looks wonderful in it—just as he should,' he said, admiring it. 'He must have a wonderful office.' He ruminated for a little while, and said, 'Brite detergent—he owns it, doesn't he, behanji?' 'He doesn't own it,' said Mrs Chatterjee, tolerant but short. 'He runs it.' The guru nodded, not entirely convinced of the distinction.

He continued to give her new songs, by the blind poet Surdas, and by Meera, who would accept no other Lord but Krishna. During these lessons, he came to know, between songs, in snatches of conversation, that Mr Chatterjee had got his two-year extension at

the helm of the company. He took this news home with him, and
related it proudly to his wife.

Two days later, he brought a box of ladoos with him. 'These
aren't from a shop—' he pointed out importunately. 'My wife made
them!'

Mrs Chatterjee looked at them as if they'd fallen from outer
space. There they sat, eight orbs inside a box, the wife's handiwork.

'Is there a festival?' asked Mrs Chatterjee. In the background,
John, the old servant, dusted, as he did at this time of the day, the
curios in the drawing room.

'No, no,' said the guru, smiling at her naivety and shaking his
head. 'She made them for you—just eat them and see.'

She wasn't sure if she wanted to touch them; they looked
quite rich.

'I'll have one in the evening,' she consoled him. 'When Chatterjee
saheb comes. He'll like them with his tea.'

But, in the evening, Mr Chatterjee demurred.

'This'll give me indigestion,' he said; but he was distracted as
well. No sooner had he been given his extension than a bickering
had started among a section of the directors about it; not in his
presence, of course, but he was aware of it. At such times, he couldn't
quite focus on his wife's music lessons, or on the guru; the guru was
like a figure who'd just obtruded upon Mr Chatterjee's line of vision,
but whom he just missed seeing. 'You know sweets like these don't
agree with me.' The sweets were an irrelevance; if the two directors—
one of whom, indeed, he'd appointed himself—succeeded in fanning
a trivial resentment, it would be a nuisance, his position might even
be in slight danger; he must be clear about that. You worked hard,
with care and foresight, but a little lack of foresight—which was what
appointing Sengupta to the board had turned out to be—could go
against you. Sometimes, he knew from experience and from
observing others, what you did to cement your position was precisely
what led to undoing it.

Mrs Chatterjee felt a twinge of pity for Mohanji. As if in
recompense, she ate half a ladoo herself. Then, unable to have any
more, she asked John to distribute them among the cook, the
maidservant, and himself. 'They're very good,' she told them. She

could see her husband was preoccupied, and whispered her instructions.

Sensing a tension for the next couple of weeks, which was unexpected since it came at the time of the extension being granted, a time, surely, for personal celebration, she herself grew unmindful, and withdrew into conversations with a couple of friends she felt she could trust. Once or twice, the guru asked her, full of enthusiasm, what she'd thought of the ladoos, but never got a proper answer. 'Oh, those were nice,' she said absently, leaving him hungry for praise. A slight doubt had been cast upon the extension, although it was trivial and this was most probably an ephemeral crisis; still, she felt a little cheated that it should happen now. It also made her occasionally maudlin with the guru, less interested in the lesson than in putting unanswerable questions to him.

'Mohan bhai, what's the good of my singing and doing all this hard work? Who will listen?'

How quickly their moods change, he thought. There you are, he thought, with your ready-made audience of colleagues and colleagues' wives; what more do you want? The questions she'd asked chafed him, but he skirted round them, like a person avoiding something unpleasant in his path. One day, however, he was feeling quite tired (because of a bad night he'd had) and lacked his usual patience; he said: 'One mustn't try to be what one can't, behanji. You have everything. You should be happy you can sing a little, and keep your husband and your friends happy. You can't be a professional singer, behanji, and you shouldn't try to be one.'

Mrs Chatterjee was silenced briefly by his audacity, and wondered what had made him say it. For the first time in days, she saw him through the haze of her personal anxieties; for a few moments she said nothing. Then she said: 'Perhaps you're right.' Her eyes, though, had tears in them.

When Mr Chatterjee heard of this exchange, however, he was very angry. In spite of all they had, he'd never felt he'd given his wife enough. And because she sang, and sometimes sang before him, it was as if she gave him back something extra in their life together, and always had. It wasn't as if she had the presence or the personality

or the charm that some of the wives in her position had; it wasn't
as if she were an asset to the society they moved about in. Her singing
was her weakness, and it was that weakness that made him love her
more than he otherwise would have.

'How dare he say such a thing?' he said, genuinely outraged.
He was angry enough to forget, temporarily, the little factions that
had come into being in the company. 'I will speak to him. As if he
can get away just like that, disclaiming all responsibility.' Without
really meaning it, he added, 'You can always get another teacher,
you know.'

Two days later, he delayed setting out for his office, and
deliberately waited for the guru to arrive. Barely had the music lesson
begun, and the recognizable sounds of voice and harmonium emerged
from the room, than he looked in, fully suited, and ready to go. The
guru, seeing him, this vision of executive energy, bowed his head
quickly in mid-song, privileged that the Managing Director should
have stopped to listen to him for a few moments. Mr Chatterjee was
impatient today, and wasn't taking in the Surdas bhajan; he had a
meeting with the Board.

'Ji saab,' said the guru, stopping.

'Guruji,' said Mr Chatterjee, 'please don't say things that will
upset my wife. That is not your job. You are here to give her songs
and improve her singing. If you can't do that properly...'

'What did I say, Chatterjee saab?' asked the guru, interrupting
him, and noticeably concerned. 'Saab, she has ten new songs now...'

'Don't evade the issue,' snapped Mr Chatterjee. 'You told her,
didn't you, that she could never be a real singer. What is your
responsibility, then? Do you take a hundred rupees a turn just to sit
here and listen to her?'

The guru's hands had grown clammy. 'I won't listen to such
nonsense again,' said Mr Chatterjee, shutting the door behind him.
'Please switch off the air conditioner, behanji,' the guru said after Mr
Chatterjee had gone. 'I'm feeling cold.'

It wasn't as if the guru began to dislike Mr Chatterjee after this.
He took his words, in part, as a childish outburst, and they couldn't
quite hurt him. One thing he understood anew was how little Mr

Chatterjee knew about music, about the kind of ardour and talent it required. But why should he? Mr Chatterjee's lack of knowledge of music seemed apposite to his position. If he'd been a musician, he wouldn't be Mr Chatterjee.

The guru knew that if he wasn't careful, the Chatterjees might discard him; Mrs Chatterjee might find herself someone else. He'd also begun to feel a little sorry for her, because of what he'd said; he could have replied, perhaps, that, given the right training from early childhood, she might have been a better-known singer, or, if she'd been in the right place at the right time, she might have become one; there had been no need to quite expose her like that.

For the following two days, Mrs Chatterjee, going around in her chauffeur-driven car from the club to the shops in the mornings, couldn't bring herself to hum or sing even once; the driver noted her silence. She'd suddenly realized that her need to sing had been a minor delusion, that both she and her husband and the world could get by without it—she hadn't been honest with herself; and no one had been honest with her. She remained polite with the guru when he came—they'd started to watch each other warily now, in secret—but went through the new bhajans with him without any real involvement, glancing again and again at her watch until the hour was up. Then, after a few more days, she realized she was taking herself too seriously, the force of the guru's words diminished, and she began to, once more, look forward to the lesson.

In the meanwhile, Mr Chatterjee had dealt with the problem at his end, after making, first of all, several late-night telephone calls to some of the foreign shareholders and directors. He had to shout to make himself heard, sometimes keeping his wife from sleep. 'Are you sure, Humphrey?' he asked, putting the onus of responsibility on the Englishman. And, then, 'Yes, I can see there's no other way...'

Two days later, he met Sengupta, the man he'd employed four years ago, and appointed to the Board last year, face to face across the large rosewood table. 'R. C.,' he said, referring to him by his initials (he himself was 'A. K.'—Amiya Kumar—to his colleagues) 'you know why we're here. If there was any dissatisfaction or disagreement, we could have thrashed it out between ourselves. But that was not to be.' As if digressing philosophically, he observed, 'Brite has had a grand history, it has a present, and a future. No person is more important than that future.' Interrupting himself, he sighed. 'Anyway, I've spoken to Dick and Humphrey, and they agree that even the project that was your undertaking is going to fold up. It shows no signs of promise. It was a mistake.'

Sengupta had said nothing so far, not because he felt he was in the wrong, but because he thought his position, because of what he'd done and the way he'd done it, was a weak one; changes were necessary, but he could see now that he should have gone about looking for them in a more knowing way.

'One thing I want to say before I resign, A. K.,' interjected Sengupta, looking at the bright space outside the large glass windows, 'is that I've had a wonderful few years at Brite, and I regret it couldn't be for longer. However, I don't always agree with the company's style of functioning—it's not democratic.'

'Companies aren't democracies, R. C.,' said Mr Chatterjee, with the exaggerated patience of a man who was getting his way. 'You weren't elected to the Board, I appointed you to it. The election was a formality. Anyway, if you wanted to effect some changes, you should have waited a couple of years. You were certainly in the running.'

Sengupta shook his head and smiled. 'I don't know about that. Some of us make it, some of us don't—it's both a bit of luck and a bit of merit, and a bit of something else.' He looked at his hands. 'I know my opportunity won't come again; that's all right. But— another thing—I don't think our personal world should encroach upon our business world, should it? I'm a great admirer of Ruma, a simple soul, a very pure person, but do you think that those costly parties with all that music and singing are necessary?'

'Social gatherings and parties have always been part of company policy; they raise its profile and perform all kinds of functions, you know that. The music came at no extra cost,' Mr Chatterjee observed firmly.

R. C. Sengupta waved a hand. 'You're right, you're right, of course! But the teacher, excellent singer, what's his name, I heard you were going to sponsor some show or performance to showcase him.

Of course, I don't know if what I've heard...'

Mr Chatterjee bristled. 'Who told you that? That's absolute rubbish. He teaches my wife—I think it's unfair to draw either of them into this.' He paused and reflected. 'An idea may have been floated at one time, as such things are, but it was revoked.' He straightened some papers on the table. 'I personally thought it was a good idea. More and more companies are doing it, you know. Music is a great but neglected thing, a great part of our tradition. We should extend patronage where it's due. It can do Brite no harm.' He looked at his watch. 'We're late for lunch,' he said.

The guru collapsed on the street, not far from his house, one afternoon, when he was on his way home. One moment he was squinting at the sun, and trying to avoid someone's shoulder brushing past him, and the next moment, almost inadvertently, without quite realizing it, he'd crumpled—bent and fallen over. A few passers-by and loiterers ran towards him; he was familiar to them as the one who taught music, and from the window of whose ground-floor chawl they could sometimes hear singing. He wasn't unconscious, but had had a temporary blackout; he kept saying, 'Theek hai bhai, koi baat nahi, it's all right, it's fine,' as they helped him up, and one of the people, a sixteen-year-old boy who knew the way to his home, insisted on accompanying him, holding him by the arm during the slow progress homeward.

'Dadiji,' said the boy to Mohanji's mother, who'd been unprepared for what greeted her, 'Panditji fell down. He should rest for a while.' He sounded conciliatory, as if he didn't want to alarm her.

'Haan, haan, rest; I've been telling him to rest,' said the mother, as Mohanji, saying, 'Theek hai, beta,' to his companion, lay down on the divan and put one arm across his eyes.

His wife was not at home, nor were his two children; they'd gone to visit his wife's father in another part of the city. This chawl was where he'd grown up, and where he'd also got married. His father, who was a teacher and singer himself (he'd died eleven years ago) had moved here thirty years ago, and they'd had no intention, or opportunity, of moving out since. Gradually the house had come to be known in the chawl as 'Panditji's house'. It was here, when he was nine or ten years old, that his father had taught him kheyal and tappa and other forms of classical music.

'Mohanji,' said Mrs Chatterjee, 'what happened to you?' It wasn't as if she'd been worried; it was just that she abhorred practising alone—she preferred him there when she sang.

'I don't know what happened, behanji,' said the guru with a look of ingenuous puzzlement. 'I fell ill.'

'I heard,' said Mrs Chatterjee, nodding slightly. 'Mrs Raheja told me...she told me you fell down.'

The guru looked discomfited, as if he'd been caught doing something inappropriate. At the same time, he looked somewhat triumphant.

'It might be low blood pressure.'

She took him to her doctor—Dr Dastur, a middle-aged physician. He saw his patients in a room on the second storey of a building in Marine Lines. Mrs Chatterjee sat with Mohanji in a waiting room with three other patients, waiting to be called in. Half an hour later, when they went inside, Dr Dastur greeted her with:

'Arrey, Mrs Chatterjee, how are you? How is your husband—his name is everywhere these days?'

'Dr Dastur,' she said, 'this is my music teacher. He sings beautifully.'

Dr Dastur couldn't remember having seen a music teacher at close quarters before. Not that he was uninterested in music—his daughter now played Chopin and Bach's simpler compositions on the piano; but he himself was inordinately proud of the Indian classical tradition about which he knew as little as most of his contemporaries.

'Masterji,' he said, bequeathing this title upon Mohanji in an impromptu way, 'it's a pleasure meeting you.'

Dr Dastur prescribed him medication, but Mohanji didn't take the pills with any regularity. Indeed, he had an antipathy towards pills, as if they were alive. Instead, he kept a photograph of his spiritual guru—the 'Baba'—close to him.

He kept his blackout from his other students. The ghazal was in boom: everyone wanted to sing songs about some imminent but unrealizable beloved. Mohanji, in keeping with this, taught Neha Kapur on the eleventh floor songs by Ghalib and more recent poets; almost every week, he, sitting at his harmonium, hummed under his breath and composed a tune.

Bhajans, too, had become big business of late; women wore their best saris and diamonds and went to the concert halls to listen to the new singers. And, somehow, everyone felt that they too could sing, and be singers, and be famous. Even Mrs Kapur had a dream that her voice be heard. And it took so little to achieve it—a bit of money could buy one an auditorium for a night, and a 'show' could be held. Even the guru had come to believe in the simplicity of this rather uncomplicated faith.

Although he was keeping indifferent health, he'd begun to sing more and more at businessmen's mehfils, and wedding parties; someone, moved by his singing, might come up to him in the middle of a song and shyly but passionately press a hundred-rupee note to his hand. Unaccounted-for money circulated in these gatherings; they were different from the parties in the corporate world, but, in a way, these people, always ostentatious with both money and emotion, seemed to care more for the music, and, moved by the pathos of some memory, shook their heads from side to side as he sang his ghazals.

These mehfils lasted late into the night, and sometimes Mohanji and the members of his family who'd accompanied him would return home in a taxi at two or half past two in the morning. Late night, and the heat of the day would have gone, and they'd be sleepy and exhausted but still know they were a thousand rupees richer. By this time, the housewives who'd heard him sing too would be setting aside their large gold necklaces and yawning and going to bed.

This year, when the ghazal was in boom, had been a better year than most for the guru. He'd gone round from home to home, patiently teaching new songs to housewives about the wave of long hair and sudden gestures and sidelong glances, singing at small baithaks, or even bhajans at temples before Sindhi businessmen if they so demanded it. This would leave him tired and moody, though, when he visited Mrs Chatterjee. She couldn't decide whether he was unhappy for some personal reason, or because he still hadn't made a name as some other singers had.

As the guru's health worsened, he began to sleep for more and more of the time. Sometimes the phone might ring in his small room, and he might speak for a few moments to a student who was enquiring after where he was. When he made the effort of going into the city, he slept on the train, carried along by its rhythm; and sometimes Mrs Chatterjee, finding him tired, would feel sorry for him and let him fall asleep after a lesson on one of the wicker sofas on the balcony, overlooking the Arabian Sea and the office buildings on Nariman Point. As he rested, she might be getting ready, to go out, once her husband returned, for dinner. Now and again, she'd go to the veranda to check how the guru was, put her hand on his forehead, and shake her head well-meaningly and say, 'No fever.' She would glance towards the traffic on Marine Drive, because it was from that direction that her husband would be approaching.

At such times, the guru was like a pet, or a child, left to himself and intermittently tended to. As Mrs Chatterjee and her husband prepared to go out they would talk about him as if he were a child they were leaving behind. Occasionally, if he heard her humming a song he'd taught her as she went out, he'd open his eyes, smile slightly, and close them again. □

Persian Love   Alan Warner

Over twenty years ago, when I was fifteen, I would pin posters and articles to my bedroom wall. In the spring of 1980, I read an interview with the bass player, Jah Wobble, who was at that time playing in my favourite group, John Lydon's post-Sex Pistols band, Public Image Ltd. I filleted the interview and tacked it to the wallpaper.

Wobble had been overwhelmed by a composition from a German musician with the magical name of Holger Czukay. He talked of a piece of music called 'Persian Love', on Czukay's recent album, *Movies*, which EMI had just released. What struck me so forcibly was his comment, 'The voices on it are so beautiful, I thought to myself, I will never, never try to sing again!'

In those days, in the Highlands of Scotland, the only way to obtain unusual music was through mail order. The album arrived packed in brown cardboard one sun-filled morning and before I caught the school bus, I'd directed the needle of my bedroom record player directly to 'Persian Love'.

Twenty-one years on and, as I write, I'm still listening to this same record. Often, when dark times rob me of my taste for beauty, I've walked away from it for months on end. But, in between the Messiaen and the Gagaku court music, the punk rock and the Puccini; like all art that has touched you deeply, and to which your heart first opens, I keep returning to 'Persian Love'. In many ways, this record and this musician remain my touchstone, in all arts. Literature as well. I subsequently dedicated my first novel, *Morvern Callar*, to Holger; we became friends and I am undergoing proceedings to have him adopt me, so I will inherit his vast wealth.

Holger, a former student of Karlheinz Stockhausen, is a master of unorthodox studio technique. He invented sampling, through 1976–78, taping down thousands of hours of high-resolution sounds from shortwave radio on to large, old magnetic tape spools. One late night in his Cologne laboratory he picked up the compelling and erotic voices of two Radio Tehran singers performing a love duet. One male and one female, seductive undertones and lisps, and those soaring minaret vocalizings.

Holger is also a wonderful guitar player, technically brilliant but he underplays in a style that's something between Kenyan 'high life' and jazzer Barney Kessel. It reminds me of Miles Davis's concept:

'Play like you don't know how to play'! Holger's guitar plays through warm-sounding valve amplifiers that produce a honeyed tone and date from the Third Reich. He used to purchase them from the basement of his local undertaker! He added spangling guitar lines in counterpoint to the keening, unearthly voices, at first sounding in ecstasy, then in heartbreak.

Holger edited the album by hand; months of work, splicing individual guitar notes from the master tape and adding others: a kind of movie editing (hence the title) and also a time travel of single notes. He manipulated the tape speeds to send his shimmering guitar sound far up into the high register of the love singers. Finally, with the virtuoso drummer Jaki Liebezeit, he added live rock drums and his own darting bass. A skipping, sinuous, waltz tempo of a song, 'Persian Love' has none of the seriousness or angularity associated with the avant garde. It is 6:22 of what beauty and life's joy there is to extract, tempered by consequential sadness, lover's caution and also the whole album's atmosphere of compressed mystery, suggestive in the found tape snatches of old movies, a bebop saxophone bursting out over an old operetta singer, a tuba soloing up in the mountains, ascending guitars that glint like suns breasting ridges.

In May, I was staying in Claridges' hotel, that historic pile which Patrick Kavanagh once described as the most expensive nursing home in London. At Onassis's old alcove table, Holger, an amiable Dr Who, was explaining how he was a childhood refugee of ruined Danzig, like his then neighbour, Gunter Grass. And how he danced at Rio in a (stolen) Brazilian admiral's uniform. And how his lifelong search for an exceedingly wealthy wife led him, direct from Herr Stockhausen, to teaching music in an exclusive Swiss girls' school; Beethoven's Seventh, mainly!

Holger and I were celebrating. Lynne Ramsay's movie of *Morvern Callar* was going to use Holger's music on the soundtrack. It felt very strange: all those years since I was a schoolboy and now we had his music in this movie. 'Not so strange,' said Holger, 'Like those voices on "Persian Love": I did not find them, they came to me! It's destiny. And destiny, dear Alan, is never strange.' □

Call for Submissions

THE KENYON REVIEW
ON
CULTURE AND PLACE

The Kenyon Review's double Summer/Fall 2003 will be a special international issue exploring the dynamic relationship between culture and place. How do different cultures imagine place? What does "nature" mean? How does the divine manifest itself in the physical world? How do different cultures use language to represent their relationships to the physical world?

The editors hope to receive diverse submissions of poetry, fiction, and nonfiction that reflect the experiences of, for example, cultures that have long been settled in specific regions; "nomadic" peoples whose sense of place will be very different from sedentary societies; and individuals who identify themselves in postcolonial, international, or diasporic terms, and who may feel variously "at home" in Calcutta, London, New York—or no where.

Send manuscripts by June 1, 2002, to
David Lynn, Editor
The Kenyon Review,
102 College Dr., Gambier, OH 43022-9623.
(No electronic or simultaneous submissions, please.)
Visit us on the web at www.kenyonreview.org.
Telephone: 740-427-5208

AMERICAN FOLK
Griel Marcus

Harry Smith in 1955

JOANNE ZIPRIN

I live in Berkeley, California. Almost every day for nearly twenty years I've walked up the same steep, winding hill, up a stretch of pavement named Panoramic Way, which begins right behind the University of California football stadium. A few years back, when my fascination with Harry Smith's *Anthology of American Folk Music*—a fascination that began around 1970—was turning into obsession, I began to imagine that Smith had lived on this street.

I knew that Smith was born in 1923 in Portland, Oregon, and grew up in and around Seattle, Washington; that as a teenager he had recorded the ceremonies and chants of local Indian tribes, and in 1940 had begun to collect commercially released blues and country 78s from the 1920s and 1930s. In 1952, in New York City, when his collection ran into the tens of thousands, he assembled eighty-four discs by mostly forgotten performers as an anthology he at first called simply, or arrogantly, *American Folk Music*: a dubiously legal bootleg of recordings originally issued by such still-active labels as Columbia, Brunswick and Victor. Released that year by Folkways Records as three double LPs, what was soon retitled the *Anthology of American Folk Music* became the foundation stone for the American folk music revival of the late 1950s and the 1960s.

Slowly at first, Smith's set found its way into beatnik enclaves, collegiate bohemias and the nascent folk scenes in Greenwich Village, Chicago, Philadelphia, Berkeley and Detroit. By the early 1960s the *Anthology* had become a kind of lingua franca, or a password: for the likes of Roger McGuinn, later of the Byrds, or Jerry Garcia, founder of the Grateful Dead, for folk musicians such as Dave Van Ronk, Rick Von Schmidt and John Fahey, for poet Allen Ginsberg, it was the secret text of a secret country. In 1960, John Pankake and others who were part of the folk milieu at the University of Minnesota in Minneapolis initiated a nineteen-year-old Bob Dylan into what Pankake would later call 'the brotherhood of the *Anthology*'; the presence of Smith's music in Dylan's has been a template for the presence of that music in the country, and the world, at large. From then to now verses, melodies, images and choruses from the *Anthology*, and most deeply the *Anthology*'s insistence on an occult, Gothic America of terror and deliverance inside the official America of anxiety and success—as Smith placed murder ballads, explosions of religious ecstasy, moral warnings and hedonistic revels on the same plane of value and meaning—have been one step behind Dylan's own music, and one step ahead.

As Smith said in 1991, with fifty years of experimental film-making, jazz painting, shamanistic teaching and most of all dereliction behind him, accepting a Lifetime Achievement Award at the ceremonies of the American Academy of Recording Arts & Sciences, he had lived to 'see America changed by music'. He died in 1994.

Three years later, when his anthology was reissued as a six-CD boxed set by Smithsonian Folkways Records, its uncanny portrayal of the American ethos would unsettle the country all over again. But that event had yet to take place when I started musing about Harry Smith and Panoramic Way. I knew that Smith had lived in Berkeley in the mid-to-late 1940s, and that he'd done most of his record collecting there. Well, he had to live somewhere, and Panoramic, I decided, looked like where he would have lived.

It's a crumbling old street, with unpredictable, William Morris-inspired Arts and Crafts touches on the brown-shingle and stucco houses—a weird collection of chimneys on one, on another a fountain in the shape of a gorgon's face, sculpted out of a concrete wall, so that water comes out of the mouth, drips down, and, over the decades, has left the gorgon with a long, green beard of moss.

Most of the houses on the downside of the hill are hidden from view. You almost never see anyone out of doors. No sidewalks. Deer in the daytime; raccoon, possums, even coyotes at night. Berries, plums, loquats, wild rosemary and fennel everywhere. Woods and warrens, stone stairways cutting the hill from the bottom to the top. An always-dark pathway shrouded by huge redwoods. The giant curve of the foundation of a house built by Frank Lloyd Wright. A street where, you could imagine, something odd, seductive, forbidden or unspeakable was taking place behind every door. Absolute Bohemian, absolute pack rat—where else would Harry Smith live if he lived in Berkeley?

I'd read that Harry Smith had lived for a time in the basement apartment of Bertrand Bronson, Professor of Anthropology at the University of California, ballad scholar and record collector, so I looked for basement apartments that seemed right. I settled on one, in a dramatic house that looked as if it had grown out of the ground, surrounded by a wild garden dotted with ceramic monsters and a replica of the Kremlin, just off of one of the stone stairways. Then I forgot the whole thing.

A couple of years later I was in a San Francisco bookstore, doing a reading from a book I'd written that had a chapter on Smith's *Anthology* at its centre. Afterwards a man with a long white beard came up to me and started talking about Harry Smith, record collecting, a warehouse in Richmond that closed just days before they got the money to buy it out, the Bop City nightclub in the Filmore district, one of its walls covered by Smith's giant bebop mural, a painting of notes, not performers—I couldn't keep up.

I barely caught the man's name, and only because I'd heard it before: Lou Kemnitzer. 'That little apartment,' he said, 'that's where we were, on Panoramic Way in Berkeley—' 'Wait a minute,' I said. 'Harry Smith lived on Panoramic?' It didn't seem real; Kemnitzer began to look like the Panoramic gorgon. I got up my nerve. 'Do you *remember*,' I said to Kemnitzer, who now seemed much older than he had appeared a minute or two before, 'what the *number* of Harry Smith's apartment was?' Kemnitzer looked at me as if I'd asked him if he remembered where he was living now—if he could, you know, find his way home. 'Five and a half,' he said.

By then it was late—on Panoramic, much too dark to look for a number. I could hardly wait for the next morning. And of course there it was: a dull, white door in grey stucco; tiny windows; a cell. Maybe ten steps across from the place I'd picked out.

Every day since, as I've walked up the Panoramic hill past Harry Smith's place and then down past it, I've wanted to knock on the door and tell whoever is living there—in four years, I've seen no one, typical for Panoramic—who *once* lived there. Who once lived there, and who surely left behind a ghost, if not a whole crew of them. 'WANTED,' ran a tiny ad in the September 1946 issue of *Record Changer* magazine:

Pre-War Race and Hillbilly Vocals.
Bascom Lamar Lunsford, Jilson Setters, Uncle Eck Dunford, Clarence Ashley, Dock Boggs, Grayson and Whittier, Bukka White, Robert Johnson, Roosevelt Graves, Julius Daniels, Rev. D. C. Rice,

Lonnie McIntorsh, Tommy McClennan, and many others.
HARRY E. SMITH, 5½ Panoramic, Berkeley 4, California.

They were still in that little room—they had to be. They
sounded like ghosts on their own records, twenty years before Harry
Smith began looking for them; deprived of their black 78 rpm bodies,
they were certain to sound more like ghosts now.

I began to fantasize how I might explain. There's a plaque a few
steps from the door of 5½, dedicated to Henry Atkins, the designer
who created the neighbourhood in 1909. So I would say, 'Hello. I
wonder if you know who used to live in your apartment. See that
plaque over there—well, there ought to be a plaque for this man. You
see, he did—remarkable things.' No, that wasn't going to work. It
already sounded as if I was recruiting for a new cult. A better idea:
take a copy of the thing. Hold it up. 'This is a collection of old
American music. Just this year,' I could say (referring to the London
art curator Mark Francis), 'a man speaking in Paris said that only
James Joyce could remotely touch this collection as a key to modern
memory. And it all came together right here, in your apartment. I
just wanted to let whoever was living here now know that.'

After a few weeks this fantasy took a turn and tripped me up.
I'd offer the *Anthology*, then walk away, good deed accomplished—
but then the person would ask a question. 'Sounds really interesting,'
she'd say. 'What's it about?'

Well, what is it about? How do you explain—not only to
someone who's never heard the *Anthology*, never heard *of* it, but to
yourself, especially if you've been listening to Smith's book of spells
for years or decades? An answer came right out of the air: 'Dead
presidents,' I'd say. 'Dead dogs, dead children, dead lovers, dead
murderers, dead heroes, and how good it is to be alive.'

That sounded right the first time it ran through my head; it
sounded ridiculously slick after that. I realized I had no idea what
Harry Smith's collection was about. When, in the fall of 2000, I
taught a faculty seminar on the *Anthology*, including what for
decades had seemed the apocryphal *Volume 4*, Smith's assemblage
of mostly Depression-era records, finally released in 2000 on the late

John Fahey's Revenant label, I realized I had no idea what it was.

A group of professors—from the English, German, Philosophy, Music, History, American Studies and Art History departments—sat around a table. Their assignment had been to listen to the CDs; I asked each to pick the song he or she most liked. 'The song about the dog,' one woman said, referring to Jim Jackson's 1928 'Old Dog Blue'. 'Why?' I asked. 'I don't know,' she said, just like any listener. 'I played the records when I was doing the dishes, and that one just stuck.' There were several votes for 'the Cajun songs'—for Delma Lachney and Blind Uncle Gaspard's 'La Danseuse', Columbus Fruge's 'Saut Crapaud', both from 1929, and Breaux Freres's 1933 'Home Sweet Home'—names and titles that in thirty years of listening to the original anthology—but, obviously, not altogether hearing it— I'd never registered.

To these new listeners, these performances—all from the part of the set Smith named 'Social Music', the part that in the 1960s people usually found least appealing—leaped right out. I was disappointed no one mentioned Bascom Lamar Lunsford's 1928 'I Wish I Was a Mole in the Ground', the most seductively unsolvable song I've ever heard, or Richard 'Rabbit' Brown's 1927 'James Alley Blues', which I think is the greatest record ever made. Well, I thought, there's no accounting for taste. And they don't really *know* this stuff—it's not like I got it the first time through. I did mention 'James Alley Blues', though. 'You mean the one that sounds like Cat Stevens?' someone said. I was horrified. I dropped the subject.

The discussion picked up when I asked each person around the table to name the performance he or she most hated. There was a Philosophy professor who, when in later meetings we took up Smith's *Volume 4*, insisted on the instantly unarguable lineage between the Bradley Kincaid of the 1933 'Dog and Gun' and anything by Pat Boone. His first contribution to the seminar was to note 'the startling echoes of the Stonemans'—in their 1926 'The Mountaineer's Courtship' and 1930 'The Spanish Merchant's Daughter'—'in the early work of the Captain and Tennile.' 'Hattie Stoneman,' responded an Art History professor, 'ought to be drowned.'

An English professor confessed she really couldn't stand the 'flatness of the voices'—she meant the Appalachian voices, Clarence

Ashley, Dock Boggs, the Carter Family, G. B. Grayson, Charlie Poole, Lunsford. 'What's that about?' she said. 'What's it for?' 'Maybe it's a kind of disinterest,' a young Musicology professor said. 'Everybody knows these songs, they've heard them all their lives. So they're bored with them.' 'It's like they don't care if anyone's listening or not,' said the first professor. 'Maybe that's what I don't like. As if we're not needed.' 'I don't think that's it,' said a German professor, who, it turned out, had grown up in the Kentucky mountains. 'It's fatalism. It's powerlessness. It's the belief that nothing you can do will ever change anything, including singing a song. So you're right, in a way—it doesn't matter if you're listening or not. The world won't be different when the song is over no matter how the song is sung, or how many people hear it.'

'Uncle Dave Macon isn't like that,' someone said of the Grand Ole Opry's favourite uncle. 'No,' the let's-drown-Hattie-Stoneman professor said, 'he's *satanic*.'

I realized I was completely out of my depth—or that Harry Smith's *Anthology of American Folk Music* had opened up into a country altogether different from any I'd ever found in it. 'It's that "Kill yourself!"', another person said, picking up on the notion, and quickly it seemed as if everyone in the room saw horns coming out of the head of the kindly old banjo player, saw his buck-dancer's clogs replaced by cloven hoofs. They were talking about his 1926 'Way Down the Old Plank Road', one of the most celebratory, ecstatic, unburdened shouts America has ever thrown up. Where's the devil?

'Kill yourself!' Uncle Dave Macon yells in the middle of the song, after a verse, taken from 'The Coo Coo', about building a scaffold on a mountain just to see the girls pass by, after a commonplace verse about how his wife died on Friday and he got married again on Monday. 'Kill yourself!' He meant, it had always seemed obvious to me—well, actually, it was never obvious. He meant when life is this good it can't get any better so you might as well—kill yourself? Does that follow? Maybe he's saying nothing more than 'Scream and shout, knock yourself out,' 'Shake it don't break it,' or, for that matter, 'Love conquers all.'

That's not how he sounds, though. He sounds huge, like some pagan god rising over whatever scene he's describing, not master of the revels but a judge. 'Uncle Dave seems much too *satisfied* about the prospect of apocalypse,' the agent-of-satan advocate said. Everyone was nodding, and for a moment I heard it too: Uncle Dave Macon wants you dead. I heard what was really satanic about the moment: when Macon says 'Kill yourself!' it sounds like a good idea—really *fun*. And you can hear the same thing in 'The Wreck of the Tennessee Gravy Train', which Harry Smith slotted into *Volume 4* of his *Anthology*. It was 1930, and Macon compressed as much journalistic information as there is in Bob Dylan's 'Hurricane' into just over a third of the time, dancing through the financial ruins of his state—the phony bond issue, the collapsed banks, the stolen funds—while crying 'Follow me, good people, we're bound for the Promised Land' over and over. 'Kill yourself!'— this is what the devil would sound like singing 'Sympathy for the Devil': *correct*.

Hearing Macon this way was like hearing Bob Dylan's one-time sidekick Bob Neuwirth's version of 'I Wish I Was a Mole in the Ground'. In London in 1999, at the first of the series of Harry Smith tribute concerts the record producer Hal Willner continues to put on, Neuwirth sang the song's most mysterious line, 'I wish I was a lizard in the spring', as 'I wish I was a lizard in your spring'. Oh. Right. Sure. Obvious.

In most of the vast amount of commentary that greeted the reissue of the *Anthology of American Folk Music* in 1997, the music was taken as a canon, and the performers as exemplars of the folk. Neither of these notions had reached the room we were in. There people were arguing with Uncle Dave Macon, not with whatever tradition he might represent. It was Hattie Stoneman who had to be drowned, not white Virginia country women in general. There was no need to be respectful of a song if you didn't like it.

In 1940, folklorists Frank and Anne Warner taped the North Carolina singer Frank Proffitt's offering of a local Wilkes Country ballad called 'Tom Dooley', about the nineteenth-century murder of one Laura Foster by her former lover, Tom Dula, and his new lover, Annie Melton. The song travelled, and in 1958 a collegiate trio from Menlo Park, California—my home town, as it happened, and in 1958 the most comfortable, cruising-the-strip postwar suburb town imaginable—made the song number one in the country. The whole story is in Robert Cantwell's book on the folk revival, *When We Were Good*—or at least the story up to 1996, when the book was published.

In 2000, Appleseed Records released *Nothing Seems Better to Me*, a volume of field recordings made by the Warners, featuring Frank Proffitt. The liner notes featured a letter from Proffitt, written in 1959. 'I got a television set for the kids,' he wrote.

> One night I was a-setting looking at some foolishness when three fellers stepped out with guitar and banjer and went to singing Tom Dooly and they clowned and hipswinged. I began to feel sorty sick, like I'd lost a loved one. Tears came to my eyes, yes, I went out and balled on the Ridge, looking toward old Wilkes, land of Tom Dooly...I looked up across the mountains and said Lord, couldn't they leave me the good memories...Then Frank Warner wrote, he tells me that some way our song got picked up. The shock was over. I went back to my work. I began to see the world was bigger than our mountains of Wilkes and Watauga. Folks was brothers, they all liked the plain ways. I begin to pity them that hadn't dozed on the hearthstone...Life was sharing different thinking, different ways. I looked in the mirror of my heart—You hain't a boy no longer. Give folks like Frank Warner all you got. Quit thinking Ridge to Ridge, think of oceans to oceans.

This is the classic Sixties account of what folk music is, how it works, how it is seized by the dominant discourse of the time and turned into a soulless commodity—the classic account of who the folk are, of how even when everything they have is taken from them, their essential goodness remains. As Faulkner put it at the end of *The Sound and the Fury*, summing up the fate of his characters, naming the black servant Dilsey but at the same time dissolving her into her people, her kind of folk: 'They endured.'

There wasn't any *they* in the seminar room as the Smith records were passed around the table. The all-encompassing piety of Frank Proffitt's letter—a letter which, I have to say, I don't believe for a moment, which reads as if it could have been cooked up by a Popular Front folklorist in 1937, which is just too ideologically perfect to be true—would never have survived the discussion that took place there. It wouldn't have gotten a word in.

I went home and put the *Anthology* on. I had read somewhere that, in the Fifties, the photographer and film-maker Robert Frank used to listen to the twentieth song on the 'Social Music' discs, the Memphis Sanctified Singers' 1929 'He Got Better Things for You', over and over, as if there didn't need to be any other music in the world. I'd tried to hear something of what he must have heard; I never could. But this day it was all there—as if, again, it had all been obvious.

Smith hadn't credited the singers individually, no doubt because he couldn't find their names. In the supplemental notes to the 1997 reissue by the folklorist Jeff Place, you find them: Bessie Johnson, leading, followed by Melinda Taylor and Sally Sumner, with Will Shade, of the Memphis Jug Band, on guitar. Johnson starts out deliberately, with small, measured steps. 'Kind friends, I want to tell you,' she says in a friendly way. Then her almost mannish vibrato deepens; it's getting rougher, harder, with every pace. When she says 'Jesus Christ, my saviour,' he's hers, not yours. Her throat seems to shred. With that roughness, and the roughness of the words that follow—'He got the Holy Ghost and the fire'—right away it's an angry God that's staring you in the face. Uncle Dave Macon, agent of Satan? This is much scarier. But then, as the first verse is ending, the whole performance, the whole world, seems to drop back, to drop down, to almost take it all back, the threat, the rebuke, the condemnation. Every word is made to stand out starkly, right up to the point of the title phrase. 'He got better things for you'—the phrase seems to slide off Bessie Johnson's tongue, to disappear in the air, leaving only the suggestion that if you listened all the way into this song your life would be completely transformed.

The *Anthology of American Folk Music* had been turned upside down and inside out, that was for sure. I was still certain that Rabbit Brown's 'James Alley Blues' was the greatest record ever made, but now another performance I'd never really noticed before, the Alabama Sacred Heart Singers' 1928 'Rocky Road', suddenly stood out. It wasn't a record, it was a children's crusade. On the *Anthology*, the spiritual 'Present Days', the same group's recording from the same year, has a deep, mature bass, a reedy lead by a man you can see as the town pharmacist, then a farmer or a preacher taking the most expansive moments of the tune, their wives filling out the music. The piece goes on too long—you hear how well they know the number, how complete it is, how finished. It's a professional piece of work. But in 'Rocky Road'—'Ohhhhhh—La la/La la/La la la', ten or twenty or a hundred kids seem to be chanting while circle-dancing in a field on the edge of a cliff. As if it were something by Little Richard and I was eleven, I didn't hear an English word, or want to. You didn't need to know a language to hear this music; it taught you. Not that it had ever taught me a thing before. You have to be *ready* to accept God, songs like this say; you have to be ready to hear songs.

When you're listening to old records, or looking at old photographs, the more beautiful, the more lifelike the sensations they give off, the more difficult it is not to realize that the people you are hearing or seeing are dead. They appeared upon the earth and left it, and it can seem as if their survival in representations is altogether an accident—as if, as the Apocrypha quoted by James Agee at the end of *Let Us Now Praise Famous Men* reads, in truth 'they perished, as though they had never been; and are become as though they had never been born'. But that's not what the Alabama Sacred Heart Singers sound like on 'Rocky Road'. Here the persons singing are getting younger and younger with every line. By the end they are just emerging from the womb. Play the song over and over, and you hear them grow up—but only so far. You hear them born again, again and again.

It's impossible to imagine that these people can ever die. That's what they're saying, of course—that's their text. Thousands and thousands of people, over thousands of years, have said exactly the same thing. But they haven't *done* it.

Harry Smith once said that his primary interest in American folk music was the 'patterning' that occurred within it. It isn't likely he meant what other record collectors would have meant: the stereotypically male, adolescent interest in classification, adding it up: trainspotting. Sorting it all out by region, style, genre, instrumentation, song-family, and, most of all, race.

Smith's placement of recordings and performers make patterns all through his anthologies. Some of these patterns are easy enough to follow, such as the string of murders, assassinations, train wrecks, sinking ships and pestilence that ends his original 'Ballads' section. Some patterns are utterly spectral—you simply sense that two songs which in any formal sense could not be more dissimilar have been commissioned by the same god. But in no case is the performer imprisoned by his or her performance—by the expectations the audience might have brought to it, or that the performer himself or herself might have brought to it. One singer is sly, a con man; another singer has already gone over to the other side, past death, past any possibility of surprise; a third laughs in the second singer's face.

It's interesting that most of the songs collected on Smith's first *Anthology*, and many of those found on his *Volume 4*—the testimony of killers and saints, tales of escape and imprisonment, calls for justice and revenge, visitations of weather and the supernatural; songs that, overall, leave the listener with a sense of jeopardy, uncertainty, a morbid sense of past and future—had been sung for generations before Smith's recordings were made. But the recordings he chose testify to the ability of certain artists to present themselves, as bodies, as will, as desire, as saved, as damned, as love, as hate—as if their singularity has removed them from the musical historiographies and economic sociologies where scholars have always laboured to maintain them.

In folk music, as it was conventionally understood when Smith did his work, the song sung the singer. But Smith's work is modernist: the singer sings the song. The singer, in a line the actress Louise Brooks liked to quote about art, offers 'a subjective epic composition in which the artist begs leave to treat the world according to his point of view. It is only a question, therefore, whether he has a point of view.'

The people to whom Smith was attracted had a point of view. His anthologies are a dramatization of subjectivity—a dramatization of what it might be like to live in a town, or a country, where everyone you meet has a point of view, and nobody ever shuts up.

Such a society does not merely decline to ask for a canon, it repels it. Look at the supposed canon-maker. Smith spoke of 'the universal hatred' he brought upon himself. He dressed as a tramp and often lived as one. He claimed to be a serial killer. He denied he had ever had sexual intercourse with another person, and many people who knew him have agreed they could never imagine that he had. Enemies and even friends described him as a cripple, a dope fiend, a freak, a bum. 'When I was younger,' Smith said in a lonely moment in 1976, speaking to a college student who had called him on the phone for help with a paper, 'I thought that the feelings that went through me were—that I would outgrow them, that the anxiety or panic or whatever it is called would disappear, but you sort of suspect it at thirty-five, [and] when you get to be fifty you definitely know you're stuck with your neuroses, or whatever you want to classify them as— demons, completed ceremonies, any old damn thing.'

A canon? What you have behind the anthologies is a man who himself never shut up—a young man in his late twenties in 1952, from the West Coast, now in New York City, who was imposing his own oddness, his own status as one who didn't belong and who may not have wanted to, his own identity as someone unlike anyone else and as someone no one else would want to be, on the country itself.

It was his version of the folk process. He would presuppose a nation, a common predicament, a promise and a curse no citizen could escape; he would presuppose a national identity, and then rewrite it. He would rewrite it by whim, by taste—in terms of what he, the editor (as he credited himself) responded to.

No pieties about folk music, about authenticity, about who the folk really are and who they are not, about whose work is respectful of the past and whose exploitive, can survive such a stance—and that may be why Smith's project has proved so fecund, so generative. He suggests to Americans that their culture is in fact *theirs*—which means they can do whatever they like with it.

No one has taken up Smith's offering more fully, and with a more complete sense of the necessary oddness of the shared voice, than the still little-known Handsome Family of Albuquerque, New Mexico, a husband-and-wife duo whose original songs—lyrics by Rennie Sparks, words that in their everyday surrealism have no parallel in contemporary writing, vocals and music by Brett Sparks— mine the deep veins of fatalism in the Appalachian voice. Singing in a drone, wielding a dulled knife that can, somehow, cut anything,

Brett Sparks likes to keep his voice not so much flat as flattening, depressed, in the psychological sense but in the physical sense, too—you can feel whatever it is that is weighing him down.

On the Handsome Family albums—*Odessa, Through the Trees, Milk and Scissors, In the Air* and *Twilight*—all recorded over the last eight years, there is the terrifying murder ballad 'Arlene', which is itself nothing compared to 'My Sister's Tiny Hands', the story of twins, a boy and a girl, of death and madness, a rewrite both of the eighteenth-century New England folk song 'Springfield Mountain' and 'The Fall of the House of Usher', a song so exquisitely balanced and unrushed, so flooded with love, that it is as hard to listen to as it is not to immediately play again as soon as it ends. There is 'I Know You Are There,' a suicide orchestrated as a waltz and declaimed as if it were a patriotic address from 1914, and 'Emily Shore 1819–1839', precious in its title, not in the lines Rennie Sparks finds for tuberculosis, lines you know would have been on Smith's collections if anyone, in the past, had known where to look: 'At night her heart pounded holes in her chest/Death like a bird was building its nest.' Brett Sparks sings the words as slowly as he can, the chords of his guitar cutting back at his voice so that the song seems to slow down against itself. There is 'Last Night I Went Out Walking', as generically complete an American folk song as 'In the Pines'—'In the Pines' as sung by Lead Belly or by Kurt Cobain—a song that in its affirmations of love, fidelity and a cleansed soul summons a dread you know will follow the singer as long as he lives.

And there is 'Winnebago Skeletons', the Handsome Family's national anthem, the number that insists that the whole history of the country, its beginnings and its end, is buried beneath the singer's town, along with its skyscrapers, traffic lights, wiffle bats, beer cans, conveyor belts, steam whistles and old multi-purpose recreational vehicles. It opens with a fuzztone on the guitar that varies its ugly, monolithic cadence only to be followed by a guitar solo that soars like a great funeral oration. 'There's a fish in my stomach a thousand years old,' the singer says in the first line, the fuzztone pushing him up a hill he knows it's pointless to climb, and for the moment nothing could seem more realistic. That's what the old American fatalism is for, the Handsome Family has learned from

Greil Marcus

Dock Boggs, Blind Lemon Jefferson, Rabbit Brown—to make you understand that nothing is impossible, that the worst is yet to come. Where else would a thousand-year-old fish be but in the stomach of a man who sounds like the man who's singing now?

In the seminar I taught on Harry Smith's anthologies of American folk music, I brought up the notion of the characters in all the performances—the characters named and shaped in the ballads about historical events as well as those only implicit and anonymous in the fiddle pieces and calls for deliverance, those representative fictional men and women in the tales told as if they really happened— as peopling a town, a community. If the songs did indeed make up such a town, what townspeople-like roles would those around the table assign the various performers on the anthologies? This did not go over very well. 'Well,' someone said finally, 'I can see Uncle Dave as the town dentist.' 'If this is a community,' another person said, 'it's not one I'd want to be part of.' 'Of course no one wants to be part of this community,' a librarian said after class, frustrated and angry. 'All of these people are poor!'

But no one is just like anybody else. No one, in fact, is even who he or she was ever supposed to be. No one was supposed to step out from their fellows and stand alone to say their piece, to thrill those who stand and listen with the notion that they, too, might have a voice, to shame those who stand and listen because they lack the courage to do more than that.

I think it's a great victory, a victory over decades of losing those who had the courage to speak out in the sociologies of their poverty, that anyone can now hear these men and women, and those they sing about, as singular, as people whose voices no particular set of circumstances could ever ensure would be heard. But once that perspective is gained, it has to be reversed. If we now see the artists Harry Smith found gazing on a common predicament, each from their own perspective, it may be time to return them, not to the sociologies that once ignored them, but to their republic, where each is a moral actor: a citizen.

This republic is not a town, but a train—a train that, at least as a song, left the station only a short time ago. 'You know you won't be back,' Bruce Springsteen says at the beginning of his recent song 'Land of Hope and Dreams'—take what you can carry. 'This train,' he says—reversing the pious American folk train that 'don't carry no gamblers'—'Carries saints and sinners/This train/Carries losers and winners/This train/Carries whores and gamblers.' 'This train,' he sings, as the voices of the members of his band circle him like shades, 'Carries lost soul ramblers/This train carries broken hearted/Thieves and souls departed/This train/Carries fools and jails.'

I doubt if this song would have been written or sung had Harry Smith not, like those once-forgotten artists he placed on his records, stepped forward to tell what the country looked like to him. Right now, Springsteen's song seems to complete Smith's work. Smith might not have liked it himself, but the lesson he taught in his anthologies is that you have to choose for yourself. □

Unfinished Sympathy Julie Burchill

First come the drums—then the cymbals and the glockenspiel. They sound jangled and edgy, like callow teens eyeing each other up at a dance hall, each waiting for the other to make the first move. And then comes the hand, flicking the switch or pulling out the plug—whatever's quickest. It's my favourite song, 'Unfinished Sympathy' by Massive Attack. It's my favourite song, and I don't want to hear it, not ever again.

Well, it was always a bit of an embarrassment, liking *that song* so much, I reason with myself. Released in 1991, it has many times been voted the nation's favourite pop single ever; loving it above all others is tantamount to saying that *Citizen Kane* is your favourite film or strawberry your favourite Opal Fruit. It won't be any great loss. And now I'm rid of it, I can search out some really obscure song by a German gabba techno group and have that as my favourite instead.

I don't ever want to hear that song again because, for the first time in my life, I want my life to stay exactly the way it is. And I know, pathetically, that certain pop songs—this one above all others—have the power to make me want nothing more than to smash up everything of value in my life just to see the pretty pattern the pieces fall into. Pop songs have the power to make me behave badly, and for the first time in my life I want to do the right thing; I'm forty-two, for goodness' sake. I don't do self-loathing, never have, but recently when I'm alone, I've begun to feel uneasy, as though there's a nutter in the room who wants to do me permanent damage. And more than anything else, I want to get away from that person.

To paraphrase Nick Hornby in *High Fidelity*, was I sexually restless all my life because I listened to pop music, or did I listen to pop music because I was sexually restless? Whatever, from the minute the hormones kicked in when I was twelve, sex and pop were wrapped around each other in my mind tighter than a tourniquet. And since then all my favourite pop songs—'Fast Love' by George Michael, 'U Sure Do' by Strike, 'Gotta Tell You' by Samantha Mumba, 'Finally' by Kings Of Tomorrow, 'Since I Left You' by the Avalanches—have been about either ditching an old love or starting up a new one. I don't think I've ever liked one song which deals with the permanence of love. I'm starting to see a pattern here.

So I turn off the radio, and think that maybe those rednecks who burned Elvis records were right, and that it really is the Devil's music. Anyway, I'm not taking any chances. For a moment I savour the silence. And then *that song* starts up inside my head! And then I know there really is no way out. ☐

STATEMENT OF OWNERSHIP, MANAGEMENT, AND CIRCULATION
1. Publication Title: Granta
2. Publication No. 0000–508
3. Filing Date: 5 October 2001
4. Issue Frequency: Quarterly (4 times per year)
5. Number of Issues Published Annually: 4
6. Annual Subscription Price: $37.00
7. Complete Mailing Address of Known Office of Publication: 1755 Broadway, 5th Floor, New York, NY 10019-3780
8. Complete Mailing Address of Headquarters of General Business Office of Publisher: 1755 Broadway, 5th Floor, New York, NY 10019-3780
9. Full Names and Complete Mailing Addresses of Publisher, Editor, and Managing Editor: Publisher: Rea S. Hederman, 1755 Broadway, 5th Floor, New York, NY 10019–3780; Editor: Ian Jack, 2/3 Hanover Yard, Noel Road, London N1 8BE; Managing Editor: Sophie Harrison, 2/3 Hanover Yard, Noel Road, London N1 8BE
10. Owners: Granta USA LLC, 1755 Broadway, 5th Floor, New York, NY 10019-3780; NYREV, Inc., 1755 Broadway, 5th Floor, New York, NY 10019-3780; The Morningside Partnership, 625 N. State Street, Jackson, MS39202
11. Known Bondholders, Mortgagees, and Other Security Holders: None
12. Tax Status: Has Not Changed
13. Publication Title: Granta
14. Issue Date for Circulation Data: Fall 2001
15. Extent and Nature of Circulation: Average No. Copies Each Issue During Preceding 12 Months:
a. Total No. of Copies: 68,114
b. Paid and/or Requested Circulation:
1. Paid/Requested Outside-County Mail Subscriptions Stated on Form 3541: 22,893
2. Paid In-County Subscriptions Stated on Form 3541: 0
3. Sales Through Dealers and Carriers, Street Vendors, Counter Sales and Other Non-USPS Paid Distribution: 31,754
4. Other Classes Mailed Through the USPS: 2,511
c. Total Paid and/or Requested Circulation: 57,158

d. Free Distribution by Mail:
1. Outside-County as Stated on Form 3541: 0
2. In-County as Stated on Form 3541: 0
3. Other Classes Mailed Through the USPS: 300
e. Free Distribution Outside the Mail: 0
f. Total Free Distribution: 300
g. Total Distribution: 57,458
h. Copies not Distributed: 10,656
i. Total: 68,114
j. Percent Paid and/or Requested Circulation: 99.5%
Extent and Nature of Circulation: No. Copies of Single Issue Published Nearest to Filing Date:
a. Total No. of Copies: 66,994
b. Paid and/or Requested Circulation:
1. Paid/Requested Outside-County Mail Subscriptions Stated on Form 3541: 24,742
2. Paid In-County Subscriptions Stated on Form 3541: 0
3. Sales Through Dealers and Carriers, Street Vendors, Counter Sales and Other Non-USPS Paid Distribution: 34,395
4. Other Classes Mailed Through the USPS: 992
c. Total Paid and/or Requested Circulation: 60,129
d. Free Distribution by Mail:
1. Outside-County as Stated on Form 3541: 0
2. In-County as Stated on Form 3541: 0
3. Other Classes Mailed Through the USPS: 300
e. Free Distribution Outside the Mail: 0
f. Total Free Distribution: 300
g. Total Distribution: 60,429
h. Copies not Distributed: 6,565
i. Total: 66,994
j. Percent Paid and/or Requested Circulation: 99.5%
16. Publication of Statement of Ownership will be printed in the Winter 2001 issue of this publication.
17. Signature and Title of Editor, Publisher, Business Manager, or Owner: I certify that all information furnished on this form is true and complete. Rea S. Hederman, Publisher

NOTES ON CONTRIBUTORS

Nicholson Baker has published five novels, including *Vox* (Granta/Vintage) and *The Everlasting Story of Nory* (Vintage), and three works of non-fiction, the most recent of which is *Double Fold: Libraries and the Assault on Paper* (Random House). He directs the American Newspaper Repository.

Julian Barnes is the author of nine novels, most recently *Love, etc* (Picador/Knopf). His collection of essays about France, *Something to Declare*, will be published by Picador in January 2002.

Craig Brown writes columns for *Private Eye* and the *Daily Telegraph*. His novel, *The Marsh–Marlowe Letters*, has just been reissued by Prion Books in the UK, and is published in the US by The Akadine Press.

Julie Burchill began her career on the *New Musical Express* in 1976. She writes a column for the *Guardian*.

Amit Chaudhuri has written four novels, most recently *A New World* (Picador/Knopf), and edited *The Picador Book of Modern Indian Literature*. A collection of stories, *Real Time*, will be published in 2002 (Picador/Farrar, Straus & Giroux).

Nik Cohn's most recent book is *Yes We Have No*, published by Secker & Warburg/Knopf. He is currently working on a novel set in New Orleans and is producing bounce records.

Michael Collins is a writer and photographer. His seascapes, which measure 122x152.5cm, are from a body of work made around Mangerton in West Dorset, where he lives.

Robyn Davidson's recent books are *The Picador Book of Journeys*, and *Desert Places* (Penguin)—an account of her travels with pastoral nomads in India. She lives in London.

Sir John Eliot Gardiner is founder and artistic director of the Monteverdi Choir, the English Baroque Soloists and the Orchestre Révolutionnaire et Romantique. He is writing a biography of Bach, to be published by Penguin in 2004.

Janice Galloway has written five books, including *The Trick Is to Keep Breathing* (Minerva/Dalkey Archive) and *Where You Find It* (Vintage/Simon and Schuster). Her awards include the American Academy of Arts and Letters E. M. Forster Award. She has a son and lives in Glasgow. 'Clara' is taken from work-in-progress of a novel based on the life of Clara Wieck Schumann, to be published by Jonathan Cape in 2002.

Ian Jack is the editor of *Granta*.

Philip Hensher's novels include *Kitchen Venom* (Penguin) which won the Somerset Maugham Award, and *Pleasured* (Vintage). His new novel, *The*

Mulberry Empire, about the British invasion of Afghanistan in 1838, is published in April 2002 by Harper Collins.

Mark Holborn is an editor and publisher who has worked with a number of leading photographers. He has a particular interest in the music of the American South and is developing a book and exhibition on the painting, sculpture and photography of the South.

Nick Hornby is the author of, among others, *High Fidelity*, *About a Boy*, and *How to be Good* (Penguin/Riverhead). He lives in London.

Andrew O'Hagan is the author of *The Missing* (Picador/The New Press) and *Our Fathers* (Faber/Harvest Books). His most recent book is *The End of British Farming* (Profile Books).

Greil Marcus's most recent book is *Double Trouble: Bill Clinton and Elvis Presley in a Land of No Alternatives*, (Faber/Picador). He is working on a book about *The Manchurian Candidate* for the British Film Institute.

Blake Morrison is the author of *And When Did You Last See Your Father?* and *As If*, both published by Granta Books in the UK and Picador in the US. His most recent book, *The Justification of Johann Gutenberg* is published by Vintage in the UK and later next year by William Morrow in the US.

David Oates is an artist whose paintings and drawings have been shown regularly in solo and group exhibitions in Britain and internationally since 1983. He lives and works in London.

Philip Pullman's novels include *Northern Lights* (US title: *The Golden Compass*), *The Subtle Knife* and *The Amber Spyglass*, published in the UK by Scholastic and by Knopf in the US. He has won, among other prizes, the British Booksellers Association Author of the Year Award, 2001, the Carnegie Medal and the *Guardian* Children's Book Award.

Alan Rusbridger is the editor of the *Guardian*.

John Ryle is Chair of the Rift Valley Institute, a research and educational association providing services for the African Rift Valley region (institute@riftvalley.net).

Richard Sennett was formerly a cellist and conductor. He is now Chairman of the Cities Programme at the London School of Economics.

Alan Warner's novels are *Morvern Callar* (Vintage/Anchor), *These Demented Lands* (Vintage/Anchor), and *The Sopranos* (Vintage/Harvest Books). A new novel, *The Man Who Walks*, will be published in April 2002 by Vintage UK.

Richard Williams writes for the *Guardian*. A collection of his music pieces, *Long Distance Call*, is published by Aurum Press. His biography of Enzo Ferrari is published by Yellow Jersey Press.

David Oates: lyrics
p.266 from VISIONS OF JOHANNA by Bob Dylan (frame by frame)
Ain't it/just/like/the night/to play/tricks/when you're/trying/to be s/o q/uiet/?
We sit here/stranded,/though/we're/all/doing our
best/to deny it./
p.267 from YOU'RE THE TOP by Cole Porter
p.268 from OH, CAROL by Chuck Berry
p.269 from HONEYSUCKLE ROSE by Fats Waller
The editors of *Granta* would like to reward the hard
work of readers by at this point publishing the lyrics
which these pictures represent. But publishing the
lyrics to every one of these tunes proved to be
impossibly expensive.

Acknowledgements are due to the following publishers and recording
companies for permission to quote from:
'G-Code' and 'Da Magnolia' © Copyright 1999, Take Fo' Records. 'Bling
Bling' © Copyright 1997, Mack Money Music. *The Rape of Lucretia* ©
Copyright 1946, 1947 by Hawkes & Son (London) Ltd. Reproduced by
permission of Boosey & Hawkes Music Publishers Ltd. *On Not Being Able
to Paint* by Marion Milner © Copyright 1957. Reprinted by permission of
International Universities Press, Inc. and Heinemann Educational Books.
'Visions of Johanna' © Copyright 1966, Dwarf Music (SEFAC), words and
music by Bob Dylan. Caetano Veloso © Copyright Caetano Veloso.
Reproduced by permission of Natasha Music Publishing, Rio de Janeiro and
Nonesuch Records, New York. Frank Proffitt © Copyright Frank Proffitt,
Courtesy Appleseed Records.

Ian Jack: acknowledgements
Books consulted for 'Klever Kaff' include: *The Life of Kathleen Ferrier* by
Winifred Ferrier (Hamish Hamilton, 1955); *Kathleen Ferrier, A Memoir*
edited by Neville Cardus (Hamish Hamilton, 1954); *Kathleen, The Life of
Kathleen Ferrier, 1912–1953*, by Maurice Leonard (Hutchinson, 1988). The
author would also like to thank Maurice Leonard, the Kathleen Ferrier
Society, and Stephen Whittle and the staff of Blackburn Museum.